NO CHILD LEFT BEHIND AND THE
TRANSFORMATION OF FEDERAL
EDUCATION POLICY, 1965–2005

STUDIES IN GOVERNMENT AND PUBLIC POLICY

NO CHILD LEFT BEHIND AND THE TRANSFORMATION OF FEDERAL EDUCATION POLICY, 1965–2005

Patrick J. McGuinn

 University Press of Kansas

KH

To the three ladies at the center of my life:
my wife, Ilana, and our daughters, Bailey and Carigan

Published by the University Press of Kansas (Lawrence, Kansas 66045), which was organized by the Kansas Board of Regents and is operated and funded by Emporia State University, Fort Hays State University, Kansas State University, Pittsburg State University, the University of Kansas, and Wichita State University

Library of Congress Cataloging-in-Publication Data

McGuinn, Patrick J.

No Child Left Behind and the transformation of federal education policy, 1965–2005 / Patrick J. McGuinn.

   p. cm. — (Studies in government and public policy)

Includes bibliographical references and index.

ISBN 0-7006-1442-7 (cloth : alk. paper) — ISBN 0-7006-1443-5 (pbk. : alk. paper)

1. Education and state—United States—History—20th century. 2. Education and state—United States—History—21st century. 3. United States. No Child Left Behind Act of 2001. I. Title. II. Series.

LC89.M48 2006

379.73—dc22   2006006836

British Library Cataloguing-in-Publication Data is available.

Printed in the United States of America

10 9 8 7 6 5 4 3 2

The paper used in this publication meets the minimum requirements of the American National Standard for Permanence of Paper for Printed Library Materials Z39.48-1992.

3/16/07

CONTENTS

PREFACE AND ACKNOWLEDGMENTS

In the fall of 1994 I began a three-year stint as a high school government and history teacher in a suburb of Washington, D.C. Little did I know at the time that my entrance into teaching would coincide with the intensification of a national debate over school reform that had begun in the wake of the 1983 report *A Nation at Risk*. That the problems identified by that report—large socioeconomic and racial achievement gaps and concerns that even the country's "good" schools were not good enough—continued to persist ten years later was not the subject of much dispute. The particular source of the country's educational maladies and the best prescription to remedy them, however, engendered enormous disagreement among educators, researchers, citizens, and politicians. The issue of school reform—and in particular the proper size and scope of the federal role in it—received a tremendous amount of attention in Washington during 1994 as Congress deliberated over President Bill Clinton's proposals to refocus and reenergize federal efforts to improve student achievement. Working on a daily basis with students in the classroom while a national debate raged over the kinds of pedagogical and governance reforms that could improve teaching and learning was a fascinating experience. So too was sitting in (as an intern) on strategy meetings of the Center on Education Funding during the summer of 1995 as education groups plotted how to repel the newly elected Republican Congress's attacks on the U.S. Department of Education and federal education spending.

My high school teaching experience left me with a profound sense of the enormous possibilities and challenges of education and an intense desire to better understand the factors that shaped the way our national political and policymaking institutions confronted the issue of school reform. When I arrived in graduate school in the late 1990s and surveyed the scholarly literature I was surprised to find that, despite the increasing prominence of education in national politics and the growing federal influence on education policy, remarkably little contemporary research existed on this subject. By the time I left graduate school in 2003 the passage of the No Child Left Behind Act (NCLB) had dramatically transformed and expanded the federal role in schools and made my investigation all the more intriguing.

This study offers a political analysis of the evolution of federal elementary and secondary education policy between 1965 and 2005. It is animated by the following questions: What factors have enabled the federal government to assume such an active role in schools in recent years, despite the country's strong tradition of local control in education? Why did most Republicans and Democrats ultimately come to support federal standards, accountability, and choice reforms when both parties (for different reasons) had long opposed them? What were the political dynamics that enabled the No Child Left Behind law to pass, and which shaped its particular provisions? Are the conditions favorable to an active federal role in schools likely to persist over time? To answer these questions, I analyze the historical evolution of the federal role in schools and place it within the context of broader institutional, ideational, and political changes in American politics between 1965 and 2005.

More broadly, I demonstrate how the struggle to define the federal role in school reform played a central role in national electoral politics and in inter- and intraparty debates during the 1980s and 1990s over the appropriate role of the national government in promoting opportunity and social welfare. I develop a framework that can be utilized to examine the evolution of policymaking in a particular issue area over time and use the case of education to analyze how national politicians and political parties use salient policy issues in the pursuit of electoral advantage. I argue that a comprehensive understanding of major policy change—such as that in the No Child Left Behind law—requires a historical approach that draws from the American political development tradition and weaves together the complex interplay among a variety of political forces in a policy area over time.

The first chapter of the book provides a more detailed introduction to the questions that guide the study, places recent developments in federal education policy in historical perspective, and surveys the existing literature on the subject. Chapter 2 places the evolution of federal education policy into the context of broader theoretical debates in political science about the nature of the American policymaking system. It presents the idea of a policy regimes framework as an alternative to the punctuated equilibrium model that is widely utilized in contemporary research on public policy. Chapter 3 provides a brief overview of the early federal role in U.S. schools (up to 1988) and emphasizes the powerful traditions of local control and decentralization in our nation's educational policymaking. It also documents the forces that began to challenge the principle of local control in the second half of the twentieth century and that led to the creation (in 1965) and subsequent expansion of the first major federal education program, the Elementary and Secondary Education Act (ESEA).

The release of *A Nation at Risk* in 1983 cast doubt on ESEA's effectiveness and on the performance of the U.S. public school system more generally and initiated a prolonged reassessment of the proper federal role in education reform. Chapters 4 through 8 examine how and why federal education policy evolved during the next twenty years. The central premise underlying these chapters is that federal education policy cannot be understood without placing it in the context of broader political developments, particularly those surrounding partisan electoral competition, ideological debates, public opinion, and institutions. Chapter 4 traces the un-successful effort of George H. W. Bush to shift the focus of federal education policy to standards-based reform with America 2000. Chapter 5 examines the important role that education played in Bill Clinton's centrist New Democrat philosophy and his success in laying the ideational foundation of a new federal education policy regime. Goals 2000 and the 1994 changes to ESEA shifted the focus of federal policy from resources to student achievement and encouraged states to adopt standards and accountability reforms.

The entrance of the federal government into new areas of education policy, however, led to an aggressive effort—described in Chapter 6—by a newly empowered Republican congressional majority to eliminate the U.S. Department of Education and roll back federal influence over schools through decentralization and privatization. But the emergence of education as a crucial electoral issue in the mid-1990s ultimately led GOP leaders to shift their focus from eliminating the federal role to reforming it. Chapter 7 discusses how the Republican shift—combined with many Democrats' increasing frustration with the slow pace of educational improvement—produced a growing convergence between the parties around standards, accountability, and choice. Chapter 8 describes the central role education played in the 2000 presidential election and the influence the election, in turn, had on federal education policy. Chapter 9 details the negotiations over the No Child Left Behind Act, the forces that shaped its final provisions, and the ways in which the law constitutes a new federal education policy regime. It also analyzes the first few years of the implementation of the new law by states and school districts and the status of public and elite opinion about it. The conclusion, Chapter 10, first summarizes the key moments in the evolution of federal education policy, and then uses the case of education to generalize about the nature of contemporary American politics and policymaking, and in particular about the increased responsiveness of policymakers to public opinion on salient issues.

Education is a fascinating and complex subject because it is intimately connected to children, jobs, taxes, religion, race, and class—in other words, to many of the most important and vexing issues confronting government and society. Since the founding of the United States, public education has been identified as the central means by which the country can promote social cohesion, civic virtue, and economic development. In the twenty-first century, social fissures, civic apathy, and the competitive pressures of the global economy have only enhanced the importance of education to our nation's well-being. Our public schools are still regarded as having deep problems, despite enormous amounts of federal attention and spending—and this book hopes to illuminate why the increased federal role in promoting reform has not been more effective. Only by understanding the unique dynamics of federal education politics will reformers be able to craft a more effective national role in school reform. And if the United States is to more fully realize its ideal of being the land of opportunity, improving public education is clearly a necessary, if not sufficient, condition.

This book began as a doctoral dissertation in government at the University of Virginia and would not have been possible without the guidance and support of many wonderful and remarkable people. Jim Ceaser, my adviser at the University of Virginia, has been a dedicated mentor, a true mensch, and a steadfast friend, and I consider it an honor and a privilege to have had the opportunity to learn from him and to know him. I have been repeatedly amazed at the incredible breadth and depth of his knowledge and his passion for all things political. Sid Milkis and Martha Derthick provided invaluable guidance from the beginning of the project, drawing on their extensive knowledge and scholarship in politics, policy, and history. I was also very fortunate to study under and research with Rick Hess, one of the most astute scholars of the politics of education, and someone who inspired and equipped me to think critically about school reform. Brian Balogh and Gareth Davies read the entire manuscript and provided an invaluable historical perspective on my research, and Larry Sabato helped me to remember that "politics is a good thing."

I am extremely grateful for the research support that I received from the University of Virginia Faculty Senate and from a predoctoral fellowship in American Political Development at the Miller Center for Public Affairs. The Miller Center arranged for Maris Vinovskis from the University of Michigan to be a dissertation mentor, and I continue to benefit tremendously from his intellect and guidance. A postdoctoral fellowship at the Taubman Center for Public Policy and American Institutions at Brown University provided the time and resources to revise the manuscript and prepare it for publication. I am very grateful to the Taubman Center's director, Darrell West, for his guidance and support and to Carl Kaestle for sharing his immense knowledge and insights about education policy with me. Sandy Maisel and the faculty in the political science department at Colby College helped me to refine the work's central arguments during the year I spent there as a visiting professor. My colleagues in political science at Drew University provide a stimulating and supportive intellectual community for which I am extremely appreciative.

Jeff Henig and Katie McDermott gave generously of their time and insight while reviewing the book for the University Press of Kansas, and I am enormously grateful for their queries and suggestions, which greatly improved the project. Fred Woodward was a strong advocate for the book at Kansas, and a very kind, supportive, and patient editor throughout the entire process. I am also grateful to Susan McRory and Susan Schott at the press for their considerable efforts in producing and marketing the book. I would like to thank the many people in education policy whom I interviewed for this project for sharing their experiences and views with me. My gratitude also goes out to the many stimulating teachers and engaging students whom I have been blessed to work with throughout my life—it is in large measure because of them that I have chosen to enter academia and why I find my job enormously invigorating and rewarding.

And last, I would like to thank my family for all of their love, encouragement, and support, and for providing me with the kind of educational opportunities that I hope one day are available to all. This book is dedicated to the three ladies at the center of my life: my brilliant and devoted wife, Ilana, who is my biggest champion and my best friend; and our two incredible daughters, Bailey and Carigan, who are the greatest blessing and a daily inspiration to improve the world that our children will inherit.

1. Introduction—
Federal Education Policy
in Historical Perspective

For most of our nation's history, control of public education has been left almost entirely in the hands of state and local governments. A limited federal role in providing supplemental funds and categorical programs was created in the 1950s and 1960s, but the national government abstained from involvement in core academic and governance issues until the 1990s. On January 8, 2002, however, President George W. Bush signed into law the No Child Left Behind (NCLB) Act, which dramatically changed and expanded the federal role in elementary and secondary education policy. The new law represents the consolidation of a reform movement that began in the wake of the 1983 *A Nation at Risk* report; it was the most sweeping transformation of federal education policy since the Elementary and Secondary Education Act (ESEA) of 1965.

The original ESEA was narrowly targeted (to disadvantaged students), focused on inputs (providing additional resources to schools), and contained few federal mandates. In contrast, NCLB embraces a much broader scope (it applies to all schools and students), is focused on outputs (measuring academic performance), and is remarkably prescriptive. The law significantly increased federal education spending, mandates that states design and administer proficiency tests to all students in grades three through eight, requires states to put a qualified teacher in every classroom, and promises to hold states accountable for the performance of their public schools by mandating a variety of corrective measures for schools that do not make adequate yearly progress toward 100 percent student proficiency.

Elementary and secondary education policy is now widely considered—by the American public and key elements of both major political parties—to be an important *federal* responsibility, a remarkable contrast with the decentralized and even individualistic views of schooling that were dominant before the Great Society and ESEA. Though the funding and day-to-day administrative control of U.S. public schools remain decentralized, the politics of education has been nationalized to a degree unprecedented in the country's history, and the federal government's influence over education policy has never been greater. Whereas the Republican Party traditionally fought against the encroachment of the national government on states' rights, President Bush made a robust federal role in education the centerpiece of his campaign for office and his administration's domestic program. Forty years after a major political battle was fought over whether the federal government should give aid to education, and less than ten years after the very existence of a federal Department of Education was fiercely debated, schools are now subject to detailed federal regulations encompassing a wide range of areas and actions.

UNDERSTANDING THE EVOLUTION OF FEDERAL EDUCATION POLICY

The federal role in education is sizable and increasing; voters report that education is one of their top concerns, and education has become a central issue in national politics and elections. Political scientists, however, have devoted relatively little scholarly attention to education policy generally and even less to understanding the evolution of the federal role in education and its influence on partisan politics. As Mary McGuire has observed, "There appears to be less emphasis on political science research of education policy issues than their prominence in American political discourse would warrant. . . . Important political science journals show significantly more coverage of health policy issues and social welfare policy issues than they do of education policy issues."[1] Two recent collections of essays on U.S. public policy in the 1990s by prominent scholars, for example, essentially ignore the issue of education. *The Social Divide,* edited by Margaret Weir (1998), focuses on social policymaking and political parties at the national level and contains chapters on health care, wages and jobs, crime, welfare, race, and urban policy but none on education. (Indeed, a search of the index finds only two references to education in the book's 550 pages.) *Seeking the Center,* edited by Martin Levin, Marc Landy, and Martin Shapiro (2001), focuses on national politics and policy-making in the twenty-first century but barely mentions education in its 450 pages. In twelve chapters devoted to a wide variety of policy areas—what the book jacket called "every important policy area over the past several years"—there is no chapter on education. Political scientists have researched education policy at the state and local levels and in recent years have devoted a great deal of attention to school choice, but the existing body of research on federal education policy is sparse and makes little attempt to analyze the political dynamics that have shaped federal education policies.

The few studies of federal educational policymaking that do exist tend to be apolitical (by viewing debates over education reform divorced from their wider political context), ahistorical (by viewing debates over particular education re-forms divorced from their wider historical context), and atheoretical (by offering descriptions but not explanations for changes in education policymaking). As a result, in 2004 Jennifer Hochschild declared that "political scientists have paid too little attention to the politics and policy of education in the United States" and that the passage of NCLB was one of

> three puzzles in search of an answer from political scientists. . . .
>
> Why would elected officials endorse such a reform, and beg voters to hold them accountable for achieving its goals? . . . Political science gives us few theories to explain why these changes have occurred; in fact, it is much better at explaining why they should not have done so. . . . [Why] would Democratic members of Congress and state legislatures promulgate a policy that teachers' unions hate, and why would Republican members of Congress and a conservative Republican president promote a law (NCLB) to enhance the federal role in education, and to prod schools into helping poor, black, and immigrant children—not exactly Republican constituents? . . . Whatever the explanation for the bipartisan movement toward standards-based reform with high-stakes tests, it stands badly in need of some careful analysis by sophisticated political scientists.[2]

In this book I provide such an analysis. More specifically, the passage of NCLB and the development of such a sizable and reform-oriented federal role in elementary and secondary education policy present three distinct puzzles, the investigation of which will frame the analytical inquiries of this book. The first puzzle relates to the politics of education: why did liberals and conservatives come together in 2002 to support an active reform-oriented federal role in education centered on standards, accountability, and choice that they had each opposed for many years? NCLB is extraordinary given the longstanding opposition of conservatives and states' rights advocates to federal influence over schools and the desire of many liberals to keep the federal role narrowly focused on providing funds and supplemental programs, particularly for disadvantaged students.

The second puzzle concerns governmental activism, for NCLB is also remarkable when placed in the context of the nation's history of decentralized school governance. Why did this new, expanded role in federal education emerge, particularly during a period of deregulation and decentralization in which even Democrats such as Bill Clinton declared the era of big government to be over? The conditions—both in education and in the broader political environment—seemed aligned against a major expansion of the federal role in education. As a result, most observers in the late 1980s and early 1990s believed that the rollback of federal influence in education that occurred during Ronald Reagan's presidency (1981–1989) would be permanent and that the future prospects for an expanded role in school reform were dim. David Clark and Terry Astuto, for example, wrote in 1990 that "the best prediction for federal educational policy, programs, and funds over the next decade is low priority, few initiatives, and declining fiscal support."[3] Just four years prior to the passage of NCLB, Jack Jennings emphasized that the "sharp partisan divisions and a rupturing of support for national programs aiding public schools" that he observed in Congress in the mid-1990s boded poorly for a vibrant federal role.[4] At about the same time, Frederick Wirt and Michael Kirst predicted that "the future of federal [education] aid appears to be policy incrementalism," noting that "there are no dramatic new proposals emanating from President Clinton or congressional leaders to expand the federal role substantially."[5] The predictions of these scholars ended up being remarkably incorrect—why?

The third puzzle is a theoretical one: how can we account for major policy change such as that of NCLB given the large body of political science literature that emphasizes the many institutional obstacles to policy change, and the ability of interest groups and narrow party constituencies to block public demands for policy reform. In particular, how can we explain major policy change that does not fit the dominant model of punctuated equilibrium (established by Frank Baumgartner and Bryan Jones and detailed in Chapter 2)? I will argue that NCLB can best be understood through the use of a *policy regimes framework* that places contemporary political and policy developments in their historical context and explains how reformers were able to overcome both institutional and political obstacles to policy change.[6]

The concept of a policy regime derives from the American political development literature and consists of a particular conception of the ends and means of government programs, an institutional arrangement that structures policymaking in that area, and a political configuration that defends the regime from reformers (see Chapter 2). A central argument here is that the evolution of federal education policy cannot be understood apart from broader developments in U.S. politics and that our understanding of contemporary U.S. politics must accord a prominent role to education. This analysis will show that education has held a central position in partisan conflict—both in the electorate and in government—since 1983 because the issue resonated powerfully with key constituent groups in both parties and with the public at large.

The Republican and Democratic parties attempted to capitalize on the increasing salience of school reform with voters in the 1980s and 1990s and to use the issue of education to reposition themselves ideologically and to appeal to moderate voters. Bill Clinton and, later, George W. Bush made the issue a lynchpin of their efforts to craft new, politically more appealing public philosophies for their parties following the demise of the New Deal and Reagan coalitions. Both leaders seized on the issue of education for its own sake and because of its ability to advance their wider efforts to appear more moderate on social policy and to appeal to crucial swing voters in an era of partisan parity. Clinton used education to emphasize the New Democratic commitment to opportunity over entitlement and to distance his party from the discredited policies of the welfare state. Bush highlighted education to emphasize that conservatism could be compassionate and would address the problems of the poor and disadvantaged. These electoral appeals further increased the salience of education with voters and led to additional public pressure on national policymakers to enact increasingly more comprehensive reforms and thus to expand federal involvement in school governance.

However, it would be a mistake to view the expansion of the federal role in education or the shape that role ultimately took as inevitable. Those who sought to reform federal education policies and to refocus the national government's role on promoting academic achievement faced many obstacles. They had to overcome the numerous inertial forces in the U.S. political system that block policy change and to undo a policy regime that had dominated policymaking in education for more than twenty years. The many institutional checks and balances built into the political system provide multiple veto points for organized interests to block efforts to create or reform programs that go against their preferences. As a result, government programs and policies often become path dependent and resistant to change. In the case of education, strong forces on both the left and the right opposed using the federal government to promote rigorous school reform; this led to a number of intense fights over federal education policy throughout the 1980s and 1990s. The development of an active and reform-oriented federal role in education proceeded in fits and starts and was strongly influenced by wider political developments.

The story of the evolution and expansion of the federal role in education is in many ways a story of how the Democratic and Republican parties overcame (or ignored) the opposition of key constituent groups to adopt new positions on school reform. We can learn much about contemporary American politics by better understanding the circumstances that favor closed, interest group–driven policymaking and those that encourage a more open, public opinion–driven process. Because the former arrangement will often favor the status quo and the latter will tend to be more reform-oriented, an exploration of the role of interest groups in policymaking and the nature of policy change at the beginning of the twenty-first century also can provide insights into questions of governmental efficiency and democratic representation.

The reform movement that culminated in the 2002 No Child Left Behind law dramatically transformed and expanded the federal role in elementary and secondary education and did so in ways that had long been opposed by powerful constituent groups within the Democratic and Republican parties. Liberal interest groups such as the National Education Association (NEA) and the National Association for the Advancement of Colored People (NAACP)—which represent two of the most important electoral blocks in the Democratic Party—had long resisted standards, testing, and accountability measures such as choice and had sought to keep the federal role narrowly focused on providing funds for new programs and services, primarily for disadvantaged students. Religious, antigovernment, and states' rights conservatives, meanwhile—represented by groups such as the Christian Coalition, the Heritage Foundation, and Empower America—had fought efforts to expand the federal government's role in education and had even sought during the 1980s and 1990s to eliminate that role altogether.

Remarkably, NCLB significantly expanded the federal role in school reform and did so by mandating that states adopt standards, testing, and accountability measures including choice. NCLB thus transformed the federal role in education in ways that powerful liberal and conservative groups opposed. Although many of these groups actively fought against the bill itself, it not only survived the legislative process but also did so with bipartisan support. Understanding how and why this occurred is essential not only for educational reformers but also for political scientists.

In recent years several different interpretations of NCLB have emerged. These interpretations, however, have painted an incomplete—and in some cases inaccurate—picture of the evolution of federal education policy, which has important consequences for our understanding of the law's origins and future. Most journalistic coverage of NCLB, for example, has ignored the historical roots of the law and implied that support for it among national policymakers was tentative. In this view, Democratic and Republican agreement on NCLB was largely due to the convergence of a variety of short-term and contingent factors.[7] Rather than resulting from any major shifts in the positions of the parties on school reform or in educational federalism, NCLB's passage reflected such things as the pressure on Republicans to support their new president on his first legislative proposal and the desire of Democrats to secure additional federal money for schools. Though such issues were not insignificant, the focus on short-term factors ignores important longer-term developments in school reform, electoral politics, and partisan views on federal education policy, which had by 2000 produced a strong bipartisan consensus about the need for an active, reformed federal role in education centered on standards, accountability, and choice.

Other interpretations of NCLB have acknowledged that the law was made possible by longer-term developments but claim that it largely represents a continuation of earlier state and federal reform efforts. Some scholars have argued that NCLB does not represent a major shift in federal education policy but rather is simply an incremental extension of the 1994 reforms contained in Goals 2000 and the Improving America's Schools Act. Lorraine McDonnell, for example, has written that "although NCLB has expanded federal regulation, this newest version [of ESEA] reflects an evolution of the federal role rather than a radical redefinition."[8]

Whereas McDonnell sees NCLB largely as a continuation of earlier federal education reforms, Paul Manna has emphasized its derivation from earlier *state* education reform efforts. He has advanced what he calls a "bottom-up agenda setting" model to explain the passage of NCLB and argues that state activity on education reform put pressure on the federal government to embrace standards, accountability, and choice.[9]

Although McDonnell is certainly correct that NCLB has roots in the national standards-based reforms begun in 1994, the addition of tough federal timetables and mandatory outcome-based accountability in NCLB are so different and significant as to constitute a revolution in federal education policy. Put another way, the 1994 reforms to ESEA marked an important shift in ideas, but those reforms were largely toothless and unenforced. As a result, by the spring of 2002, shortly after the passage of NCLB, only sixteen states had fully met the requirements of the 1994 law. In essence, then, Goals 2000 *encouraged* states to create standards, testing, and accountability systems, but NCLB *requires* it. The Education Commission of the States summarizes the difference between the 1994 and 2002 reforms in this way:

> NCLB . . . represents a more systemic approach to achieving reform and improvement, tying together a variety of requirements and incentives in areas ranging from student testing, school safety and reading instruction, to professional development for teachers to technical assistance for low-performing schools. Second, it significantly raises the stakes—for states, districts, and schools—for failure to make steady, demonstrable progress toward improving student achievement.[10]

And though Manna's work illuminates the important role that state school reform activity played in pushing education to the top of the federal agenda, it is less useful in understanding the particular policy outcomes that emerged once the issue pierced the federal agenda. The widespread adoption of standards and accountability reforms in the states during the 1980s and 1990s clearly played an important role in legitimizing these reforms and building elite and public support for them at the national level. As noted previously, however, NCLB contained a number of elements that were strongly opposed by states, factions of the Republican and Democratic parties, and powerful interest groups. States have always welcomed federal education funding, but they have fought vigorously to protect their policymaking autonomy over schools. Yet NCLB forces states to change their education policies in a number of major ways. For example, though forty-eight states had standards and tests in place in 2000, only thirteen states were testing students every year in reading and math between the third and eighth grades, as NCLB now requires, and even fewer had strong accountability systems of the sort mandated by the new law. Thus, prior to NCLB, even in the states that had standards and tests in place there were few consequences for schools that failed to perform well. NCLB's significance is in mandating that *all* states adopt a standards and testing regime, that they conform to federal timetables for achieving student proficiency, and that they suffer real consequences for failing to do so. The numerous policy mandates contained in NCLB were thus far from the states' preferred type of federal education policy at the time of passage. In addition, some of the strongest opposition to the law has come from those states (such as Virginia) that had most aggressively adopted standards-base reforms prior to 2002.

The interpretations of NCLB as merely a continuation or incremental expansion of previous education reforms are consequential because they underestimate the impact that the requirements of the new law are having on schools across the nation as well as the magnitude of the shift in national education politics that occurred between 1994 and 2002. Clinton's 1994 education reforms created an important ideational foundation upon which NCLB was later built. If, however, NCLB is essentially a continuation of Clinton's Democratic education reforms embraced strategically by a Republican presidential candidate to appeal to swing voters, it is reasonable to presume that the GOP's commitment to supporting and implementing the law would be weak. Similarly, if Democrats remain wedded to an equity approach and merely agreed to support NCLB in exchange for greater federal funding for schools, then we should not expect them to be particularly devoted to the law's reforms and mandates.

In addition, a focus on state education politics and reform efforts can lead to the mistaken impression that it will be state policymakers alone who ultimately determine the fate of NCLB. It is important to recognize that the law's future rests in equal measure on political developments at the national level and that these developments are only partly related to state preferences and pressures. In a 1994 analysis of Goals 2000, Michael Mintrom and Sandra Vergari concluded that "state and local education interests have the political capacity to shape federal programs to their liking."[11] Although that may have been true in the mid-1990s, when the national Republican Party was engaged in a vigorous defense of states' rights and decentralization in education, it seems much less true today given changes in the politics of educational federalism.

Many commentators expressed shock at the GOP's support of NCLB because of the party's perceived abandonment of its longstanding support for states' rights. Some have even predicted that these principles will inevitably resurface and that the party will back away from NCLB and federal activism in education. This analysis ignores that Republicans in Congress embraced federal activism in education in the late 1990s *before* George W. Bush and for political and policy reasons that are deeper—and less mutable—than often supposed. That Republicans abandoned their defense of states' rights in education when the political costs became too high should not surprise scholars of federalism. Timothy Conlan surveyed federalism in the Nixon and Reagan administrations and in the 104th Congress and found that "those holding power in Washington will naturally seek to use it. . . . Conservative Republicans are often tempted to use and even expand federal authority when they have the opportunity to do so."[12] Overall, he concluded that "neither party, it would seem, is willing to sacrifice the opportunity for federal involvement in state and local activities that hold political appeal."[13] This fundamental political dynamic of federalism remains in place today. As a result, state implementation challenges and protestations about NCLB—while important—will not by themselves be determinative in debates over the future of the federal role in education.

In sum, all three of these interpretations of the origins of NCLB underestimate the cause and extent of the political shifts in the Democratic and Republican parties that enabled the law to be passed and that are likely to sustain federal activism in education over the long term. If NCLB was really just a response to short-term political factors, did not reflect a new bipartisan consensus on federal education policy, or is dependent on state preferences, then the law's political future—and its ability to survive what will be a long and painful implementation process—would clearly be suspect. But the act represents a transformative shift in federal education policy—not merely a new policy but a new policy regime as it embodies a different set of ideas, interests, and institutions for federal education policy. The origins and future prospects of this regime can only be fully understood in the context of a variety of developments in education, electoral politics, and federalism that have unfolded over time and in a way that make it unlikely that this new regime will be replaced in the near future.

EDUCATION AND CONTEMPORARY AMERICAN POLITICS
AND POLICYMAKING

This book provides an in-depth historical and political analysis of an important but understudied time period in American national educational policymaking to enhance our understanding of the interaction between American educational reform movements and the country's policymaking institutions. As Frederick Wirt and Michael Kirst noted in their recent survey of the literature in this area, "The [current] gaps in education politics research will hinder our ability to devise policy solutions to many urgent education problems."[14] It also hopes to increase our theoretical and substantive understanding of the nature of American politics and policymaking at the beginning of the twenty-first century. The project uses the case of federal education policy to demonstrate how a historically based policy regimes framework can illuminate the gradual shifting of ideas, interests, and institutions in a policy area over time that can ultimately bring about major policy change. The framework is based on the insights derived from the study of political regimes in the American political development literature and emphasizes that particular policy regimes are less stable than the "punctuated equilibrium" model would suggest. It argues that the policymaking process in any particular issue area is best characterized not by short bursts of dynamic reform amidst long periods of policy stasis but rather of gradual regime construction, maintenance, enervation, and reconstruction.

The policy regimes framework offers a way to analyze how national politicians and political parties use salient policy issues in the pursuit of electoral advantage, and the consequences of these efforts for public policy. The national politics of education provide an opportunity to see how an issue was raised from the periphery to the center of political discourse, when and why it rose as it did, and the effect its rise had on broader political debates. In the chapters that follow, I will explain how education became a key battleground in the war of ideas that was waged between the Democratic and Republican parties over social welfare and governmental activism during the 1980s and 1990s and how the debate over the federal role in schools has had and continues to have major repercussions in American politics.

2. The Politics of Policy Regimes

Political scientists have long debated the nature of the American political system, particularly the degree to which the federal government is amenable to major policy initiation and reform. There are two basic schools of thought on this question. One school—which we will call the *stasis school*—argues that the system is highly resistant to major change. The other school of policymaking—which we will call the *dynamic school*—emphasizes the openness and responsiveness of our political system and the relative ease of generating reform at the national level. Although the stasis and dynamic schools are helpful in explaining systemic tendencies and the influence of particular forces on the policy process, they are less useful in illuminating the evolution of governmental policymaking in a single issue area over time.

Dynamic approaches correctly identify the *potential* for policy change in the political system, but history validates the stasis school's claim that extensive reform within a particular issue area is, in reality, quite infrequent. It does nonetheless take place, and this chapter will draw from both schools in articulating a policy regimes framework that specifies the mechanisms by which major policy change occurs *within a specific policy arena*. By "major change" we do not mean the perpetual fine-tuning and incremental ebb and flow of policymaking but the more fundamental reshaping of policy ends and means, such as one finds in the 2002 No Child Left Behind (NCLB) education law.

A policy regime is the set of ideas, interests, and institutions that structures governmental activity in a particular issue area (such as health care, transportation, etc.) and that tends to be quite durable over time. A policy regimes framework draws on the insights of the stasis school to understand the factors that allow policies to withstand pressures for major change for many years, but it relies more heavily on the dynamic school to comprehend how inertial forces are eventually overcome and a new regime constructed. It offers an alternative to the "punctuated equilibrium" model, developed by Frank Baumgartner and Bryan Jones, in which major policy change is seen as resulting from short bursts of rapid reform after a long period of hegemony by a policy monopoly. The policy regimes framework draws from the American political development literature's study of *political* regimes to argue that individual policy regimes are less stable—and change, when it occurs, less rapid—than the "policy monopoly" model would suggest.

THE STASIS SCHOOL AND THE POLITICS
OF THE STATUS QUO

Political scientists have frequently observed that the American political system contains numerous inertial forces that reinforce the status quo and limit major policy change. The stasis school does not say that major change *never* occurs, but it emphasizes the forces that make policymaking configurations and policies highly durable and stable over time. It has several variants. One places the emphasis on American political culture and strong public support for free enterprise, limited government, and local control, which make efforts to create national programs and regulations difficult.[1] Another stresses the character of the U.S. constitutional system and, in particular, the fragmentation of its policymaking institutions. Federalism, separation of powers, and checks and balances create a system of multiple veto points that opponents can use to protect existing policy arrangements and thwart reform proposals.[2] Other variants of the stasis school add to the systemic explanation something more general about the character of policymaking itself. Incremental and bureaucratic models, for example, emphasize the limitations on decisionmaking and implementation processes that incline complex systems toward only minor change.[3]

A large and powerful class of interest-group actors can utilize these veto points and their influence over the bureaucracy to block initiatives that threaten their interests.[4] Together with politicians and bureaucrats, these groups establish "iron triangles" that reinforce the status quo and make major policy creation or change extremely difficult. The general apathy and inattention of the general public to politics, meanwhile, largely permits a "power elite" to control government unimpeded by citizen vigilance.[5] Citizens generally have low levels of political information and interest, and politicians can mask their unresponsiveness through procedural mechanisms or shift public attention to other issues. As a result, policymakers are more likely to be responsive to mobilized interest groups or party activists than to the public at large.[6]

In this environment, elites work to create "policy monopolies" around issues— political alliances, institutional configurations, and conceptual understandings that structure the participation and policymaking in that area for many years.[7] Policies generate patterns of political mobilization, citizens' ways of thinking about the issue, and institutional structures that become "sticky" and "locked in" and very difficult to change. Initial policymaking in a particular area often generates "positive feedback" and "increasing returns" and becomes "self-reinforcing" over time. These subsystems gain public acceptance of (or at least deference to) a favorable conception of their issue that they then utilize to dominate their particular policy area by limiting access and proposals for radical change. These causal stories or buttressing policy ideas are generally connected to core political values (such as progress, fairness, and economic growth) that are sold to the public through the use of image and rhetoric.[8]

The generally inattentive nature of the American public means that public mobilization on behalf of policy reform is rare and infrequent. The overwhelming number of issues facing Congress and the public at any one time also ensures that Congress will often delegate much discretion to policy subsystems and that few issues stay on the public agenda for long.[9] It is in this vacuum of public, media, and congressional attention that policy monopolies thrive.[10] Beneficiaries of the policy defend the status quo against reforms that threaten their interests, and it becomes difficult—if not impossible—to change the direction of the program or to eliminate it. As a result, government policies and programs tend to become path dependent.[11] Paul Pierson has argued that "most policies are remarkably durable" and that "political arrangements are unusually hard to change." He continues, "Key features of political life, both public policies and (especially) formal institutions, are change-resistant. . . . Formal barriers to reform are thus often extremely high . . . [as the] institutional stickiness characteristic of political systems reinforces the already considerable obstacles to movement off of an established path."[12]

For these reasons, major change in federal programs is difficult to bring about and tends to come only slowly and incrementally.[13] In her study of social security policymaking, for example, Martha Derthick has demonstrated how the program was long viewed as politically untouchable and how established interest groups worked with policymakers and administrative officials to protect and gradually expand it. "The nature of policymaking did little to correct, but instead reinforced, a complacent, poorly informed acceptance of the program—participation was so narrowly confined; expert, proprietary dominance was so complete; debate was so limited . . . and the forward steps seemed so small . . . conflict was muted and narrowly contained. Other courses of action than orthodox, incremental measures of expansion received little attention."[14] In the interest group, path dependency, and incrementalist approaches, policymaking becomes a closed and static process characterized by iron triangles, subgovernments, issue networks, or policy monopolies, with policies modified only in minor ways, if at all. This view of the American policymaking system helps to explain why major policy change is rare, but it is less useful in understanding those cases, such as federal education policy, in which the ends and means of government policies are fundamentally altered.

THE DYNAMIC SCHOOL AND THE POLITICS
OF POLICY CHANGE

How is major policy change possible in a system with such strong and varied inertial forces? Even political scientists who emphasize the closed or unresponsive nature of the American policymaking process recognize that policies sometimes change. Pierson, for example, has written about path dependence theory that "asserting that the social landscape can be permanently frozen hardly is credible . . . and that is not the claim. Change continues but it is bounded change—until something erodes or swamps the mechanisms of reproduction that generate continuity."[15] This formulation, however, simply begs the question, What factors lead the mechanisms of reproduction to be "swamped"?

The dynamic school emphasizes that the keys to understanding policy change are electoral competition and public pressure. Politicians in a republic with frequent elections have strong incentives to be mindful of the "electoral connection" by responding to changing public policy demands.[16] The result, as James Stimson, Michael MacKuen, and Robert Erikson concluded in their study of a wide range of domestic policies, is that politicians behave "like antelopes in an open field. . . . When politicians perceive public opinion change, they adapt their behavior to please their constituency."[17] Although the general political apathy of the American public often permits policy monopolies to exist unimpeded for long periods of time, an apathetic public is always a latent political force. As E. E. Schattschneider has noted, "many conflicts are narrowly confined by a variety of devices," but "there is usually nothing to keep the audience from getting into the game."[18] The mobilization of public pressure behind policy change effectively expands the "scope of conflict" and can have a major impact on policy outcomes.[19]

Party competition provides a natural and recurring incentive for the expansion of conflict—for drawing public attention to policy issues. Anthony Downs has observed that strategically minded party leaders try to raise new issues that cross party lines or "trespass" on the issues of the other party in order to expand their electoral coalition.[20] Policy entrepreneurs inside and outside of government also spur policy change by "going public"—bringing problems to the attention of the media and citizens to generate political support for new ways of thinking about old issues.[21] Exogenous shocks to the political system can also lead to policy change by drawing public and elite attention to the failure of existing programs or their inappropriateness to new conditions.[22] Disasters, wars, economic crises, scandals, and even the release of new research can challenge the status quo and create conditions favorable to policy change.[23] The fragmentation of the American political system, meanwhile, offers many opportunities for reformers to redefine issues or seek change through an alternate institutional venue. Proposals for policy change that are rejected in one institutional setting, for example, can be reintro-duced in another.

Electoral competition ensures that existing policy approaches will be frequently challenged and that political leaders will seek public support for the creation of new policies or the reform of existing ones. Public pressure for reform can be a powerful agent for policy change when it reaches a "critical mass" that can overcome the stasis orientation of the policymaking system.[24] Some scholars have even argued that secular changes in the American political system since the 1980s have reduced the power of inertial forces in policymaking and made major policy change in the contemporary era easier to accomplish.[25] The stasis school's emphasis on the power of interest groups and other inertial forces misses the important reality that politi-cians and policy entrepreneurs often have incentives to expand the scope of con-flict and to challenge existing policies. Clearly, however, there are many obstacles to policy reform, and the outcome of any individual reform effort will depend on the status of the dominant policy approach, the political strength of the status quo coalition, and the relationship of the policy issue to broader partisan conflict.

A POLICY REGIMES FRAMEWORK

Political scientists have generally focused on periods of relative stability or pe-riods of rapid change in policy areas and have devoted less effort to explaining the transition from one to the other. Studies of policy change also tend to focus either on aggregate change across all issue areas or on the influence of particular institutions, actors, or events in driving change. In order to understand the origins of policy change in a particular issue area, however, it is necessary to develop a framework that weaves together the complex interplay among ideas, interests, and institutions over time and that analyzes the impact of public opinion and elec-toral pressures on political strategy and partisan competition.[26] What is needed is a more *integrative* approach to studying policymaking—one that synthesizes the insights of both the stasis and dynamic approaches and that incorporates the institutional insights of political science with the ideational and group focus of sociologists and the longer temporal reach of historians.

Such a framework must be based on the recognition that the national policy-making process exhibits very different characteristics across time and space. At cer-tain moments and on certain types of issues, politicians are generally quite respon-sive to reform pressures; at other times and on other issues, the forces of the status quo are likely to defeat the forces of change. This is not to say that a general theory of policy change is unobtainable, but rather that it must carefully specify how the American political system can produce both long periods of policy stability and periods of extensive policy change. Such an approach must also dispense with attempts to quantify the influence of single causal variables on policymaking. Policymaking is a complex process involving a wide variety of actors, institutions, and forces, and the crucial question is not which element is the most important but rather how they interact to produce policy change. Similarly, the macro-level debate over whether the anti- or pro-change view of policymaking is more accurate is less useful than specifying the conditions under which policies are amenable to change and when they are not.

The recent work of Baumgartner and Jones on agenda-setting offers the most promising effort to date in explaining policy change.[27] They argue that whereas no general equilibrium is possible in the policymaking process, it is best described as a system of punctuated equilibria featuring long periods of policy stability and short periods of rapid and dramatic change. Baumgartner and Jones's contribution to our understanding of the dynamics of policy change has been enormous, but their work focuses largely on agenda setting, and they devote less attention to exploring what happens after policy monopolies are destroyed and issues opened up for reconsideration. As they note in their more recent work,

> The punctuated equilibrium perspective directs our attention to how governmental institutions and policy ideas interact—sometimes yielding stability, sometimes yielding punctuations. But the particular network of causation has not been fully analyzed. More than anything else, we need case studies of particular policy arenas cast within a framework that is sensitive to institutional constraints and incentives and the nature of ideas and arguments put forward by the participants.[28]

In addition, Baumgartner and Jones's work emphasizes that the American policymaking system tends toward equilibrium—and that when this equilibrium is occasionally punctured by an issue that rises to the public agenda, a new policy monopoly will arise and enforce a new status quo that will, in turn, persist for many years.

The punctuated equilibrium view has long gone unchallenged in the political science and public policy literature, but it seems to underestimate the importance of history—and in particular the long-term shifting of ideas, interests, and institutions both within policy areas and in the broader political environment. In part, this may reflect a general reluctance on the part of political science to integrate historical approaches into the empirical analysis of politics and policymaking in a systematic way. This has begun to change in recent years, however, with the publication of Paul Pierson's *Politics in Time*, Karen Orren and Stephen Skowronek's *The Search for American Political Development* (both 2004), and a series of articles in the *Journal of Policy History* and *American Political Development*.[29] Pierson has argued that we must reintegrate history into political science and move away from the current focus on isolating individual causal variables because the significance of such variables is frequently distorted when they are ripped from their temporal context. While most contemporary social scientists take a "snapshot" view of political life, there is often a strong case to be made for shifting from snapshots to moving pictures. This means systematically situating particular moments (including the present) in a temporal sequence of events and processes stretching over extended periods. Placing politics in time can greatly enrich our understanding of complex social dynamics.[30]

The concept of regimes that has been articulated in the American political development literature seems to provide the basis for a new way of incorporating history into the study of public policy and for understanding the politics of policy change. This regimes approach has been utilized by scholars in international relations and comparative politics to study historical shifts in governing coalitions and by economists to examine different eras of financial policy. Recently, Americanists such as Stephen Skowronek have used the idea of regime building in their exploration of the dynamics of presidential politics (1993) and (with Karen Orren) of the origins of the New Deal (1998). Skowronek has also argued in another work (1997) that the opportunity for presidential leadership is dependent on the president's position within and relationship to the political regime cycle. His central insight— that the power of political regimes fluctuates over time and that it is this dynamic that provides the crucial context for transformational leadership—would seem to have great import for the study of the politics of *policy* change as well.

The policy regimes approach offers a systematic framework for analyzing the role of ideas, interests, and institutions in generating major policy change in a specific issue area over time. Policy regimes are organized around specific issue areas and consist of three dimensions—a policy paradigm, a power alignment, and a policymaking arrangement—that combine to produce a distinctive pattern of policymaking and policies.[31] *Power arrangements* can take many different forms but center on the alignment of interest groups and governmental actors on the issue. A *policy paradigm* refers to how the particular issue is conceptualized—how problems, target populations, and solutions are defined by elites and the public. A *policymaking arrangement* is the institutional and procedural context for making decisions about an issue and the implementation process by which these decisions are carried out. The policies created in a particular issue area will thus reflect the regime's particular conception of the ends and means of government programs, the institutional arrangement that structures policymaking in that area, and the goals of the members of the dominant political coalition. These factors play a crucial role both in the establishment of the core policies and programs in a policy area and in the defense of these policies and programs from reformers.

The most thorough application of the concept of a policy regime to the study of change in particular policy areas appears in the work of Richard Harris and

Sidney Milkis (*The Politics of Regulatory Change*, 1996) and Daniel Tichenor (*Dividing Lines: The Politics of Immigration Reform in America*, 2002). Harris and Milkis use a regime approach to examine changes in American regulatory politics and policymaking during the second half of the twentieth century.[32] They identify three components of the regulatory regime: ideas justifying government control over business activity, institutions that structured regulatory policymaking, and the actual set of policies and regulations that were imposed on businesses. Harris and Milkis emphasize that a number of "inertial forces" operated to limit change in the case of regulatory policy. "The character of bureaucracy and American political institutions," they write, "combines with the prevailing public philosophy to generate a great deal of systemic inertia. Changing a regulatory regime in the face of these inertial pressures is a formidable task indeed."[33] They demonstrate how concerns about the impact and effectiveness of regulatory policy grew during the 1980s and coalesced into calls for regulatory reform. Republicans called for deregulation as part of a larger conservative effort to limit the size and cost of government, and the public interest lobby called for new social regulations. Both views demanded a redefinition of the relationship among government, business, and society—including new institutions and policies—and challenged the regulatory status quo. A new policy regime was created, and regulatory politics "hitherto dominated by economic policies and 'special' interests that were the focus of agency action, were restructured to address 'quality of life' issues and provide more avenues for public participation."[34]

In *Dividing Lines*, Tichenor uses a policy regime framework to examine the changing politics and policymaking of immigration throughout U.S. history.[35] More specifically, he seeks to identify distinctive historical patterns of immigration policy and to account for the creation, maintenance, and destruction of immigration policy regimes across American political development. Previous analyses of immigration policy had focused on economic conditions, social interests, national values, and electoral realignments as explanatory variables, but Tichenor argues that these are not adequate to understand how and why different policies emerge. He offers what he calls a "historical-institutional analysis—one that places special emphasis on the interplay of dynamic governing institutions, policy alliances, expertise, and international crises—to illuminate broad patterns and transformations of American immigration policy over time."[36] Tichenor acknowledges "the enormous challenges and complexities of achieving major policy innovation in a fragmented political system replete with veto-points." But his work also shows how broad historical analyses that focus on interlocking political processes can "capture the possibilities of innovation in a U.S. polity whose governing institutions, social interests, and dominant political ideals are often changing."[37]

The studies by Harris and Milkis and Tichenor demonstrate the advantages of a policy regime framework, with its focus on the interplay between ideas, interests, and institutions. The political guardians of a policy regime use the established policy paradigm, power alignment, and policymaking arrangement to protect the status quo. These regimes, however, though vigorously defended and often quite durable, are under almost continuous attack by a variety of forces. Competing political actors actively seek to define and redefine issues in the pursuit of better public policy and/or electoral advantage.[38] Policy entrepreneurs seize on focusing events to draw public attention to new ideas and understandings about old problems and programs.[39] Power shifts and institutional changes within the policy regime and in the broader political system can enable reformers to force a reconsideration of existing policies. Orren and Skowronek have observed, for example, that "the ordering propensities of institutions are about so many points of access to a politics that is essentially open-ended and inherently unsettled. As institutions congeal time, so to speak, within their spheres, they decrease the probability that politics will coalesce into neatly ordered periods, if only because the institutions that constitute the polity at that time will abrade against each other and in the process drive further change."[40] Major policy change is extremely difficult and takes time to bring about because reformers must contend with the political, institutional, and policy remnants of the old regime even as they construct its replacement. Rarely, however, are the different pillars of a policy regime felled at the same time or with a single decisive assault. As a result, the tendency of the policymaking system is not toward equilibrium but toward disequilibrium.

METHODOLOGY: AN AMERICAN POLITICAL DEVELOPMENT APPROACH

This book is predicated on the belief that a comprehensive explanation of the evolution of federal policy and the passage of No Child Left Behind requires a historical analysis of politics and policymaking over an extended period of time. Such an explanation necessitates the incorporation of the wide variety of actors and factors at work in American politics and the ways in which they interact to produce policy. As a result, I have used the following sources of data: legislative histories and voting records on the authorizing, reauthorizing, and appropriations of major federal education programs between 1965–2002; journalistic coverage of education politics and policy; speeches, correspondence, and reports from the Department of Education and in presidential papers; national public opinion data; and interviews with key political actors involved in education policy in Congress, the White

House, the Department of Education, educational interest groups, and national political party organizations (see Appendix).

This kind of historical analysis cannot determine the precise causal impact of individual variables to policy change, but it can substantially enrich our understanding of the forces that interacted to shape politics and policymaking and how these forces changed over time. Orren and Skowronek have noted that American political development research is concerned primarily with "shifts in governing authority" and that such concerns require a particular kind of methodology.

> This is because the study of shifts, by definition, resists containment within predefined institutional boundaries and because relationships among variables are altered as these boundaries change over time. Whereas other research in political science characteristically looks for a causal relationship between two kinds of variables (independent variables that affect changes in dependent variables), development as shifts-in-authority presumes configurative and crosscutting effects, in which feedback and interdependency are omnipresent.[41]

A central theme of this study is that public opinion played a major role in the transformation of federal education policy and that public opinion on swing issues has become a powerful force in American politics and policymaking more generally. The public opinion literature in political science demonstrates that citizen policy preferences are neither completely endogenous nor completely malleable by political actors. I argue that politicians both responded to public opinion shifts on education *and* helped to bring them about. As such, this book incorporates a large amount of survey data with the goal of understanding shifts in public opinion on education and, in particular, public views on the performance of public schools, the level of support and opposition to specific kinds of school reforms, the salience of the education issue to voters, and assessments of the positions of parties and candidates on education issues.[42]

Because many voters do not stand to benefit directly from federal funding for elementary and secondary education—either because they do not have school-aged children or because their children attend private schools or well-performing public schools—it may seem surprising that education would have risen to the top of the national political agenda in the 1990s. Research on political behavior in the United States has found, however, that Americans assume a "sociotropic" view on certain public policy issues. There are times when voters will accord great weight to what they think is best for the community or the nation—not just by what they believe will improve their immediate personal well-being.[43] Such attitudes are especially prevalent when voters are thinking about policies that resonate with their conceptions of a just society or that impact vulnerable and sympathetic populations, as in the case of education. Political parties respond to this by taking positions and crafting messages that appeal not only to voters' self-interest but also to cultural conceptions of American values and ideals. Consequently, it is important to view the political discourse not only through the narrow lens of particular interests but also with an eye to the values that characterize the larger culture.

As noted earlier, however, there is considerable debate in political science about the extent to which public opinion influences policy outcomes in the United States.[44] But as Lawrence Jacobs and Robert Shapiro have noted, the use of public opinion data as an explanatory variable in social science research has become widely accepted.[45] Carl Kaestle remarked in his analysis of "the public schools and the public mood" that "the schools always have had plenty of critics, but widespread reform has succeeded only when there has been a general crisis of confidence in the schools and reformers have solidified public consensus about what changes are needed."[46] The interviews conducted for this book indicated that politicians and policymakers regularly monitored public opinion on education and that it was an important—and often decisive—consideration in electoral and policy discussions.

THE DEVELOPMENT OF A REFORM-ORIENTED FEDERAL EDUCATION POLICY REGIME

An examination of the evolution of federal education policy offers an opportunity to explore the politics of policy regime construction, maintenance, destruction, and reconstruction as well as its relationship to and influence on American political development more generally. The major policy change contained in the No Child Left Behind Act of 2002 is best understood as a response to gradual shifts in the policy regime and broader political environment that played out over a three-decade period. In particular, the emergence of the new federal policy regime in education cannot be understood apart from the deep and growing salience of school reform on the public agenda and its influence on the strategic calculations of political actors. The federal role in education policy has undergone major changes from the original path established in the Elementary and Secondary Education Act (ESEA) of 1965. Public and elite perceptions of a crisis in education, in tandem with changes in the wider political and electoral environment, have led politicians to alter how they look at education policy and to challenge existing arrangements in pursuit of school improvement and electoral gain.

ESEA laid the foundation for a policy regime in education that persisted for almost thirty years. At the heart of this regime was a policy paradigm, meaning a set of views about the nature of the country's educational problems and the appropriate means of government response. The core beliefs of this paradigm were that most public schools were doing fine, that problems were concentrated in schools located in poor areas, and that issues of school governance and improvement were the responsibility of local and state governments. ESEA created a narrow federal role in education and proscribed both the means and ends of national policy—providing additional resources and procedural safeguards to promote equity and access for disadvantaged students. For many years national policymaking in education was largely closed, and this view of the federal role was protected by congressional Democrats (and their majorities) and their interest-group allies, particularly civil rights groups and teachers unions. As a result, during the 1960s and 1970s, the federal role in schools expanded incrementally, though its scope and nature did not change significantly. Some political elites questioned the effectiveness of federal programs and proposed reforms, but the small size and the low salience of education reform with the public and in national politics made it difficult for reformers to gain traction on the issue.

The passage of the report *A Nation at Risk* in 1983 was a crucial focusing event, however, as it undermined the old policy paradigm in education and generated momentum for reform.[47] Led by governors, business organizations, and moderates from both parties concerned about educational opportunity and economic competitiveness, a new push for standards, accountability, and choice began to emerge. As the issue of school reform rose on the national public agenda in the 1980s and 1990s, politicians had incentives to broaden the scope of conflict—to go public—and to use the issue to appeal for political advantage. Politicians responded to the increased salience of education among voters with expanded rhetoric about the need for the federal government to promote school reform. Since the first President Bush's 1988 campaign pledge to be an "education president," education has played an increasingly important role in presidential and congressional election campaigns. As presidents have moved to capitalize on the symbolic and substantive appeal of education, they have encountered resistance not just from the opposition party but also from factions within their own parties. As successful candidates moved from the campaign trail to the White House, these struggles intensified as presidents sought to turn campaign promises into legislative action (and to thereby enhance their own future electoral prospects and those of their party). As a result, a cycle of escalating elite rhetoric, increased public expectations, and political pressure for policy action was established regarding the federal role in education reform.

Regime change would take some time, however, as the guardians of the old regime continued to defend it and both parties faced challenges in attempting to develop federal education reform agendas. The Republican Party consistently had seen education as primarily a state and local responsibility and opposed federal mandates and spending in education. When given control of Congress or the

White House during the 1980s and 1990s, Republicans sought to roll back the federal role in education by slashing programs, spending, and bureaucracy. Even as education rose on the public agenda in the 1990s and the electoral cost of opposing federal activism on education began to grow, many conservative party loyalists remained strongly opposed to it. Democrats, in contrast, with a base of minority, urban, and disadvantaged voters, were inclined to promote a more activist social agenda and expanded federal support for education. Many liberals, however, continued to believe that the key problem facing schools was a lack of sufficient resources. This view, combined with the powerful influence of teachers unions in the Democratic Party, led most Democrats to oppose reforms such as standards, accountability, and choice during the 1970s, 1980s, and 1990s and to focus on increasing federal funding. George H. W. Bush and Bill Clinton advanced reform-oriented education agendas but encountered stiff resistance from both the left and the right and achieved only marginal success in refocusing the federal role on academic achievement.

During the 1990s, however, the rise of education to the very top of the public agenda changed the political dynamics of federal education policy. It became a crucial electoral issue for both parties. With the old policy paradigm increasingly under fire from the left and the right, the parties fought over what the new federal role in schools should be. Voters rejected the preferred education agenda of both liberals and conservatives, and moderates in both parties worked toward a centrist compromise. Interest-group resistance and other inertial forces were ultimately overwhelmed by public pressures that forced Democrats to support reforms (such as accountability and choice) that teachers unions and civil rights groups had long opposed, while Republicans began to support reforms (such as increased federal leadership and spending) that limited-government, states' rights, and religious conservatives had long opposed. The passage of NCLB in 2002 fundamentally changed the ends and means of federal education policy from those put forward in the original ESEA legislation and laid the foundation for a new policy regime. As noted earlier, the old education policy regime was narrowly focused on helping disadvantaged students by promoting equity and access, and it had been governed by a largely congressional and interest group-dominated policymaking process made possible by the issue's low salience with the public. The new education policy regime embraces a broad federal commitment to promoting academic achievement for all students and features a very visible and open policymaking process that is responsive to public pressures and directed by presidential leadership.

Like earlier issues such as poverty, the environment, deregulation, and immigration, education emerged in the 1980s and 1990s from relative obscurity in national politics to assume a prominent place on the federal policymaking agenda.[48] The emergence of each of these issues was due to the development of new policy images that shattered the existing policy paradigm in each area. These new policy images fundamentally altered public and elite perceptions of the nature of the policy problem and the appropriate government response, and in so doing, they changed the political and policymaking dynamics for the issue. The transformation of the education policy regime was distinct from the transformation of the poverty, environmental, regulatory, and immigration policy regimes in at least one crucial respect, however: the debates in these other policy areas never emerged as major electoral issues. Even as they received significant attention from policymakers, their salience to voters remained relatively low. As a result, the destruction of these policy regimes had important policy consequences in defined areas but did not have a major impact on politics more generally. Education, in comparison, was by the mid-1990s viewed by voters as one of the top issues in the country and played a central role in broader debates about promoting opportunity and economic development. This had important ramifications both for how the education policy regime was reconstructed and for the outcome of larger partisan electoral conflicts.[49] Issue evolution in the areas of poverty, the environment, regulation, and immigration resulted in some important changes in policy, but the issue evolution in education reverberated throughout the political system and became one of the central questions of contemporary American electoral politics.

3. The Early Federal Role in Education (to 1988)—ESEA and the Equity Regime

The U.S. Constitution does not mention education. In fact, before the 1950s, education policymaking in our federal system was viewed primarily as a state and local responsibility. As a result, schooling in the United States—in contrast to Europe and much of the rest of the world—has historically been a very decentralized and locally run affair.[1] Education would not assume a prominent place in national politics until the Supreme Court's 1954 *Brown v. Board of Education* decision declared segregated schools unconstitutional and initiated a long and controversial effort to integrate public education. The *Brown* decision, together with the 1965 Elementary and Secondary Education Act (ESEA), initiated a new era of federal activism in education and laid the foundation of a policy regime that was to last for approximately thirty years. At the heart of the ESEA regime was a powerful equity rationale for federal government activism to promote greater economic opportunity through more equal access to more equally funded schools.

Initially ESEA was intended to provide additional resources to disadvantaged students with little federal involvement as to how the resources were utilized by state and local education authorities. Over time, however, federal legislative enactments, bureaucratic regulations, and court mandates in education became increasingly numerous and prescriptive, and federal influence over schools grew significantly. As a result, the political debate shifted from whether the federal government had an obligation to promote educational opportunity to making these efforts more effective and/or less intrusive. By the 1980s the contentious politics of desegregation and growing skepticism about the efficacy of federal education programs led to a backlash against ESEA and fueled a reform movement that promoted administrative flexibility, parental choice, and outcome standards.

THE FEDERAL ROLE IN EDUCATION PRIOR TO ESEA

Federal involvement in school governance had little public support in the eighteenth and nineteenth centuries, and states and localities jealously guarded their prerogatives in education.[2] The federal government helped spur the construction

25

of public schools with the Land Ordinance Act of 1785 and the Northwest Ordinances of 1787, which set aside proceeds from the sale of unsettled U.S. lands to fund public education.[3] After the Civil War, Congress went one step farther and required all new states admitted to the Union to establish free, nonsectarian public schools. States were slow to build public schools, however, and were even slower to establish supervision and basic regulation of them. It was not until the "common school movement" of the mid-nineteenth century that the majority of states began to develop organized systems of public schools and to institute even basic statewide regulations.[4]

The federal government became more directly involved in education—and set a precedent for grants-in-aid programs—with the passage of the Morrill Act in 1862. The act authorized the creation of a network of what became known as land-grant colleges and committed the federal government to support them financially through the sale of federally owned lands. A U.S. Office of Education was created in 1867, but it was given little staff or resources and only a very proscribed mandate: to gather statistical data on schools.[5] The federal role in education increased in 1917 with the passage of the Smith-Hughes Act, which provided the first annual federal appropriation for K–12 schooling for vocational education programs. Even as late as the first half of the twentieth century, however, the nation's school system remained extremely decentralized. The day-to-day management of schools, including such matters as personnel, curriculum, and pedagogy, remained in the hands of local authorities, with state and federal governments having little influence. Prior to World War II, candidates for national political office generally ignored the issue of education. Education played a minor role in the political affairs of a nation where, in 1930, less than a fifth of adults over age twenty-five had completed high school and where the Progressive Party had fought doggedly to convince the public that schooling decisions ought to be entrusted to "non-political" educational professionals.[6] When education did emerge as a political issue, it was typically due to religious, ethnic, or racial tensions rather than more abstract concerns about school quality.[7]

During the New Deal, however, a tremendous increase in the breadth and depth of the activities of the federal government occurred, along with a profound change in public and judicial attitudes toward the responsibilities of government. Americans began to look to the national government for solutions to their economic and social problems to an unprecedented extent. Nonetheless, the ambitious legislative agenda of the New Deal contained remarkably little on elementary and secondary education—only impact aid for school districts adversely affected by the presence of non-taxed governmental institutions. Despite the New Deal's nationalizing effect on many areas of social policy then, federal activism in education was generally confined to a few small unconditional grants to the states and support for higher education through programs such as the GI Bill (which passed in 1944).

Education gained new prominence after World War II, however, as high school completion became the norm and as the GI Bill spurred a dramatic increase in college enrollment.[8] For the first time, education became part of the lexicon of the working-class American and a key to economic and social mobility.[9] Expanding educational access also became a central objective of the civil rights movement. The Supreme Court's *Brown v. Board of Education* decision in 1954 calling for the end of segregated schools dramatically altered the politics of educational policymaking in the United States. The *Brown* decision would ultimately engage the federal government directly and forcefully in the effort to create, for the first time in the nation's history, a more equitable system of public schooling. The original *Brown* decision, while declaring that states must integrate their public schools, was silent on the crucial issues of when and how this was to be accomplished. The court's 1955 *Brown II* decision declared that integration should proceed "with all deliberate speed," but the following year 101 senators and representatives from the South signed the "Southern Manifesto," which denounced the *Brown* decisions as "contrary to established law and to the Constitution." In *Brown II* the Court again declined to set firm deadlines or methods for integration, omissions that enabled recalcitrant states such as Virginia to engage in "massive resistance" and to postpone large-scale integration efforts until the latter half of the 1960s.[10] Nonetheless, the Court's powerful statement in *Brown* on the importance of equal educational opportunity would help to give rise to a public conception of education as the birthright of a free citizenry and essential to social justice.[11]

These developments, together with the publication of a large body of social-science research during the 1950s and 1960s, created a much greater public awareness of the economic and educational inequalities facing the country's racial minorities and the poor. Work by Michael Harrington (*The Other America*), James Conant (*Slums and Suburbs*), and others highlighted the resource-and-achievement gap between students in poor schools relative to students in middle- and upper-class schools. Poor children, it was also recognized at the time, were concentrated in the inner cities and were often from racial minority groups. The consequence, as one observer noted, was that "beginning in the 1950's and continuing through the 1960's and 1970's, Americans generally were made keenly aware of the existence of a number of social injustices. Thus, there developed a climate of public opinion favorable to social reform efforts."[12] Although these developments increased public support for educational equality in the abstract, federal and judicial pressure to integrate local schools would remain enormously controversial, particularly after the courts adopted a more aggressive approach and timetable for integration in the late 1960s.

Cold War competition with the Soviet Union also provided an impetus for greater federal involvement in education in the 1950s. The Soviet launch of *Sputnik*—the world's first orbiting satellite—generated fears that the United States was falling behind in the development of new technologies and underscored the importance of education to national security. These developments provided the impetus for the passage of the National Defense Education Act (NDEA) of 1958, which provided categorical aid to states to improve math, science, and foreign-language instruction in U.S. schools. The NDEA was an important political precedent and psychological breakthrough for advocates of federal aid to education.[13] Even with the NDEA, however, as of 1960 national support for education remained quite small in absolute dollars (less than $1 billion) and as a percentage of total education spending (around 2 percent). It was also fragmented into several categorical grants with little direct federal oversight. Existing federal aid was generally devoted to narrow ends: statistics collection, specialized research and demonstration grants, vocational education assistance, the school lunch program, and impact aid.

The 1950s and early 1960s thus had a mixed legacy for the national politics of education. On the one hand, the Cold War demand for improved technical education, the greater number of Americans attending high school and college, and a growing awareness of the financial and racial inequities in the public school system combined to increase the salience of education and create significant momentum for expanded federal support for schools. Many citizens and political elites became convinced that states and localities were either unable or unwilling to address educational failures and inequities on their own. On the other hand, most Americans continued to believe that education policy decisions should be made at the state and local levels, and the period witnessed growing and often intense opposition to federal efforts to integrate public schools. As a result, as Hugh Graham has written in his classic work on the period, "to propose federal 'intrusion' into the sanctity of the state-local-private preserve of education was to stride boldly into a uniquely dangerous political minefield that pitted Democrat against Republican, liberal against conservative, Catholic against Protestant and Jew, federal power against states rights, white against black, and rich constituency against poor in mercurial cross-cutting alliances."[14] This opposition succeeded in defeating a number of proposals by Democrats for increased federal education spending in the 1940s and 1950s, as well as several by President John Kennedy's administration in the early 1960s.[15]

THE GREAT SOCIETY AND THE PASSAGE OF THE ELEMENTARY AND SECONDARY EDUCATION ACT

Kennedy's successor, his vice president and the former Senate majority leader, Lyndon Johnson, capitalized on the growing public awareness of school inequalities,

political goodwill for Kennedy's agenda following his assassination, and the large
Democratic majority in Congress following the 1964 election to push again for
an education bill.[16] LBJ declared a "war on poverty" and thrust the quest for civil
rights to the center of his domestic agenda. He considered his education proposal
to be a central component of the broader antidiscrimination efforts begun with
the Civil Rights Act of 1964 and of his antipoverty program, which had rejected
an income-transfer strategy in favor of an emphasis on job training and education. Johnson believed that "very often, a lack of jobs and money is not the cause
of poverty, but the symptom. The cause may lie deeper—in our failure to give our
fellow citizens a fair chance to develop their own capacities in a lack of education
and training."[17] If education was the key to social mobility, however, it was clear
that too many schools lacked the resources to provide the necessary skills to students from disadvantaged backgrounds. As one observer noted, "the architects of
the Great Society have found the school systems, for the most part, ill-prepared
and ill-equipped to meet the educational challenges to be encountered in building
the Great Society. Furthermore, they learned that most localities today are hard
pressed to finance the schools on which success depends."[18]

When LBJ introduced his education plan in 1965, the former schoolteacher
argued that "nothing matters more to the future of our country; not our military
preparedness, for armed might is worthless if we lack brainpower to build a world
of peace; not our productive economy, for we cannot sustain growth without
trained manpower; [and] not our democratic system of government, for freedom
is fragile if citizens are ignorant."[19] Johnson also saw federal leadership in education as a logical—and essential—extension of the New Deal. During a "State of Education" address in February 1968, Johnson remarked that "on January 6, 1941, President
Franklin D. Roosevelt set forth to Congress and the people four essential freedoms
for which America stands. . . . Today, wealthier, more powerful, and more able than
ever before in our history, our nation can declare another essential freedom—the fifth
freedom is freedom from ignorance."[20] Johnson's activism on education can be
seen in his frequent use of the bully pulpit on the issue (see Table 3.1).

From the outset, however, Johnson and his advisers were cognizant of the political obstacles that had defeated previous attempts to expand the federal role in
education. What had become known as the new "three R's"—race, religion, and
the reds (opposition to government support for integration and Catholic schools,
and bureaucratic centralization)—remained a substantial barrier. The passage of
the Civil Rights Act in 1964—and particularly Title VI, which outlawed the allocation of federal funds to segregated programs—would prevent federal education bills from becoming entangled with racial issues as they had in 1956 and
1960.[21] Johnson's commissioner of education, Francis Keppel, warned in a 1964
memo, however, that the other two R's remained. Any plan to provide substantial

Table 3.1. Presidential Attention to Education

Years	President	Total Number of Speeches with Word "Education"	Annual Average Number of Speeches with Word "Education"
1789–1913	Washington–Taft	226	2
1929–1933	Hoover	148	37
1933–1945	Roosevelt	382	29
1945–1953	Truman	667	74
1953–1961	Eisenhower	771	96
1961–1963	Kennedy	777	259
1963–1969	Johnson	3,104	621
1969–1974	Nixon	1,428	238
1974–1977	Ford	830	277
1977–1981	Carter	2,055	514
1981–1988	Reagan	2,497	312
1989–1992	George H. W. Bush	2,656	664

Source: Analysis conducted by author using the Public Papers of the Presidents of the United States, accessed online at http://www.gpo.gov/nara/pubpaps/srchpaps.html.

new federal aid to schools, he observed, would still meet with intense opposition from states' rights and antigovernment conservatives as well as from two important Democratic constituencies, Catholics and the National Education Association (NEA).[22] Catholics opposed any bill that would direct federal money to public but not private schools, whereas the NEA opposed any diversion of federal education aid to private schools.

Keppel devised an ingenious compromise solution that provided the basis for the Elementary and Secondary Education Act. His plan was to target federal aid to poor *children* regardless of the type of school they attended (whether public or private). This plan had the advantage of spreading money around to a majority of congressional districts, to public and private school children, and to state education agencies for implementation purposes, thereby undercutting most of the potential political opposition to the aid. Keppel also recommended linking ESEA to the existing impact-aid program, which had been established fourteen years earlier and enjoyed strong congressional support. By all accounts, President Johnson's legislative savvy and active lobbying on the bill's behalf were crucial to its passage. As Harold Howe (who succeeded Keppel as commissioner of education in 1965) remarked, "Johnson asserted a very personal influence. . . . The 89th Congress voted all the new education legislation through, literally *pushed* by him."[23] The bill was supported by large majorities in both chambers, passing by a vote of 263–153 in the House and 73–18 in the Senate.[24] Johnson signed the measure into law in front of his former elementary school in Texas and declared that "I believe deeply no law I have signed or will ever sign means more to the future of America."[25]

ESEA was intended to be primarily a redistributive bill, to put a floor under spending in the nation's poorest communities and to lend federal muscle to efforts to innovate and improve educational services. The centerpiece of this effort and of the legislation itself was the Title I program, which received $1.06 billion of the initial $1.3 billion appropriated for ESEA.[26] The text of Title I stated that "the Congress hereby declares it to be the policy of the United States to provide financial assistance . . . to expand and improve . . . educational programs by various means . . . which contribute particularly to meeting the special educational needs of educationally deprived children."[27] Title I was designed to assist communities with a high concentration of low-income families (then defined as families earning less than $2,000 annually) by raising per-pupil expenditures. The nature of the legislative process, however, meant that the redistributive edge of ESEA got rubbed off as money was spread around in exchange for political support. In the end, the funding formula was designed to maximize the number of school districts (and thus the number of congressional districts) that would be eligible, and the restrictions on how the money would be spent were loosened considerably. Ninety-four percent of all school districts ultimately received ESEA funds, and the act allowed Title I funds to be used for a variety of purposes—including hiring additional staff, purchasing classroom equipment, and improving classroom instruction.[28] The result was that ESEA would, despite Johnson's initial desire, remain a hybrid program, both distributive and redistributive in its design and impact.[29] The political incentives for local school authorities and state policymakers—and at times national politicians—to disperse education funding broadly would lead to a long-standing struggle over its focus on disadvantaged students.

ESEA was premised on the idea that the federal government should intervene in what was increasingly seen as an educational crisis among poor and minority children. There remained a great deal of disagreement, however, over the causes of poverty and educational inequality and what the government should do to address them. Researchers and policymakers disagreed about the most important factors influencing educational achievement and what kind of educational reforms were likely to work for disadvantaged students. In addition, a great ideological rift existed between conservatives and liberals about whether the issue of disadvantaged students should be approached from a deficit perspective, a structural perspective, or something else entirely. Conservatives argued that disadvantaged students suffered from a "culture of poverty" and that they could only succeed if they were taught middle-class values.[30] Liberals countered that the primary problem facing poor students was that they attended resource-poor schools. In this view, the structure of the American social, political, and economic systems resulted in inequalities that the schools largely served to replicate. In addition to these debates over educational strategy, policymakers disagreed about which level of government (federal, state, or local) was best suited to achieve school reform.

The mix of programs established under ESEA reflected the substantial disagreement over the precise cause of educational inequalities among poor children and over the best strategies for eradicating them. As educational historian Diane Ravitch has noted, "the vigorous advocacy of differing theories obscured the fact that educators did not know how best to educate poor children or even whether it was possible to eliminate the achievement gap between poor and middle-income children."[31] As a result, ESEA funds were allocated to support a wide variety of programs in local school systems, including teaching innovations, cultural and social enrichment programs, library improvements, parental involvement activities, nutrition programs, and social and medical services. How best to fight poverty and its effects in schools was thus unclear, and there was no consensus even among child development and educational experts on how government aid might be used most effectively to that end. This uncertainty would prove to be a major obstacle in the implementation of ESEA.

The design as well as the substance of ESEA were to have important consequences for American education policy. One of the most significant features of ESEA was what it did *not* do—it did not provide general federal aid to public schools. Instead, ESEA provided "categorical" aid that was targeted to a specific student population: disadvantaged students. As Paul Peterson and Barry Rabe would later note, "passage of the ESEA . . . provided for greatly increased support for public education, but it hardly took the form that traditional education interest groups had long advocated. Instead of a program of general aid, the legislation concentrated resources on educationally disadvantaged children living in low-income areas."[32] And, as will be discussed in more detail, the creation of federal categorical programs required that federal educational institutions shift from what had been largely an information-gathering and -disseminating role to a more supervisory role in the administration of the new federal funds and programs. Given the political opposition to federal "control" in education, however, it had been impossible to include rigorous compliance provisions in ESEA, or even the kind of requirements that were normally attached to categorical grants.

Many supporters of expanding federal aid for education and of expanding opportunity for the poor were concerned that ESEA's failings—poor targeting, conflicting educational philosophies, and ambiguous implementing authority—greatly limited the potential impact of the legislation. As one liberal Democratic U.S. representative commented,

In 1965, the issue was not good education policy versus bad. The question Congress had to settle in 1965 was whether there was ever going to be federal aid to the elementary and secondary schools of this nation. . . . The 1965 bill, in all candor, does not make much sense educationally; but it makes a hell of a lot of sense legally, politically, and constitutionally. This was a battle of principle, not substance, and that is the main reason I voted for it. If I could have written a bill that would have included provisions to meet the national interest in the education field it would not have been 89–10 [ESEA].[33]

It was thus clear from the start—even to its supporters—that the implementation of ESEA would present many challenges.

Many observers at the time nonetheless recognized the symbolic significance of ESEA for national education policy: an important threshold had been crossed and an important federal role in education policy cemented. President Johnson remarked at the time that in one year Congress "did more for the wonderful cause of education in America than all the previous 176 regular sessions of Congress did, put together."[34] And as both the supporters and opponents of federal aid to education acknowledged, the federal role in education was likely to expand after ESEA despite continuing opposition on some fronts. Rep. John Williams (R-DE), for example, remarked after the passage of ESEA that "this bill . . . is merely the beginning. It contains within it the seeds of the first federal education system which will be nurtured by its supporters in the years to come long after the current excuse of aiding the poverty stricken is forgotten. . . . The needy are being used as a wedge to open the floodgates, and you may be absolutely certain that the flood of federal control is ready to sweep the land."[35] Together, NDEA and ESEA were to dramatically increase federal funding for education, both in absolute terms and as a proportion of total education spending. Between 1958 and 1968, for example, federal spending on education multiplied more than ten times, from $375 million to $4.2 billion, and the federal share expanded from less than 3 percent to about 10 percent of all school funding.

The policy paradigm, policymaking arrangement, and power alignment at the heart of ESEA formed the basis for an equity policy regime that would persist into the 1980s. The policy paradigm undergirding this equity regime was that the majority of schools were doing fine, that federal education reform efforts should target schools with high concentrations of poor and minority students, and that the primary problem facing these schools was a lack of integration and/or adequate funding. As a result, the early orientation of ESEA and federal education policy was toward using federal grants and judicial decrees to promote equal educational opportunity, with progress measured by the pace of state integration efforts and the size and distribution of school resources. This particular set of ends and means—along with the decision to deliver ESEA funds through categorical pro-grams rather than general aid—had important consequences for the institutional arrangements that would make and administer ESEA policies and programs. Cat-egorical programs required congressional and bureaucratic oversight and necessi-tated the creation of new federal and state administrative capacities to oversee the administration of the programs and ensure state compliance. And once the federal role in education policy had been institutionalized, it became more difficult for opponents of that role to substantially reduce or change it.[36]

The fundamental feature of the equity regime's power alignment was the strength of the New Deal coalition—both in Washington and among voters at large—that enabled Democrats to dominate Congress for most of the 1960s, 1970s, and 1980s and united the party in support of federal social welfare programs and efforts to equalize educational access and funding. Federal spending for educa-tion—particularly when it was dispersed widely and came with few mandates or accountability measures—was also popular among state politicians and education agencies, as well as powerful parent and education groups. These beneficiaries of federal aid to education quickly became a powerful political force in Washington, an "education-industrial complex" that fought hard to protect existing programs and to create new ones. As Hugh Graham has noted, "by the end of the Johnson administration, the very proliferation of Great Society programs . . . reinforced the growing triangular networks with a vested interest in maximizing their benefits by pressing willing congressional authorizing committees to exceed by large margins the president's budget requests, especially in education."[37] Although the political survival of ESEA seemed assured by the end of the 1960s, concern was growing in many quarters about the implementation of federal education programs and their effectiveness in promoting equal educational opportunity.

THE IMPLEMENTATION AND EXPANSION OF ESEA

Policymaking and implementation in education are inherently difficult given the vagaries, conflicting goals, and ambiguities that characterize schooling. It quickly became clear that the implementation challenges surrounding ESEA were espe-cially difficult and that the compromises required to gain congressional approval of ESEA in many ways compromised the legislation's original goal of improving educational opportunities for poor children. First, the legislation itself (as dis-cussed earlier) incorporated multiple goals and methods, some of which were in-compatible with one another. Second, the original ESEA gave federal administra-tors few tools to force compliance with federal directives and goals in the use of ESEA funds. Third, even if such tools had been available, the agency charged with implementing ESEA—the U.S. Office of Education—was for several years after its passage disinclined or unable to make use of such compliance tools. Fourth, lingering opposition to federal control of education ensured that attempts to rigorously administer ESEA would generate a strong political backlash. Fifth, and finally, the politics and implementation of ESEA were greatly complicated by the addition of new purposes and programs and increasingly contentious racial politics in the years following 1965.

Though the goal of ESEA—to improve educational opportunity for the poor—was clear, the legislation was vague on how this goal was to be achieved. ESEA distributed funds to school districts according to the number of poor children enrolled, but it did not specify which services districts should provide to "educationally deprived" children.[38] The consequence of ESEA's initial flexibility was that federal funds were used in a wide variety of ways and for a wide variety of purposes, and local districts often diverted funds away from redistributive programs.[39] As Hugh Graham observed, "the upshot of all this is that when Title I was implemented, it produced not *a* Title I program, but something more like 30 thousand separate and different Title I programs."[40] The original ESEA legislation gave the Office of Education little power to coerce states to comply with federal regulations or goals or to punish states and school districts that failed to do so. The large amount of discretion accorded to states and school districts in spending the new federal money ensured that compliance with federal goals was spotty at best. In his examination of the implementation of ESEA, Joel Berke noted that "federal aid is channeled into an existing state political system and pattern of policy, and a blend distilled of federal priorities and the frequently different state priorities emerges. . . . Federal money is a stream that must pass through a state capitol; at the state level, the federal government is rarely able—through its guidelines and regulations—radically to divert the stream or reverse the current."[41]

Initially the U.S. Office of Education relied on the assurances of state education officials that they were in compliance with federal guidelines.[42] But one of the fundamental premises behind the idea of compensatory education, and of ESEA more generally, was that state and local education authorities had failed to ensure equal educational opportunities for their students and that they could not be trusted to do so in the future without federal intervention. The distrust of local education authorities—and mounting evidence that states and localities were diverting federal funds to purposes for which they were not intended—ultimately led Congress and federal bureaucrats to increase the regulation and supervision of federal aid. By the 1970s, the additional resources available to the Office of Education and the agency's gradual adjustment to its new administrative role led the office to more aggressively enforce federal education mandates.[43] As Diane Ravitch has observed, "in this atmosphere of discord and distrust, those with grievances turned naturally to the courts and the federal government to enforce their rights against local school boards. . . . Programs, regulations, and court orders began to reflect the strong suspicion that those in control of American institutions were not to be trusted with any discretion where minorities, women, or other aggrieved groups were concerned."[44]

The implementation of ESEA thus quickly became enmeshed in the highly charged struggles over integration and busing that were fought across the country during the 1960s and 1970s. Though it was the 1964 Civil Rights Act that declared that federal funds could not be allocated to support segregated institutions or programs, it was ESEA funding that became a key carrot (and stick) for federal integration efforts. States that failed to comply with court integration decrees would lose their share of federal education funds, which, as noted earlier, were very sizable after the creation of ESEA. And the initial flexibility and discretion that the Supreme Court accorded state desegregation efforts came to an end with the 1968 *Green v. County School Board of Kent County, Virginia* case when the Court declared that school boards must develop integration plans that promise "realistically to work *now*."[45] Opposition to this ruling—and to the widespread busing of students that lower courts increasingly mandated to carry it out—was strong across the country and was bitterly attacked by conservatives George Wallace and Richard Nixon during the 1968 presidential election campaign. In this and subsequent elections, Republican presidential candidates would successfully use opposition to school busing and integration as a key part of their "southern strategy" to appeal to conservative Democratic voters and their assault on federal government activism more generally. Several scholars have argued that race—and particularly the debate over school integration—became the decisive issue in U.S. politics during the second half of the twentieth century and led to the unraveling of the coalition that had supported the Great Society and the war on poverty, and ultimately, a partisan electoral realignment.[46]

Despite these developments and reservations about ESEA's implementation and effectiveness, it quickly developed formidable political constituencies and allies in Washington, which successfully pushed for incremental expansions in the size and scope of federal education programs. Continuing opposition to federal micromanagement in education and the lack of consensus on how to measure the effectiveness of school reform efforts, however, led federal administrators to focus on school districts' spending patterns and administrative compliance. The result was that large numbers of bureaucratic regulations were created during the 1970s without any kind of concomitant focus on student or school results—everything was judged by procedure and process. In the 1980s, John Chubb would note that "in federal programs that are not explicitly regulatory, as well as those that are, policy has come to be carried out by increasingly detailed, prescriptive, legalistic, and authoritative means."[47] Between 1964 and 1976, for example, the number of pages of federal legislation affecting education increased from 80 to 360, and the number of federal regulations increased from 92 in 1965 to nearly 1,000 in 1977.[48]

One of the most significant consequences of ESEA was thus the bureaucratization and centralization of education policymaking from the local level to the state and federal levels. From 1965 to 1975, federal funds for elementary and secondary education more than doubled (with a 210 percent increase in inflation-adjusted dollars).[49] In addition, between 1960 and 1985, the percentage of total education spending provided by the national government grew from 8 percent to 16 percent. Over the same period, the share of local spending dipped from 51 percent to 31 percent and the state share increased from 41 percent to 55 percent.[50] Eligibility for federal education funds was often conditioned on the provision of state matching funds, the creation of central implementing offices, and the collection of a variety of statistical information that necessitated that state education agencies expand their size and activities and become more institutionalized. This was a clear objective of ESEA, as the original legislation contained funding for the agencies to build up their administrative capacity so that they would be better equipped to handle their new federally imposed responsibilities. The result, as Paul Hill has noted, was that state education agencies often became so dependent on federal funding and pliable to federal direction that they were effectively "colonized."[51]

In addition, the number of independent school districts in the United States dropped from approximately 150,000 in 1900 to 15,000 in 1993; the concurrent administrative centralization at the state level ultimately made education more susceptible to federal regulation.[52] In practice, centralization also meant that local decision-makers had less and less flexibility in how they ran their schools. Diane Ravitch observed that "during the decade after 1965, political pressures converged on schools . . . in ways that undermined their authority to direct their own affairs. . . . Congress, the courts, federal agencies, and state legislatures devised burdensome and costly new mandates. In elementary and secondary schools, almost no area of administrative discretion was left uncontested."[53]

As opponents of federal control of education had feared, the passage of ESEA had given a crucial beachhead to those who sought to further increase the federal role in education policy. ESEA had been based on the idea that the federal government had the obligation to assist "disadvantaged" students and that such assistance would be efficacious. Once this rationale had been enshrined in federal law and court precedent, a number of education-related interest groups worked hard to protect it and to expand the number and type of students considered "disadvantaged" and thus eligible to receive federal Title I aid. These groups included the National Advisory Council for the Education of Disadvantaged Children, the National Welfare Rights Organization, the Legal Standards and Education Project of the

NAACP, the Lawyers Committee for Civil Rights Under Law, and the National Association of Administrators of State and Federally Assisted Education Programs.

With the support of these and other organizations, a number of disadvantaged groups were able (often with the assistance of the courts and the U.S. Office for Civil Rights) to secure additional federal spending and protections in schools. Amendments to the ESEA in 1968 provided funding and new federal programs for disadvantaged students in rural areas, for dropout prevention programs, and for the support of bilingual programs. Congress strengthened the act in 1974 and reauthorized it in 1978 by wide bipartisan margins. (The $50 billion five-year reauthorization in 1978, for example, passed 86–7 in the Senate and 350–20 in the House.) The education proposals of the Nixon and Carter administrations largely continued in the path established by LBJ by adding more than 100 new categorical programs in education. Migrant children, children for whom English was a second language, delinquent and neglected children, and children with mental and physical handicaps would all eventually be added to Title I. Writing in the 1990s, Michelle Fine noted that "the language of 'risk' is upon us, piercing daily consciousness, educational practices, and bureaucratic policymaking. We have all been quick to name, identify, and ossify those who presumably suffer at the mercy of 'risk factors.'"[54]

The creation and growth of the special education program within ESEA demonstrates how the scope of the act was expanded and some of the consequences of this expansion. A 1966 amendment to ESEA created a new title (Title VI) to provide grants for programs for "handicapped" children. This new program—like ESEA itself—continued to expand over time as the definition of "handicapped" was broadened to cover more and more students. In 1970, for example, Title VI was broken off from ESEA and expanded to form a separate Education of the Handicapped Act. This later became the Education for All Handicapped Children Act (1975) and, in 1997, the Individuals with Disabilities Education Act (IDEA). Despite a decline in the total public school population between 1968 and 1986, the number of children in special education programs in the United States during that period increased from 2.3 million to 4.3 million. Special education programs became the fastest-growing part of the state and local education budget and the second-largest federal education program.[55]

The increasing power of the National Education Association (NEA), the nation's largest teachers union, in national politics and the Democratic Party during the 1970s and 1980s was another driving force behind the expansion of ESEA. Liberal Democrats joined with the unions in vigorously defending the equity regime at the heart of ESEA. They argued that the only education "reform" that was needed to improve bad schools was additional federal funding and regulation and new categorical programs to serve disadvantaged students. Democratic president

Jimmy Carter continued the institutionalization of the federal role in education when he created a cabinet-level Department of Education in 1979.[56] Conservatives and states' rights advocates opposed the new department on the grounds that education was a state and local responsibility and that the federal role had been intrusive and counterproductive.[57] Once created, the new department quickly became a powerful symbol to both proponents and opponents of federal involvement in education.

By 1980 federal spending and influence on schooling had expanded dramatically, and ESEA had facilitated the centralization, bureaucratization, and judicialization of education policymaking. The case of special education policy represented an extension of the ESEA logic—that the federal government needed to defend the worst off or most vulnerable from local majorities or inequities in the larger state and local systems. The result was increasing federal involvement in education but also increasingly inflexible and copious regulations and increasingly intrusive court involvement—by 1980 the Department of Education administered approximately 500 different federal education programs.[58] But the federal focus remained on access and equity issues rather than on improving schools' or students' academic performance, and there was little effort to measure the educational progress of students who received federal funds or protection. This fueled the growing perception in the 1970s that federal education policy—like many other federal policies from the Great Society—had become more about providing entitlements and protecting rights than about enhancing opportunity or demanding responsibility. This situation led to growing discontent among Republicans, states' rights advocates, and even some Democrats about the nature and effectiveness of federal education aid and set the stage for a backlash against ESEA.

A NATION AT RISK?

The growing negative response to federal education policy coalesced around two complaints: that it had become too prescriptive and intrusive, and that it had been ineffective in improving school quality or student performance. The unpopularity of school busing during the late 1960s and 1970s played a major role in this reaction. In addition, a number of prominent studies published during this period argued that ESEA funds and programs had largely failed to improve educational opportunity for disadvantaged students.[59] Joel Berke and Michael Kirst, for example, analyzed data from more than 500 school districts and concluded that ESEA aid had done little to redress the large inequality in per-pupil expenditures between rich and poor districts. They found that though Title I—which was explicitly focused on disadvantaged students—had a somewhat redistributive effect, this was erased by the effects of the other titles of ESEA and vocational aid, which went disproportionately to wealthier districts.[60] By dispersing ESEA funds widely across school districts, not only was federal assistance poorly targeted to its intended beneficiaries, but the additional resources that came to any particular school were limited.

In addition, because ESEA was premised on the provision of additional resources rather than the promotion of school reform, federal education aid generally went to support existing state and local programs. This approach came under fire over time as the additional resources failed to generate improvement in student achievement. In a September 1970 speech whose themes would be widely repeated in the following years, Republican president Richard Nixon argued that increased spending on education would not improve educational opportunity unless more fundamental changes in schools were required. Congress had been, he noted, "extraordinarily generous in its support of education . . . [and] much of this activity was based on the familiar premise that if only the resources available for education were increased, the amount youngsters learn would increase." It was time, he argued, to recognize that existing education "programs and strategies . . . are . . . based on faulty assumptions and inadequate knowledge."[61] Nonetheless, as Table 3.1 shows, presidents Nixon and Ford did not devote much attention to the issue of school reform, in part because the issue (as opposed to integration and busing) remained quite low on the public agenda at that point. Table 3.2 demonstrates that between 1964 and 1972, education reform remained at the bottom (literally) of voters' lists of the most-important issues facing the country; as a result there was little incentive for politicians to seize on the issue.

By the 1970s, the Great Society was under fire from both conservative and liberal politicians. As Gareth Davies has noted, "the former was increasingly certain that the poor did not deserve the War on Poverty's largesse, and the latter was equally adamant that they were entitled to far more."[62] As a result of the questionable benefits and unintended consequences of ESEA, public support for it and many of the other social welfare programs born during the Great Society began to wane in the 1970s and particularly in the 1980s. There was a growing perception that many programs that had begun as an effort to promote opportunity and self-reliance had morphed into entitlements that encouraged dependency—that opportunity liberalism had transformed into what Davies calls "entitlement liberalism."[63] As Marshall Kaplan and Peggy Cuciti have noted, "Although the very visible War on Poverty program appeared to be aimed at assisting the poor to find a competitive place in the system . . . the entitlement programs that evolved seemed premised on a commitment to assist a poverty population that could not, should not, or would not compete."[64] Typical of the growing backlash against the Great Society was Charles Murray's widely publicized book *Losing Ground: American*

Table 3.2. Public Perceptions of the Nation's Most Important Problem in
Presidential Election Years, 1960–1988

Year	Candidates	Most Important Issue	Rank of Education
1960	Kennedy/Nixon	Foreign relations	14th out of 20
1964	Johnson/Goldwater	Civil rights	24th out of 24
1968	Humphrey/Nixon	Vietnam	17th out of 17
1972	McGovern/Nixon	Vietnam	26th out of 26
1976	Carter/Ford	Inflation	Not listed
1980	Carter/Reagan	Inflation	23d out of 41
1984	Mondale/Reagan	Recession	17th out of 51
1988	Dukakis/Bush	Drugs	8th out of 26

Note: Respondents were asked, "What do you think is the most important problem facing this country today?" All surveys were conducted within two months of the presidential election except for 1988
(July) and 2000 (June).

Source: Roper Center at University of Connecticut, Public Opinion Online, http://web.lexis-nexis.
com/universe/form/academic/s_roper.html. Accessed June 25, 2001.

Social Policy 1950–1980, which argued that the poor were worse off after the Great
Society than they had been before it.[65]

As ESEA continued to expand in size and to cover more and more disadvantaged groups despite its apparent failure to deliver on its promise to enhance
educational opportunity, support for a fundamental reconsideration of the federal role in education gained momentum. Many conservative Republicans—who
strongly opposed the growth of federal spending and influence in education as
a violation of states' rights—seized on the reports as evidence that far from providing constructive leadership, federal influence had contributed to the declining performance of U.S. schools. In the 1980 presidential election, Ronald Reagan,
a champion of conservative Republicans, was able to take advantage of growing
public opposition to the federal role in education and the expansion of the welfare
state more generally to defeat Democratic incumbent Jimmy Carter. Reagan en-
ergized the Republican Party and mobilized it behind a conservative agenda that
centered on cutting taxes and rolling back the size of the federal government and
the scope of its activities.[66]

The 1980 Republican platform called for "deregulation by the federal government of public education and . . . the elimination of the federal Department of
Education." The platform fretted that "parents are losing control of their children's
schooling" and that Democratic education policy had produced "huge new bureaucracies to misspend our taxes."[67] During the campaign, Reagan tried to appear sensitive to the need for a level playing field while calling for less government
spending by arguing that the federal government obstructed social and economic
progress and that the states were better equipped to safeguard opportunity for all.

In the end, Reagan lost the education issue, with Democrats enjoying a nine-point advantage over Republicans on it in 1979. This was of little significance, however, given Reagan's broad appeal and the relatively low priority given to education in the election, with voters on one survey ranking it as only the twenty-third most important issue (out of forty-one).

Once in office, President Reagan argued that "it's time to bury the myth that bigger government brings more opportunity and compassion."[68] As part of his "New Federalism" program, Reagan gained passage in 1981 of the Education Consolidation and Improvement Act (ECIA), which dramatically reformed many of the provisions of ESEA. The changes reduced the amount of federal funding for education by almost 20 percent, simplified eligibility requirements, and increased flexibility for states in the use of federal education funds. One scholar estimated that the number of regulatory mandates imposed on states through federal education programs was reduced by 85 percent during the Reagan administration.[69] Reagan hoped either to eliminate the federal role in schools or to redefine the nature of the federal education policy regime by making privatization, choice, and competition—rather than equity—its guiding principles.[70]

States' rights advocates celebrated what they thought was the beginning of a new era (or perhaps more accurately, a return to an old era) in which the federal government would leave education policymaking to the states. As Hugh Graham observed at the time, however, "the Reaganite hostility to a strong federal role in education (beyond defense-related R&D) is not shared by a congressional majority that clings with surprising tenacity to the consensus forged during the Kennedy-Johnson years, which survived and even prospered under the Nixon and Ford administrations, and which was strongly reinforced under Carter."[71] By 1980, ESEA and the federal role in education had been institutionalized and were vigorously defended by teachers' unions, state education agencies, and parent groups. The result was that, as Diane Ravitch has noted, "the new politics of the schools rotated about a state-federal axis rather than a local-state axis."[72]

Republican efforts to roll back federal influence in education in the 1980s also ran smack into fresh evidence that U.S. schools were in very poor shape and the subsequent increase in public and media attention to the issue. The 1983 report of the National Commission on Excellence in Education was crucial in this regard and marked a milestone in the history of federal education policy. The commission that was formed to examine the state of American education was appointed not by Reagan, as is often assumed, but rather by his education secretary, Terrell Bell. Bell had become unpopular within the administration because of his support for public schools and his opposition to eliminating the Department of Education. Apparently Bell appointed the commission because he thought that it would conclude that public schools were doing a satisfactory job and that this finding would end conservative calls for radical reform.[73] Reagan had very different ideas, however, and his marching orders to the commission members were (as recollected by a member) to "focus on five fundamental points that would bring excellence back to education: bring God back into the classroom. Encourage tuition tax credits for families using private schools. Support vouchers. Leave the primary responsibility for education to parents. And please abolish that abomination, the Department of Education."[74]

The commission's final report did not conform to either Bell's or Reagan's expectations. Entitled *A Nation at Risk: The Imperative for Educational Reform*, it painted a dire portrait of the country's public schools and highlighted how far American students lagged behind their foreign counterparts on academic achievement tests. The report's title also emphasized the authors' conclusion that although education had long been primarily a *state* issue, the dire performance of American students had become a *national* problem. This point was also cast—as it had been in the years following *Sputnik*—as a matter of national security in our Cold War struggle with the Soviet Union and in our competition in the global economy. The report's conclusion that the American public school system was in a state of crisis obviously did not deliver the positive endorsement of public education for which Bell had hoped. Ironically, however, the report did succeed in tempering the conservative assault on public schools, at least in the short term. This was because the report did not endorse the Reagan administration's calls for the elimination of the Department of Education or for the creation of vouchers or tuition tax credits to support private schools. Instead, it advocated a number of new public school reforms, such as increased teacher pay, strengthened curricula, and standards, and emphasized the importance of federal efforts to improving schools. The federal government, the report declared, has "the primary responsibility to identify the national interest in education. It should also help fund and support efforts to protect and promote that interest . . . and provide the national leadership."[75]

The Reagan White House was initially at a loss as to how to respond to the report. Some of his moderate advisers (such as Jim Baker and Mike Deaver) urged the president to endorse it, whereas conservatives such as Ed Meese recommended that he denounce it strongly; others argued that he should simply ignore it. In fact, requests by the commission to present the report formally to the president at the White House were initially rejected. In the end, however, Reagan received the report at a Rose Garden ceremony in which he praised the report for its call to eliminate the Department of Education and for its support of vouchers, tuition tax credits, and school prayer, none of which the report actually endorsed.[76] But the report's striking tone and conclusions ignited a frenzy of media attention to education, and the issue began to rise on the public agenda. As a result, Reagan and his staff decided to tone down their direct attacks on the Department of Education and their calls for support for private schools and instead sought, as Bell has noted in his memoir, "to get the greatest possible mileage from the commission report."[77] Reagan began to talk more about the importance of education and to encourage states and localities to adopt aggressive school reforms. Although Reagan did not introduce any legislation to expand the federal role in education—and indeed continued to fight Democratic proposals to do so—this rhetorical campaign clearly reinforced the sense that education was a national issue that demanded national leadership.

The salience of education was further increased by the release of several other high-profile reports declaring an educational crisis in the weeks after the appearance of *A Nation at Risk*. That May, the Education Commission of the States—comprised of governors and business executives—released a report entitled *Action for Excellence: A Comprehensive Plan to Improve Our Nation's Schools*. The report reflected growing concern about the poor state of American public schools among state leaders who believed that education was essential to worker productivity, international competitiveness, and economic growth. Soon thereafter, two additional reports—the Twentieth Century Foundation's *Making the Grade* and the Carnegie Foundation's *High School*—further stoked calls for a reassessment of school policy. Two best-selling books that appeared in 1987—Allan Bloom's *Closing of the American Mind* and E. D. Hirsch's *Cultural Literacy*—also brought added attention to the need for education reform.

The Reagan administration highlighted the reports' findings as evidence that the growth of federal involvement since the 1960s had been ineffective. Secretary Bell epitomized this view in a 1983 interview, remarking,

> Education is a foremost responsibility of state governments. Recent reports show that state governments haven't been doing a very good job of handling education over the last couple of decades. But the federal government ought not to be mandating curriculum and standards. We could ask Congress to make it a violation of a federal statute to graduate a student without x years of science and y years of mathematics. Or we could say that as a condition to receive federal money, states would have to set certain minimum requirements. But I don't think we should do that. The National Commission on Excellence has heightened the decline. Now it is the responsibility of state and local governments to do something about it.[78]

Bell also began a very visible (and controversial) effort to prod state education reform by providing public rankings of the states according to the quality of their public education systems.

During the 1984 presidential election campaign, Reagan attacked his Democratic opponent, Walter Mondale—formerly vice president under Carter—as another apologist for welfarism. Against a backdrop of surging economic growth, increasing public satisfaction at home, confidence in American foreign policy abroad, and affection for Reagan himself, Mondale's efforts to defend federal programs and attack Reagan as callous fared poorly.[79] By 1984, the tumult generated by *A Nation at Risk* had caused the public, for the first time, to rank education in the top tier of its concerns. The 1984 Republican platform, however, once again opposed an active federal role in education reform. The platform stated that "from 1965–1980 the U.S. indulged in a disastrous experiment with centralized direction of our schools." The Republican position on education did not seem to sit well with voters, who saw Mondale as much more likely than Reagan to improve the quality of education in the United States.[80] But amidst more salient concerns about job creation and the Cold War, Democratic attacks on Republican fairness gained little traction, and Reagan defeated Mondale in a forty-nine–state landslide.

Reagan's second education secretary, Bill Bennett, traveled the country highlighting the poor condition of U.S. public education and the urgent need for reform. The Reagan administration hoped that these efforts to use the bully pulpit would achieve several objectives. First, it hoped that by exposing the poor track record of federal school reform efforts, it would generate public support for rolling back the federal role in education policy. Second, it hoped that its arguments would resonate with the strong support for local control of education in the United States and advance the party's broader quest to reduce the size of the federal government and the scope of its activities. Third, the administration wagered that its efforts to shake up the education establishment and promote choice would bring about political gain by showing that the Republican Party was concerned about education and the plight of poor and middle-class students trapped in failing schools.

In the end, however, President Reagan's efforts to convert federal education spending into vouchers or block grants and to dismantle the U.S. Department of Education failed after meeting significant resistance from Congress, educational interest groups, and the public. As noted earlier, by the 1980s a formidable collection of interest groups had developed around federal education programs, and they lobbied actively to protect and expand federal education spending and institutions such as the Department of Education. They were aided in these efforts by evidence that the public did not support Reagan's education agenda. In a poll taken on September 25–26, 1981—in the days following Reagan's speech calling for the elimination of the department—respondents opposed the proposal by an almost two-to-one margin (63 percent to 32 percent).[81] A poll taken in August 1983 revealed that the public disapproved of Reagan's handling of education by a 49 to 31 percent margin.[82] Though Reagan's effort to disband the department was ultimately unsuccessful, his attacks succeeded in substantially reducing its staffing and budget and its regulatory authority, thereby further limiting its ability to promote educational coordination or improvement. The budget for the Department of Education was cut by 11 percent between FY1981 and FY1988 (in real dollars), and the National Institute of Education (the federal educational research and development body) lost 70 percent of its funding during the period.[83] In many important ways, however, the trend toward greater federal control in education and the nationalization of education politics continued during the 1980s despite the concerted efforts of Reagan and his conservative administration.

Perhaps the most important consequence of *A Nation at Risk* and the growing concern about the consequences of poor public education on economic development was that state governments began to play a much more active role in education reform. As part of what became known as the "excellence movement," many states increased their spending on schools and established new curricular and achievement standards in the 1980s to guide local school districts. Thomas Toch has written that "the national debate on public education produced scores of reforms. . . . Through 1984, 1985, 1986 and beyond, education was a dominant issue in state capitols nationwide. . . . In all, there were an estimated 3,000 separate school-reform measures enacted in the states during the mid-1980s."[84] Paul Manna has shown that this intense state educational activity had two major consequences for federal education policy: first, it helped to increase the visibility of education as an issue in national politics; and second, it contributed to the building of a public and elite consensus around standards-based reforms as the most efficacious foundation for national reform efforts.[85]

The flurry of state education reform activity and extensive media coverage that these efforts received contributed to the growing sense that the country was facing an education crisis that required expanded federal leadership.[86] Polls showed that the public largely rejected Reagan's argument that the best way to improve our schools was to get the federal government out of education policy and believed that the Reagan administration had done a poor job with education. Sixty percent of the respondents in a May 1987 poll concluded that the Reagan administration had tried but failed to improve education, not dealt with the problems in education, or made them worse.[87] A 1988 poll reported that 66 percent of respondents gave the administration a grade of "C" or below for its efforts over the eight years to improve the quality of education.[88]

Though the public was not supportive of Reagan's approach for reforming public education, it agreed with him that schools were in crisis and that school reform should be a priority. In 1987, for example, toward the end of Reagan's two terms in office, 64 percent of poll respondents gave the nation's public schools a grade of "C" or below, with 20 percent giving them a "B" and only 3 percent an "A."[89] By 1987, when given a list of five issues facing the national government (federal debt, education, health care, foreign competition, and national defense), respondents ranked education second in importance, behind only the federal debt.[90]

Polls also revealed strong public support for national solutions to the problems of the public education system. In a February 1987 poll, 66 percent of respondents thought that the federal government should spend more on education than Reagan had proposed in his budget.[91] Another 1987 poll found that 84 percent of Americans thought that the federal government should require state and local educational authorities to meet minimum national standards.[92] The same poll also indicated strong (74 percent) support for a national testing program for public school students.[93]

Though Reagan was not successful in eliminating the federal role in education or reducing public support for federal leadership in education reform, he was successful in challenging the effectiveness of the equity regime at the heart of ESEA and in discrediting the New Deal/Great Society welfare state more generally. The 1988 reauthorization of ESEA—which required school districts to assess the effectiveness of Chapter 1 programs and develop improvement plans for underperforming schools—represented the first, albeit small, step to shift federal education policy away from the equity approach. More generally, the legacy of the "Reagan revolution" deeply influenced the politics of the following decade. In 1985, after Reagan's second election victory, southern governors and other moderates who felt threatened by the liberalism of the national party formed the centrist Democratic Leadership Council (DLC). Offering a vision of limited government, public investment, and fiscal prudence, the DLC leadership—including such rising figures as Arkansas governor Bill Clinton and Tennessee senator Al Gore—sought to refashion the New Deal–era Democratic commitment to redistribution. Focused on finding a new way to balance responsibility and opportunity, the New Democrats found education and welfare reform to be areas of pressing need and political opportunity. They began to call for active federal leadership in education reform and increased spending but also new standards and accountability measures. At the end of Reagan's term, education thus seemed poised to assume greater prominence in national politics, and the contours of the debate over the federal role in school reform had shifted in important ways.

CONCLUSION

For most of the nation's history the federal government had little role in elementary and secondary education. The policy regime in education from the nation's founding until the first half of the twentieth century was based on a view of public schools as performing adequately and best controlled by state and local governments. During the 1960s, the civil rights movement and the war on poverty shattered this policy image. The Elementary and Secondary Education Act of 1965, though vigorously opposed in some quarters, established the ideational, political, and programmatic foundation for a new policy regime. A crucial part of the Great Society, ESEA committed the national government to the defense of civil rights and the promotion of equal opportunity. The policy paradigm at the heart of the ESEA regime continued to view public education as the appropriate domain of states and localities and to accept that public schools, on the whole, were functioning well. But it saw these lower levels of government as unable or unwilling to provide the equality of access and resources essential to promoting success in education for disadvantaged students.

ESEA established an important federal role in education, but it was a very targeted and limited role. ESEA programs were framed as temporary measures designed to address an extraordinary crisis for a specific group of disadvantaged students. Both the ends and means of federal policy were clearly circumscribed—the national government would limit its efforts to improving educational equity by providing small categorical programs and supplemental funding for poor schools and children. Strong institutional and ideological obstacles to an expansion of federal influence in education persisted long after the passage of ESEA in 1965 and a bipartisan consensus of sorts developed around these limits on the federal role. Liberals fought to keep the federal role redistributive in nature and focused on disadvantaged students. In addition, because of their alliance with teachers unions and the belief that inadequate school resources were the primary problem facing schools, Democrats also sought to keep the federal role centered on school inputs rather than on school outputs or curricular or governance issues. Conservatives, meanwhile, were willing to tolerate a small federal role in education so long as it was unobtrusive and did not threaten local control over schools. Given Democratic control of Congress for much of the period, there was little conservatives could do to eliminate or fundamentally recast the federal role in any event.

A powerful network of interest groups rose up during the 1960s and 1970s to defend federal education programs and to advocate for their incremental expansion. These groups allied with powerful congressional committees and subcommittees to lock in the original and limited view of the federal role in education and to defeat periodic reform efforts. Federal education policymaking during this early period (aside from busing issues) was a largely closed process dominated by the iron triangle of congressional staffers, interest groups, and executive bureaucrats with little influence exerted by the wider public. During the 1960s and 1970s, the American public generally saw public schools as doing a good job, and the major debate over schools centered on equity, integration, and social issues rather than concerns about academic performance. Democrats used their control of Congress during this time to gradually expand existing federal education programs for the poor and to create new ones. Crucially, federal mandates and administrative capacity in education also increased gradually as liberal Democrats sought to force recalcitrant state and local school officials to embrace congressional goals and methods. The story of the 1960s and 1970s for federal education policy, then, was one of expanded national intervention in schools—intervention that was focused on ensuring procedural compliance with integration mandates and programs for small groups of disadvantaged students.

Public and elite complacency about education began to change in the 1970s and 1980s as evidence mounted that student achievement—among both disadvantaged and mainstream students—had deteriorated. *Time* magazine reported in a 1980 cover story, for example, that "like some vast jury gradually and reluctantly arriving at a verdict, politicians, educators and especially millions of parents have come to believe that the U.S. public schools are in parlous trouble."[94] The release of the report *A Nation at Risk* in 1983 led to heightened concern about the decline of public education and its impact on the country's economic competitiveness. Both Democrats and Republicans seized on the report to argue for major changes in federal education policies, but they advocated very different visions of what reform should look like.

During this time, President Reagan and his conservative supporters in Congress led a passionate and sustained attack on the federal role in education. By the end of the 1980s, however, it was clear that their efforts had largely failed. The Department of Education had not been abolished—and public support for the agency remained high.[95] Federal regulation in education, though substantially reduced, remained significant. And federal spending on education actually *increased* over the eight years of the Reagan administration. Perhaps most important, Reagan's hands-off approach toward education proved unpopular, and the public believed that his administration had failed to improve schools. Seventy-one percent of respondents surveyed at the end of Reagan's presidency thought that the next president should start with new policies in education rather than continue in the same direction.[96]

Republican efforts to draw attention to the failure of federal policy to improve the performance of public schools had in many ways backfired. They succeeded in expanding media coverage of education and in ensuring that the media would generally portray schools in a negative light.[97] But rather than resulting in increased public support for a reduction in the federal role in education, Republican rhetoric increased the salience of education in national politics and among the electorate and helped to generate momentum for increased federal leadership in school reform.

By the middle of the 1980s it was clear that the ideational foundation of the equity policy regime created in 1965 in education had been destroyed. The liberal emphasis on improved access and resources that had been the foundation of the original ESEA was increasingly seen as insufficient to improve student performance—either for its original target population of disadvantaged students or for American students generally. The conservative attempt to eliminate the federal role had also been defeated and was unpopular with the general public. An alternative reform vision began to develop among many governors and business leaders that called for national leadership and reforms centered on academic standards. The continuing opposition of both liberals and conservatives—and key groups within the Democratic and Republican coalitions—to a reform-oriented federal role in education, however, persisted throughout the 1980s and into the 1990s. On the Democratic side, the opposition of teachers unions to reforms with teeth—such as strong standards, testing, choice, and accountability measures—prevented the federal government from adopting a more active and productive role in improving schools. The Republican Party in the 1980s, meanwhile, was heavily influenced by religious conservatives and states' rights groups, which opposed any federal role in education whatsoever.

The 1980 and 1984 presidential elections centered on foreign policy and Republican critiques of Great Society–style social welfare policies. By forcing Democratic nominees to defend an increasingly costly and unpopular federal welfare state, Reagan did not have to offer much more than a general rejection of liberalism and federal activism in areas like education. Growing public attention to school reform (and domestic issues generally) and emerging doubts about the Republican commitment to equal opportunity would eventually increase the political importance of the Democrats' advantage on the education issue and force the Republicans to develop a more substantive response. The evisceration of the original equity regime that had animated ESEA and the emergence of a new dynamic of national education politics would usher in a new era of federal school politics and policy-making in the 1990s.

4. From Devolution to National Goals in Education— George H. W. Bush and America 2000 (1988–1992)

Conservatives' high-profile attack on the federal role in education and the release of the report *A Nation at Risk* signaled the beginning of the end of the equity education policy regime that had existed since 1965. As education began to rise on the national agenda during the 1980s and 1990s, Republicans and Democrats alike had strong political incentives to respond with new federal initiatives and increased spending. Such federal government activism, while consistent with the principles of the Democratic Party, was at odds with the devotion to decentralization, deregulation, and limited government that had long been at the heart of the GOP. Despite the desire of some moderate Republicans to use federal influence to push state school reform efforts forward, major differences remained within the Republican Party over the federal role in education—and social policy more generally—and the struggle to resolve them would be a central theme of the late 1980s and 1990s. Intra- and interpartisan debates over education took on broader political significance, too, as the issue became central to both parties' attempts to adapt their public philosophies to the post–Great Society era.

George H. W. Bush would work to establish a "kinder and gentler" image for the Republican Party by embracing more moderate rhetoric and a pragmatic agenda on social policy and by pledging to be an "education president" during the 1988 presidential campaign. He abandoned the Reagan administration's proposal to eliminate the Department of Education and instead called for using federal influence to promote school improvement based on academic standards and tests. As president, Bush would contribute to the nationalization of the school reform debate by convening an unprecedented education summit with governors in Charlottesville, Virginia, and introducing legislation to establish national goals in education. But Bush's attempt to establish a new moderate policy regime in education based on national standards and assessments was ultimately defeated by liberals who remained wedded to the traditional federal focus on inputs and by conservatives who felt that any federal role in education was counterproductive and would threaten local control.

THE 1988 ELECTION AND BUSH'S PLEDGE TO BE
AN "EDUCATION PRESIDENT"

The starting point for any evaluation of Bush's approach to education policy must be the 1988 presidential election, which pitted Bush against Michael Dukakis, a three-term governor of Massachusetts.[1] As Reagan's vice president (and previously a representative in the U.S. Congress), Bush had had little involvement with educational issues—unlike Dukakis, who had worked on school reform issues as governor. *A Nation at Risk* had put education on the national agenda, however, and in 1988 education was high among the public's concerns, although it was eclipsed by the issues of defense, taxes, and crime. Polls taken during the campaign revealed that education would have a significant impact on the election, with 87 percent of respondents indicating that the issue was "very important" in deciding how they would vote.[2] As a result, the candidates devoted a great deal of rhetoric to education, with one commentator noting that "education is all the rage among the presidential candidates this year. It's the one-word answer to every tough question—how America can boost its productivity and competitiveness, how to stop the AIDS, and drug, plagues, how to lift up the underclass."[3]

Early in the campaign primary season, presidential candidates from both parties gathered for a debate focused exclusively on education, which was apparently the first such debate in U.S. history.[4] The lingering perception of an educational crisis and the flurry of state-level school reforms in the 1980s also pushed the presidential candidates in 1988 to develop more ambitious federal reform proposals. Public support for increased federal spending and involvement in education increased substantially between 1980 and 1990.[5] A 1987 Gallup survey, for example, found that 84 percent of Americans thought that the federal government should require state and local educational authorities to meet minimum national standards.[6]

Bush entered the campaign with the advantage of being associated with a popular outgoing administration and the economic growth that had occurred on its watch. But in an attempt to appeal to moderate voters, Bush sought to identify issues that would distinguish him from his predecessor and distance him from Reagan's unpopular conservative positions on social issues.[7] The Reagan administration's cutbacks in federal education funding and its attempts to eliminate the Department of Education had left Bush and the Republican Party in a vulnerable position on education. In fact, in 1988, the American public thought Democrats would do a better job of improving education than would Republicans by more than a two-to-one margin. Bush sought to address perceived Republican callousness on education and social welfare by declaring his intention to work for a "kinder, gentler nation" and to be "the education president." As Bush adviser

Charlie Kolb has noted, Bush "had to find a way to define himself differently than Reagan without undermining him. Bush used the education pledge as a friendly, subtle way of distinguishing himself from Reagan—it gave Bush something positive to stand for."[8] Bush made education one of the centerpieces of his campaign and emphasized its importance to solving many of the nation's pressing social and economic problems.

In the speech that he gave around the country, Bush stated, "I'd like to be the education president. See, I believe as I look into the future—our ability to compete around the world, our ability to solve problems of poverty that are unsolved in this country . . . whatever it is, education has got to be the priority. Better schools mean better jobs."[9] Bush repeatedly hammered on the inadequacy of the American public school system and the need for improvement. In a speech to the National Press Club in June 1988, Bush argued that "our schools are absolutely not as good as they must be . . . [and] to achieve quality results, we must set and enforce standards, provide incentives, and permit the freedom and flexibility on the local level to experiment with new ideas."[10] Bush's remarks on education were generally well received by the media and, according to polls, by the public. Bob Teeter, the Bush campaign pollster, noted that the issue was good policy and good politics and that "the more he began to talk about education publicly, the better reaction it got."[11] Republican strategists believed it was important to address family issues such as education, child care, and health care, which had traditionally been strong issues for the Democratic Party, and that Republicans had an advantage in promoting school reform because they, unlike the Democrats, were not tied to powerful education interest groups.[12]

Bush called for increasing federal spending on education and for the creation of a number of new federal education programs, which marked a clear break with the policies of the Reagan administration and the wishes of many conservatives in his party. Bush's education plan also called for public school choice, renewed efforts to deregulate schools, and the creation of more rigorous academic standards. He pledged to hold a national conference on education with governors from around the country to discuss school reform. While emphasizing the importance of education to him and to the country, however, Bush was careful to offer the disclaimer that he did not support federal control of education: "I don't want the federal government taking over. I don't want the federal government talking about the curriculum and setting all of that. . . . But I also think a role of the president ought to be using the bully pulpit to spell out excellence."[13]

Bush's more pragmatic agenda on education stemmed in part from his general ideological moderation and in part from a recognition that the federal government's role in education was not likely to disappear and, indeed, would ultimately be decisive in shaping school reform efforts. This view—which was shared by a number of moderate Republican business leaders, governors, and members of Congress—was expressed most clearly in a 1986 *National Review* article by Chester Finn, a member of the Department of Education in the Reagan and Bush I administrations. In the piece, entitled "Two Cheers for Education's G-Men," Finn emphasized that the "war of ideas" about education was increasingly being fought at the national level and warned Republicans that they should shift their efforts from eliminating the federal role in schools to reforming it.

> It is time to consider, once again, the possibility that the Federal Government could be the ally of good education.... For conservatives to abandon the effort at systematic inquiry into education or the dissemination of sound educational ideas is to leave the field firmly in the possession of the colleges of education, the NEA, the American Association of School Administrators, and other bastions of liberal establishmentarianism. Whatever our internal differences about how to repair the education system, the most shortsighted strategy imaginable would be to withdraw all our explorers from this alien territory and turn it back over to the indigenous population.[14]

The conservative wing of the Republican Party, however, saw even Bush's relatively modest campaign proposals as a dangerous federal intrusion into the prerogatives of local government. These concerns found expression in the 1988 Republican platform, which took a slightly softer tone on the federal role in education compared to 1984 but nonetheless declared that "parents have the primary right and responsibility for education."[15] The platform criticized the expansive Democratic education proposals and praised the efforts of the Reagan administration to return educational control to the states. It noted that

> for two decades before 1981, poor public policies had led to an alarming decline in performance in our schools. Unfocused federal spending seemed to worsen the situation, hamstringing education with regulations and wasting resources in faddish programs top-heavy with administrative overhead.... In the 1980s, we asserted what works: parental responsibility, community support and local control, good teachers and determined administrators, and a return to the basic values and content of the Western civilization.

Another significant development in the campaign was the shifting Republican approach to school choice. Reagan's choice rhetoric had been seen mainly as a part of his broader program of deregulation and privatization and had focused on appealing to disaffected Catholics. In 1988, however, Republicans began a tentative effort to use school choice as a way to neutralize the party's weakness on education and the equity issue. Thus the Republican platform voiced its support for federal school vouchers as a way to "empower [low-income families] to choose quality . . . schooling." School choice held a natural attraction for the Republicans by promising a way to address educational concerns without expanding the federal government's role. In this and future campaigns, however, Republicans would have a difficult time attracting minority voters, who remained strongly aligned with the Democratic Party.

Dukakis and the Democratic Party, meanwhile, faced a tremendous challenge in 1988 given Reagan's successful attacks on the welfare state and the public's overall satisfaction with eight years of Republican rule. Recognizing the need to modify the party's traditional support for federal activism in a time of large budget deficits and public skepticism of the efficacy of government programs, Democrats would use "a new political language," as one reporter called it. "Instead of talking about 'spending,' they propose 'investments in the future.' They hate the word 'taxes,' preferring, when they have to, to speak of 'new revenues.' . . . Beneath the words is a substantive, and surprising, consensus that is coming to be called the 'post-Reagan agenda.'"[16] The central components of this agenda were welfare reform and economic competitiveness, and educational improvement was proposed as a crucial means of attaining these wider goals. Dukakis attempted to run a more moderate campaign that focused on "competence" rather than "ideology," and this marked the first time a Democratic presidential nominee had explicitly sought to distance himself from the party's activist legacy. Despite these efforts, the Bush campaign was able to successfully depict Dukakis as another "tax and spend" liberal in the mold of George McGovern, Jimmy Carter, and Walter Mondale.

Democratic strategists believed that education was a winning issue for the party because polls showed that voters were concerned about the state of schools and were willing to embrace federal leadership and spending in school reform. Education also offered a way for the Democratic Party to appeal to its low-income and minority constituencies as well as to middle-class voters who were generally receptive to government support for poor children in a way that they were not for poor adults. Centrist Democrats such as Colorado governor Roy Romer warned, however, that "the party needs to send a strong message [on education] that it's not just a matter of putting more money into the programs, it's a matter of reforming the programs so we really do deliver an effective service."[17]

Though Dukakis had not been as active on education as other Democratic governors—such as Bill Clinton of Arkansas and Richard Riley of South Carolina—he emphasized his efforts to promote school reform in Massachusetts and claimed that "no issue, no concern, no institution means more to me."[18] Given the press of higher agenda items, however, Dukakis did not make education a central theme of his campaign; his education proposals were modest in size and scope and lacked the specificity of Bush's. The centerpiece of Dukakis's education plan was a $250 million National Teaching Excellence Fund. In general, however, Dukakis sought to demonstrate his support for public education by his promise to increase federal education funding and his opposition to private school choice. Like Bush, Dukakis advocated working with governors to support the creation of higher academic standards and to reward successful states with additional federal resources.

Dukakis challenged Bush's credentials on education, stating that Bush's pledge to be an education president was the product of an "election year conversion" and that Bush must have been "playing hooky" when the Reagan administration's education cutbacks were made.[19] "How can he say [he wants to be an education president] after the last seven years," Dukakis wondered, "after seven years of an administration that has slammed a door in the face of millions of youngsters looking for the chance to go to college, after seven years of treating education as if it were a product, like a sports car or a fancy living room set, as if it were a privilege for the few instead of a right?"[20] At the Democratic National Convention, the party's spokespeople contrasted Democrats' historical commitment to education with the Reagan and Bush administration's cuts in education funding. Democrats portrayed the Republican Party as more concerned with foreign policy than with domestic policy and ill-equipped to deal with the challenges facing middle- and lower-class Americans.[21]

As had by now become typical for the Democratic candidate, Dukakis received the endorsement of the nation's two major teachers unions, the National Education Association (NEA) and the American Federation of Teachers (AFT). As noted earlier, the NEA (the larger of the two unions) had allied itself firmly with the Democratic Party in 1976 as a result of Democratic president Jimmy Carter's creation of the Department of Education and congressional Democrats' steadfast support of increased federal funding. By 1988 the union had fashioned itself into a major political force, as it marshaled large quantities of the three most important political resources—money, votes, and volunteers. It invested approximately $2 million in political action committees and spent an additional $300,000 to $400,000 annually on political communications with its almost 2 million members.[22] In 1988 NEA members voted to endorse Dukakis over Bush by a huge margin (86 percent to 14 percent) and indicated that Dukakis's call for greater levels of federal education funding and his determination to end what it called "eight years of teacher-bashing" led to their support. The NEA also pledged to mobilize a half-million members to volunteer in his campaign.[23] However, the unions continued to oppose rigorous standards, accountability measures, and calls for expanded school choice, and this opposition circumscribed the reform agenda of the Democratic Party.

In part because of this overwhelming support of teachers for Dukakis, Bush's attempt to make inroads on the issue of education during the campaign was largely unsuccessful. Polls showed that despite Bush's pledge to be an education president, the public continued to view Dukakis more favorably on the issue of education by a sizeable margin.[24] One in-depth study of what it called Bush's "issue trespassing" on education in the 1988 election concluded that his efforts had failed to bring electoral gain.[25] The study demonstrated the difficulty that Bush and other Republicans would face in trying to chip away at the Democrats' longstanding advantage on the education issue. It is quite possible, however, that Bush's education rhetoric helped bolster his broader efforts to be seen as a more moderate and compassionate Republican and thus played an important indirect role in his victory.

The extensive discussions by Bush and Dukakis about education in the 1988 campaign marked a real break from earlier presidential elections in the 1970s and 1980s, when foreign policy issues often dominated the campaigns and when education was rarely discussed. Though Bush and Dukakis were responding to the perception that education had risen on voters' agenda, their expanded rhetoric no doubt helped to solidify the sense that school reform should be a priority for national policymakers. It is also likely that the national attention to education increased public support for expanded federal leadership and spending on education. Ultimately, the continued predominance of economic and foreign policy issues enabled Bush to win the 1988 election despite losing the education issue. As president, however, Bush would face mounting pressure to increase federal education funding and to bring about measurable improvement in school performance.

BUSH'S FIRST EDUCATION REFORM PLAN

Once in office, Bush worked to fulfill his pledge to be an education president by continuing to talk about the importance of school reform and by declaring the issue one of his legislative priorities. Whereas Reagan had mentioned education in (on average) 312 public speeches and statements a year, for example, Bush would do so more than twice as often, in 664 speeches and statements a year on average, during his term.[26] Education would be a touchstone issue in Bush's effort to make a "kinder, gentler America" and to move the Republican Party closer to the political center on domestic policy. According to one adviser, "his education policy . . . in many respects came to serve as the cornerstone for the rest of his domestic social agenda."[27]

Bush's positions on education were fundamentally different from his Republican predecessor's in a number of important ways. Reagan's first education secretary, Terrell Bell, commented that

> in education, there's probably a bigger difference [between Bush and Reagan] than in other aspects of government policy. I think there will be a perception about the federal role that will be different. I wouldn't say that there won't be an understanding

that education is primarily a state and local responsibility, but there will also be an understanding that there can be some federal leadership provided and more concern and compassion for disadvantaged, low-income, and handicapped children.[28]

Reagan and deputies such as Bill Bennett had blamed the teachers unions and bureaucrats for the poor performance of American schools and called for school vouchers and the elimination of the Department of Education. Bush, in contrast, praised teachers for "giving their heart and soul to their jobs," declared his opposition to public funding of private schools, and abandoned the effort to close the department.

Bush's emphasis on education raised expectations that his administration would bring about successful reform, but he faced a number of obstacles in gaining passage of his education agenda. First and foremost, many of Bush's fellow Republicans in Congress had supported President Reagan's attempts to abolish the Department of Education and reduce federal influence over schools and were wary of any new initiatives that might give Washington more control over local schools. Second, the economic recession and large budget deficit—along with Bush's campaign pledge not to raise taxes—dramatically limited the federal money available for new programs in education or elsewhere. Third, Congress was controlled by Democrats who were unlikely to support education proposals that would threaten their key allies in the teacher's unions or that might help Bush politically on a traditionally Democratic issue. Fourth, despite the collapse of the Soviet Union, the Persian Gulf War would ultimately focus the president's attention on foreign rather than domestic policy.

President Bush first outlined his education approach publicly in his "Building a Better America" speech to Congress on February 9, 1989. Emphasizing themes he had developed during the campaign, Bush stated that

> the most important competitiveness program of all is one which improves education in America. When some of our students actually have trouble locating America on a map of the world, it is time for us to map a new approach to education. We must reward excellence and cut through bureaucracy. We must help schools that need help the most. We must give choice to parents, students, teachers, and principals; and we must hold all concerned accountable. In education, we cannot tolerate mediocrity.[29]

Two months later, Bush sent education reform legislation, the Educational Excellence Act of 1989, to Congress. His plan called for reallocating $441 million from the Department of Education's budget to support several initiatives that Bush had touted during the campaign—rewards for excellent teachers and merit schools, expanded public school choice, alternative teacher certification programs, and increased drug prevention education.

The Bush proposal was, on the whole, quite modest and really more notable for what it did not contain than for what it did. The legislation did not call for significantly increased federal funding for education, private school vouchers, or national education standards and tests, which would become a prominent feature of the education debate a few years later. In presenting the plan, Bush echoed the Reagan administration argument that additional federal funding was not the answer to solving the problems that plagued the public school system. Bush remarked that "we must do more than wish we had more to spend, because the challenge of education reform suggests something much more fundamental than money."[30] He nonetheless faced an uphill struggle in convincing Democrats in Congress and the general public that school reform could be achieved without significantly increased federal investment in education. A poll taken right before Bush took office, for example, revealed that a large majority of Americans (72 percent) thought the federal government should spend more money on schools.[31]

Bush's education legislation failed to gain passage in 1989 or the following year, when it was reintroduced in virtually the same form. The bills were attacked by Democrats in Congress, who lamented that they did not allocate sufficient spending or provide enhanced federal leadership in education.[32] Though Democratic opposition was to be expected, the Bush proposal also had a frigid reception among many Republicans. Conservatives were angered that Bush had called for new federal education initiatives and had not called for private school vouchers or tuition tax credits, and this contributed to his shaky standing with the party's conservative wing.

The Democrat-controlled House and Senate passed bills that scaled down or stripped most of the reform-oriented provisions from the original Bush proposal and instead provided for increased funding for existing—and Democrat-supported—education programs. The revised bills also authorized funding for the National Board for Professional Teaching Standards (NBPTS), which drew sharp opposition from the Bush administration and conservative Republicans such as Sen. Jesse Helms (R-NC), who saw the panel as an inappropriate intrusion of the federal government into teacher licensing. The conference report passed the House, but conservative Republicans in the Senate saw the legislation as a threat to local control of education and used "holds" to prevent it from ever coming up for a vote on the Senate floor.

Had Bush's education bill passed, the president could have claimed an important legislative victory and trumpeted that he was providing national leadership for results-based education reform. The repudiation of the bill by Democrats reconfirmed the suspicion of many Republicans that Democrats were unwilling to deviate from the status quo in education. The actual demise of the bill at the hands of conservative Republicans, meanwhile, both provided grist for Democratic accusations that the Republican Party was not concerned about education and denied Bush a legislative success on one of his high-profile domestic priorities.

THE CHARLOTTESVILLE SUMMIT AND
THE NATIONAL EDUCATION GOALS

As the administration's first education bill lay stalled in Congress, Bush turned to the bully pulpit to make good on his campaign promise to be an "education president." The centerpiece of this effort was the convening of an unprecedented meeting of the nation's governors in Charlottesville, Virginia, in the fall of 1989 to discuss education reform and the idea of national standards. As Bush administration official Chester Finn has noted,

> The Charlottesville summit was a public relations effort necessitated by the fact that there wasn't anything else the administration could do on education. . . . Everything was dead in the water, and nothing was happening. Bush had said he was going to be the education president but hadn't really done anything. This sense that we needed to look like we were doing something on education led to two big symbolic efforts—PEPAC (the President's Education Policy Advisory Committee) and the Charlottesville summit.[33]

The standards movement had received strong support from the business community and had generated a great deal of momentum at the state level during the 1980s.[34] As Chester Finn has observed, "This kind of results-oriented way of thinking took over the country's education reform consciousness in the 1980s. . . . The *A Nation at Risk* report led to an obsessive focus on results, and there was mounting awareness that the federal input-based strategy hadn't achieved adequate results."[35]

Several southern governors who had been active in pushing standards at the state level—Bill Clinton (D-AK), Richard Riley (D-SC), and Lamar Alexander (R-TN)—played a prominent role at the Charlottesville conference. The central compromise of the summit was a pledge on the part of the Bush administration to give states and school districts more flexibility in the use of federal education funds in exchange for commitments to meet school performance standards. The governors agreed to support the creation of a set of national education goals and to assess the states' progress in meeting them. Which role the federal government should play in promoting and paying for reform was a major source of disagreement at the conference, but ultimately the governors agreed to support the creation of voluntary national education goals, with little resolution concerning the role of the federal government.[36]

The formal statement released by the summit participants stated that "we believe that the time has come, for the first time in U.S. history, to establish clear, national performance goals, goals that will make us internationally competitive. This agreement represents the first step in a long-term commitment to re-orient the education system and to marshal widespread support for the needed reforms."[37] In his speech at the close of the summit, Bush remarked that "this is a major step forward in education. We've reached agreement on the need for national performance goals, on the need for more flexibility and accountability, [and] the need for restructuring and choice." He added, "A social compact begins today in Charlottesville, a compact between parents, teachers, principals, superintendents, state legislators, governors, and the Administration. . . . The American people are ready for radical reforms. We must not disappoint them."[38] Democratic governors and members of Congress indicated that they intended to seek additional funds to support the education goals and would hold Bush to promises made at the summit in this regard.

Most observers hailed Bush's decision to orchestrate the education summit as a political masterstroke, for it enabled him to fulfill his pledge to be an education president without directly expanding the federal role in education. As one observer noted, "the 1989 summit meeting was a carefully orchestrated media event designed to enhance the president's image as an educational leader determined to solve the 'crisis' in education despite his focused effort to propel the federal government away from financial commitments to educational reform."[39] Both Democrats and Republicans thought that the Charlottesville summit would aid their respective school reform agendas. Republicans thought that the emphasis on school performance would shift the national education debate from a focus on school inputs to school outputs. Democrats, however, believed that the increased media and public attention to education at the national level would put pressure on Bush and the Republicans to accept increased spending on education. William Safire agreed, warning at the time that the summit could make Republican efforts to reduce the federal role in education much more difficult. "Nobody seems to sense the danger in this grand confabulation," he wrote. "If all we hear is the sounds of 50 rattling tin cups, and if all we see is the spectacle of a demand for leadership from Washington, then we will witness a voluntary power shift from the states to the national government."[40]

From the basic agreement in Charlottesville that there should be national education goals, the White House and the National Governors Association (NGA) engaged in intensive negotiations to determine exactly what those goals would be. Announced in President Bush's 1990 State of the Union address, the six goals were: (1) all children in America will start school ready to learn; (2) the high school graduation rate will increase to at least 90 percent; (3) students in grades four, eight, and twelve will be competent in English, mathematics, science, foreign languages, civics and government, economics, arts, history, and geography; (4) every school will be free of drugs, violence, firearms, and alcohol and will offer a disciplined learning environment; (5) U.S. students will be the first in the world in mathematics and science achievement; (6) every adult will be literate and will possess the knowledge and skills necessary to compete in a global economy. The goals were intentionally quite vague, calling for children in the United States to start school "ready to learn," to be "competent" in a variety of subjects, and to attend schools that were "free" of drugs and violence and that offered a "disciplined" learning environment. What specifically was meant by those terms, how states should work to meet the goals, and what, if anything, the federal government would do if the goals were not met was not clear.

Once Bush announced what the national goals were, the next—and crucial—question became determining how the progress of schools and states would be encouraged. Many became convinced that the vague national goals would have to be supplemented by more specific national standards and tests in order to push states forward in their reform efforts and to provide a yardstick against which such efforts could be measured. As Diane Ravitch has written, "The logic of the goals implied new arrangements, but at the outset, no one knew what those might be nor whether national standards could be established without also creating an intrusive federal bureaucracy."[41] Although the idea that schools should be pushed to achieve higher standards had become widely embraced by the time of the Charlottesville summit, there was little consensus on the sticky (but essential) issues of measurement and accountability. Finn has noted that "the standards-based reform movement argued that we should state what results we'd like to achieve, then establish a reliable measuring system to see if we're achieving them, and then create a behavior modification program such that if desired results are being achieved, people get rewarded, and if not, then people get whacked or punished."[42] The key issue, however, was whether the federal government would do any whacking. Democrats—and their teachers union allies—were strongly opposed to any federal accountability system that was punitive in nature or failed to provide extra resources for implementation. Republicans, meanwhile, were convinced that teachers and school administrators would not change their behavior without strong accountability measures but were wary of federal interference in local control of schools or the prospect of increased federal funding.

Democrats ultimately came to see national standards—or at least the right *kind* of standards—as a means of highlighting the need for significantly increased federal education funding. Though most Republicans in Congress continued to object to national standards and tests, some moderate Republicans were beginning to embrace them as the only way to spur needed improvements in schools. Rep. Bill Goodling (R-PA), for example, wrote in a 1990 op-ed piece that one of the problems in the past has been that the federal oversight of [education] programs has focused primarily on fiscal accountability and not on educational accountability. That is, was the money spent on the right categories of children, for the approved activities, within the proper period of time? There has not been much emphasis on what difference the funds make in the education and development of these students. . . . The federal government must support . . . a new generation of testing approaches that better measure what students know . . . and to reward improvement and excellence.[43]

Widespread public support for national education standards also gave the movement significant momentum. A 1987 Gallup poll found, for example, that 84 percent of Americans thought that the federal government should require state and local educational authorities to meet minimum national standards.[44]

The Charlottesville summit—like the earlier release of A Nation at Risk—was clearly an important turning point in the history of federal education policy. Bush Department of Education official Bruno Manno believes that it was "important both for its symbolism and for what it said. It began to shift the school reform debate to standards and the goals that we wanted for public education. There was a new focus on results and accountability and the beginning of a discussion about alternative school structures."[45] However, deep disagreements over the appropriate federal role in pushing national standards emerged after the administration created the National Education Goals Panel in the middle of 1990. The panel was intended to provide an institutional impetus to facilitate and encourage state school reform but quickly became mired in controversy over its membership and mission. In the end its role was largely limited to issuing yearly report cards on the nation's progress toward the education goals. Though support for national standards and tests continued to grow in the aftermath of the Charlottesville summit, there was little consensus over the role the federal government should play in pushing states to meet the goals or even in measuring their progress toward them. As the battle over Bush's second education reform plan would show, disagreements within and between the parties remained a major barrier to the creation of a new reform-oriented federal policy regime in education.

AMERICA 2000 AND THE FIGHT
OVER PRIVATE SCHOOL CHOICE

The Charlottesville summit was widely viewed as a public relations victory for the Bush administration, but in subsequent months the governors and the media increasingly criticized the White House for failing to follow through on the promises made at the summit. The administration was slow to move to create a national education goals panel, did not push for additional resources for education, and seemed content to confine its education reform efforts to symbolic efforts such as the "Educational Excellence for Hispanic Americans Executive Order."[46] As a result, the public view of Bush as an education president would decline significantly over the course of his administration. By February 1990, polls showed that the public was more critical than positive of Bush's handling of education by more than a two-to-one margin.[47] In an April 1990 survey, only 32 percent of respondents thought Bush was doing an "excellent" or "good" job in dealing with the country's long-term educational problems, and 61 percent rated him "fair" or "poor."[48] Surveys showed that the majority of the public believed that schools had not improved during the first two years of Bush's term, with more people seeing them as having deteriorated than improved.[49] When asked if Bush had made progress in improving schools, only 8 percent thought he had, and 72 percent believed that he had "just talked about it."[50]

Toward the end of his term, Bush and his advisers became increasingly worried about the domestic record that the president would be able to take to voters when he came up for reelection in 1992. The Persian Gulf War had dominated the headlines and the attention of the administration during 1990–1991. As the war receded in the public mind and the economy sank further into recession, public attention shifted to domestic issues, and Bush's once-high public approval ratings began to sag. An August 1991 poll, for example, asked respondents to rate the issues that should be the president's most important priority: 45 percent chose "domestic issues such as education, health care, and the environment," 36 percent picked the economy, and only 12 percent selected foreign policy.[51] Bush's advisers became increasingly concerned about the need for the president to record some domestic policy successes. As one administration official remarked at the time, "Pretty soon, it's going to be 1992 and I don't know what the President is going to run on."[52]

Bush and his advisers seized on education reform as the way to signal the president's commitment to solving domestic problems and bringing about social progress. Why education? Two of the most memorable promises that Bush had made during the 1988 presidential campaign had been his pledge to not raise taxes and to be an education president. In late 1990, however, Bush had agreed to a compromise with Democrats in Congress on the budget that included an increase in certain taxes—a decision that was roundly criticized not just by conservatives but also by many moderate Republicans. Having abandoned one of his central campaign promises, Bush and his advisers were also well aware that they had done little to deliver on the other—education reform. Education also remained high on the national agenda in December 1990, with citizens identifying it as the second-most urgent problem facing the country (after crime).[53]

The decision was made to change the public face of the Bush education team and to propose new, more aggressive reforms in the hope of gaining a legislative victory or, at least, improving public perceptions about Bush's commitment to schools. In December 1990, Bush fired his education secretary, Lauro Cavazos, and replaced him with Lamar Alexander, the former governor of Tennessee and a key participant in the Charlottesville summit.[54] The switch to Alexander marked a crucial turning point in the Bush administration's education agenda, as it began to vigorously advocate national standards and testing as well as private school choice.[55] In April 1991 President Bush introduced his America 2000 education reform plan. The centerpiece of the plan was a proposal to develop more detailed standards in the core academic subjects to encourage progress toward the national education goals. It also called for the National Education Goals Panel to create "a system of voluntary examinations" called "American Achievement Tests" for all fourth, eighth, and twelvth graders, which would be made available to governors for adoption.[56] America 2000 also proposed the creation of a quasi–private-public "New American Schools Development Corporation" to design model schools; the publication of report cards for schools, districts, and states; merit pay and alternative certification for teachers and principals; and the establishment of a number of private school choice demonstration projects. Though Bush administration officials would later claim that the voucher proposal was not intended to be the centerpiece of the reform package, it would become its most controversial component.

The legislation's ambiguous language on standards and goals reflected the contradictory philosophical and political imperatives at work within the Bush administration on education. Bush and his advisers hoped to reap political gain by demonstrating their commitment to national leadership in education while at the same time assuaging the fears among conservative Republicans that the federal government would expand its control over public schools. Out of such political pressures was born the legislation's strange phrasing about "state-level national assessments." Similarly, Bush's speech introducing the legislation attempted to walk the fine line between declaring education a national priority and proclaiming it a local responsibility. Bush called for "a true renaissance in American education," stating that "if we want America to remain a leader, a force for good in the world, we must lead the way in educational innovation. Think about every problem, every challenge we face. The solution to each starts with education." At the same time, however, Bush argued that "people who want Washington to solve their educational problems are missing the point. What happens here in Washington won't matter half as much as what happens in each school, each local community, and yes, each home."[57]

Bush—like many other Republicans during the 1980s and 1990s—would try to convince the public to draw a distinction between "national" and "federal" efforts in education reform. "America 2000," Bush wrote in transmitting the legislation to Congress, "is more than just a federal effort; it is truly a national strategy. . . . The legislative proposals included in the bill are just components, albeit very important components, of a strategy most of which would take place outside of the federal government."[58] Lesley Arsht, a Bush administration education official, added that "America 2000 was crafted not to expand the federal role but to give the feds a limited role and to work our way around Congress. . . . Our perspective was that if any of this was to work over the long term it had to be bottom-up rather than top-down."[59] Observers then and later, however, questioned whether the American public was willing or able to discern the difference between a national or a federal school reform approach or to appreciate a philosophical defense of federalism.

Vouchers aside, America 2000 was a moderate and pragmatic plan that called for active federal leadership to promote school reform through a new focus on student achievement. As a centrist plan, however, it alienated some on both the right and the left. As Arsht has noted, "Democrats hated America 2000 immediately. Liberal Democrats hated it because it wasn't enough money and it didn't go to the right places. Conservative Republicans didn't like it because they didn't want federal involvement in schools, period, and they certainly didn't want federal tests."[60] Sen. Edward Kennedy (D-MA), chair of the Senate Labor and Human Resources Committee, remarked about the legislation that

> Robbing old education programs to pay for new ones is nothing more that education strip mining. We should not . . . look only to current school programs as the source of new funds for school reforms. That's not the way we paid for the Persian Gulf War, and it's not the way we win the battle for better education. . . . By offering public dollars to private schools, including religious schools, the administration is reopening the bitter and divisive policy and constitutional debates of the past about public aid to private schools.[61]

Kennedy's comments contained all of the main criticisms that Democrats would use to attack Republican education reform proposals in the 1992 presidential election and for the rest of the 1990s.[62] Democrats would argue that educational improvement necessitated increased spending on education and highlighted Bush's (and Republicans') preference for spending on the military over domestic programs as a sign of their skewed priorities. Democrats were aided in this effort by the nation's two largest teachers unions, the NEA and the AFT, which publicly opposed the Bush education plan and portrayed Republican school voucher proposals as an attack on public education that would divert crucial resources from poor public schools.[63]

The Democratic response to the Bush initiatives regarding standards and testing—to call for converting federal education funds into unrestricted block grants—was, to say the least, ironic given the debates of the preceding twenty years. The liberal policy regime of the 1960s, 1970s, and 1980s had utilized federal mandates to force states to promote access and equity for disadvantaged and minority students. Republicans had complained that such mandates were an inappropriate and intrusive burden on schools. Bush's America 2000 plan represented the first attempt to use federal influence to promote school reform—to address the outputs of education rather than just process and inputs. This was a historic shift in the view of the federal role, and it challenged the longstanding Democratic and Republican positions on federal education policy.

In the end, the final compromise bill on America 2000 that emerged from the House-Senate conference committee did not include three of the four major elements of Bush's original proposal—school choice, "New American Schools," or national student assessments. The Democratic bill did, however, include national academic standards as well as school delivery or "opportunity to learn" standards to encourage states to set minimum levels of resources that should be provided to schools. Bush and Republicans in Congress vehemently opposed the school delivery standards because they saw them as an attempt to shift the debate over school reform away from performance and back to funding. Republicans also feared that having national standards without assessments would increase federal influence and spending on education without improving school performance or accountability. Secretary Alexander declared that the school reform bill in the House was "even worse than awful" and that the Senate bill "pokes the federal government's nose too far into local decisions," would create "new layers of unworkable bureaucracy," and "fails to help change our schools."[64] Alexander publicly called for the president to veto the bill if it reached his desk. Determined to avoid forcing the education president to veto an education bill close to the election, however, Senate Republicans filibustered the conference report after it passed the House. As a result, Bush's America 2000 bill ultimately died in Congress, and the four years of the Bush administration ended without passage of a single major school reform bill.

The debates over America 2000 revealed that increasing concerns about student performance had produced little consensus on the basis for a new education policy regime. Republicans and Democrats remained opposed to federal standards and tests in 1992, though for very different reasons. Republicans feared that they would inevitably lead to federal control of education, whereas Democrats feared that they would lead to the imposition of unfair school accountability measures and a deemphasis on the importance of increasing federal funding for education. PEPAC chairman Paul O'Neill observed that there is a strain of libertarian thought in the conservative part of the Republican party that believes the federal government should see to the national defense and make sure the post office works and that's all they should do. They viewed this [America 2000] as an overreach of the federal role, as an inappropriate intervention in national affairs. The hard left has generally been reflective of the organized education community that has argued that federal taxpayers should pay a third or more of the total elementary and secondary education funding, and anything that doesn't accomplish that is the wrong thing. The left generally was focused on increasing funding for education—[they] believed that words without money were worthless.[65]

Bush education official Manno reiterated this point, noting that "Democrats didn't want anything to do with a test, and conservatives were afraid of a national curriculum. So you had a very unusual alliance that came about with both the left and the right opposing the bill for different reasons."[66]

Bush and the Republicans blamed Democrats for the defeat of the legislation and charged that they were beholden to the teachers unions and were opposed to any reforms that might change the status quo in education.[67] In response to the rejection of his moderate reform proposals and growing discontent within the Republican Party's conservative base, Bush adopted a more confrontational education tone at the end of his term. Whereas Bush had begun his administration by praising teachers, in July 1992 he remarked that "the problem is that many that control the education establishment in Washington are in the grips of a very powerful union, the NEA."[68] Republicans portrayed themselves as fighting to take power away from bureaucrats and the unions and give it to parents to enhance choice.[69] Republican efforts to blame Democrats for "obstructionism" in Congress apparently were unsuccessful, however, as public opinion polls showed that the public continued to have considerably more faith in the ability of Democrats to handle the education issue.[70]

Despite the virulent opposition to vouchers among the unions and Democrats, Bush also put forward another, bolder school voucher plan in 1992. The GI Bill for Children, as it was called, proposed a $500 million program to give middle- and low-income parents $1,000 in new federal money to spend on the public or private school of their choice. Upon introducing the plan, Bush commented that

we need a revolution in American education, not more money to do it the same old way. . . . Choice can open up opportunities, create genuine change in our schools. For too long, we've shielded our schools from competition, allowed our schools a damaging monopoly power over our children, and this monopoly turns students into statistics and turns parents into pawns. And it is time we began thinking of a system of public education in which many providers offer a marketplace of opportunity, opportunities that give all of our children choices and access to the best education in the world.[71]

The language of economics that was so prevalent in this speech would become a centerpiece of Republican efforts to convince the American public of the efficacy of market-based education reforms.[72] The Bush administration's reversal of its position on vouchers signaled that its efforts to move the party to the middle on education had failed and that Republicans were not yet prepared to embrace active federal leadership in school reform.

The voucher plan was also clearly designed to help Bush repair his damaged relationship with the right wing of the Republican Party. Talk of a conservative challenge to Bush for the 1992 Republican Party nomination began to increase after Bush's agreement on tax increases in the 1990 budget deal. A number of prominent conservatives, including House minority whip Newt Gingrich (R-GA) and former housing and urban development secretary and 1988 presidential candidate Jack Kemp, broke with Bush publicly over taxes and domestic policy. Gingrich noted that "we are in the middle of an argument which a lot of us thought ended in 1989. There really is a fundamental difference between the managerial/accommodationist approach to the welfare state and the reform/replacement approach."[73] As Jay Diskey, special assistant to the U.S. Secretary for Education for Communications in the Bush administration, has noted,

> the Bush GI Bill voucher plan was an example of the policy tensions at work within the party. The modest America 2000 voucher proposal was designed to say to conservatives, look, we're going to keep pushing for this but in a subtle way. Bush and Alexander were moderates and weren't keen on vouchers, but the Bush White House became concerned about losing votes on the right. Beginning in November and December 1991, when the poll numbers began to go south, there was an increasing feeling that the administration needed to do something for the conservative wing of the party, and the GI Bill was the result.[74]

Education—and particularly private school choice—was a passionate issue for conservatives, and Bush and his advisers thought that embracing vouchers would help them regain conservative support while potentially also boosting the president's credentials as an education reformer.[75] Whereas Bush would use education to move to the right in 1992, the Democratic nominee, Bill Clinton, would use the issue to claim the vital political center.

There were really three separate battles wrapped up in the fight over America 2000 and federal education policy during the Bush I administration. The first battle was over the federal role in national standards and tests. Republicans continued to be wary of any legislation that could increase federal control over such major educational issues and argued that the states could solve their own educational problems. Democrats, meanwhile, wanted a strong federal presence in education to promote equity but opposed any effort to create tests that could be used as part of an accountability system that could result in punitive action against teachers or poor and minority students. The second major issue concerned school choice, with Republicans arguing that public and private school choice were necessary both to create competition to improve schools and to give parents a way to move their children out of failing schools. Democrats vehemently opposed private school choice as a dangerous diversion of public resources and feared that public school choice could lead to resegregation and was a distraction from the real funding problems that plagued traditional schools. The third key debate surrounding America 2000 and federal education policy during this period centered on whether additional federal funding was necessary to improve schools. Republicans argued that the essential problems facing schools were curricular and structural and that additional funding was not necessary, whereas Democrats argued that federal money was needed to compensate for local school funding disparities and to provide states with the extra resources to implement reforms. These three issues would continue to dominate the debates over federal education policy during the rest of the 1990s.

CONCLUSION

Despite the lack of a major new education reform law, the first Bush presidency represented an important shift in the evolution of the politics of federal education policy. Bush made his pledge to be an education president a prominent part of his 1988 presidential campaign, and the issue became the centerpiece of his domestic agenda. As Charles Kolb has noted,

> His efforts at reforming America's elementary and secondary system constituted what was probably the best-developed and most coherent of all his domestic policy efforts. Simply measuring Bush's performance by his personal "input," it was evident that he had done more education "events" than any previous president: photo ops, speeches, school visits, Rose Garden recognition and award ceremonies. From a "bully-pulpit" perspective, Bush had very definitely been an activist "education president."[76]

In contrast to Reagan, Bush embraced a federal role in education reform and helped to legitimize the idea that the country's historically decentralized public schools needed national leadership to help them improve.

Whereas Reagan had sought to decentralize control of schools, Bush pushed for the creation of a number of new federal education organizations such as the Federal Literacy Task Force, the National Education Goals Panel, the National Commission on Time and Learning, the Office of Educational Research and Improvement, and the National Commission on Education Standards and Testing.

Though the initial impact of these institutions was (by design) largely symbolic, their activities ultimately helped to further nationalize the debate over education reform. The 1989 Charlottesville summit was also an important milestone in this regard. Whereas Reagan had pushed for states to be allowed to govern their schools without federal interference, Bush gathered the nation's governors together to discuss education reform under presidential direction for the first time. Bush continued to declare his support for local control of schools, but his efforts to shift the focus of federal policy from issues of equity and access to academic performance significantly broadened the nature of federal involvement in education. As PEPAC chairman Paul O'Neill has noted, "The idea that the federal government should go beyond just a variety of financial support interventions was a major turning point. There was a threshold crossed with the national education goals; that was really different, to explicitly define national goals for education."[77]

The Bush administration represented the first concerted attempt to fundamentally shift the Republican Party's approach to federal education policy and to create a new policy regime based on federal support for standards-based school reform. Recognizing the increasing salience of education to voters and the possibility of using the issue as a symbol for his centrist approach to government, Bush largely turned away from the conservative antigovernment approach of the Reagan era. Vic Klatt, the deputy assistant secretary for congressional affairs at the Department of Education in the Bush administration, noted that

> there was a time, back in the 1980s, when Democrats controlled Congress and when education legislation would come up, Republicans would just shrug their shoulders and just go along with it. Every once in a while someone would propose school choice, but mostly they didn't do much and pretty much stayed away from the issue. Republicans began more and more to engage the issue under Bush—public opinion shifts beginning in the early 1990s showing that the issue was more and more important played a big role in this. The Reagan administration really looked at education only through a federalism perspective; Bush began to change this. He wanted to be the education president, and [we] began to see more proactive initiatives on education beyond school choice coming out of the Republican Party.[78]

Instead of pursuing the elimination of federal influence in education, Bush sought to use federal influence to reform public schools and improve student performance. As Jay Diskey recalled, "The fight over America 2000 changed the way a lot of people looked at education reform. It didn't pass, but it really kicked off the standards movement in this country. Administration education officials traveled around the country advocating standards and pushing states to adopt them, and many did so even without federal legislation."[79]

The defeat of Bush's America 2000 plan, however, was a devastating blow to his efforts to reposition the Republican Party and to capitalize on the salience of the school reform issue. Liberal Democrats opposed the focus on choice and standards and continued to argue that increased federal funding was the key to school improvement. The fight over America 2000 also revealed that the Republican Party—and particularly its conservative base—remained staunchly opposed to expanding the federal role in education, even in pursuit of enhanced school accountability. As Diane Ravitch has noted, Republicans were still "committed to the principle of decentralization and local control. . . . President Bush's championing of national standards and a national system of tests, even if voluntary, made many members of his party deeply uncomfortable."[80] The defeat of Bush's two education packages in Congress demonstrated how difficult it would be to develop the political support and policy consensus to establish a new reform-oriented policy regime.

Along with standards and assessments, choice was central to Bush's vision of education reform. The efforts to promote school choice during the Bush administration (and later in the 1990s), however, were hampered by the Republican Party's inability to convince voters of its commitment to serving the disadvantaged. Republicans tried to portray school choice as a civil rights issue by arguing that school vouchers and charter schools would give African-American and urban children trapped in inferior schools a better alternative. They sought to use growing national support for school choice—especially among African-Americans and urban residents—to dispel the perception that the Republican Party was unconcerned with the plight of the poor and minorities. However, for a variety of reasons, including the frosty reception of the established civil rights leadership, continued minority skepticism of the modern Republican Party, and the effectiveness of Democratic efforts to paint Reagan Republicanism as callous, the Republicans were unable to use this appeal to broaden their support among either minorities or swing voters. In general, public affection for the public schools, concern about the inequities inherent in market-based arrangements, and suspicion about Republican motives rendered the choice-based approach to school improvement politically ineffective.

Bush and Republicans repeatedly made the case that increased federal spending and prescriptions were not necessary to improve the country's schools. Despite the considerable amount of rhetoric expended in this effort, however, it clearly failed to convince the public. A survey taken at the end of the Bush administration, in October 1992, revealed that 68 percent of respondents believed federal education spending should be increased, with only 3 percent in favor of a decrease.[81] And in a poll conducted during the final months of the Bush administration, respondents cited inadequate financial support as the top obstacle faced by public schools.[82] Public support for increased spending on education would be a major weapon in the Democratic arsenal in future battles with Republicans over school reform. Bush's decision to give the largest increase in his 1993 budget proposal (11 percent) to the Department of Education seemed to reflect recognition of the failure of Republican arguments about school funding as well as of the importance that education was likely to have in the 1992 election. Bush's argument that the influence of the federal government over schools was limited and that reform had to be initiated by state and local governments also failed to resonate with the public. A December 1991 poll found that a majority (66 percent) thought that the president can "do a lot" to improve the quality of education in public schools; only 28 percent responded that the president can only "do a little."[83]

In the end, the lack of substantial increases in federal spending, the defeat of his legislative proposals, and support for school vouchers undermined Bush's appeal for support among moderate and minority voters on the education issue. A *Phi Delta Kappan* survey also found that the public held a very poor view of the state of America's public schools and of Bush's education record (with 52 percent giving him a grade of D or F and only 7 percent an A or B).[84] Though polls showed support for some of Bush's specific education reform proposals, such as standards and testing, he was never able to convert this support into approval of his overall education reform strategy or into credibility for the Republican Party on the education issue. This may have been due to the very public divisions within the GOP on education and Bush's shifting rhetoric and policy positions as he sought to appeal both to the conservative base of the Republican Party and to the more moderate mass public.

Despite his failure to enact a reform program or reap political gain on education, however, Bush—like Reagan before him—did much to increase media and public attention to the crisis in U.S. schools and thus helped make school reform a high-profile *national* issue. Ernest Boyer, president of the Carnegie Foundation for the Advancement of Teaching, observed during the Bush administration that a "weakening of localism" in education had resulted in "less concern about local control than national results" among parents and the general public. Boyer believed that education was in the midst of a "historic transition," with a shift from an era when "local control over schools was the only conversation we ever had" to concern over "how to balance local control with national results."[85] Bush was able to generate some momentum behind the idea of national standards and tests and to begin to shift the debate over school reform from inputs to outputs and from funding to structural reforms. Bush communications adviser Lesley Arsht has remarked that "the Bush administration was successful at one thing in education and failed at everything else. They staked the ground around standards and national goals and began a conversation that raised the profile of education. They put education on the agenda and established improving education as a high priority for the nation."[86]

In the 1988 campaign—and during the first half of his administration—Bush had adopted a moderate message on education and used the issue to present himself as a kinder, gentler Republican. This move caused some resentment with conservatives, and during the second half of his administration, fearing a conservative challenge to his renomination, Bush responded by embracing vouchers and adopting a more aggressive rhetoric toward the teachers unions and the education establishment. As some observers noted at the time, the move to the right (on education and other issues) left Bush vulnerable to a centrist Democratic challenger in 1992.[87] And the failure of the Bush administration to increase federal funding for education, to pass major education legislation, or to generate improvements in school performance left him particularly vulnerable on an issue that Bush had hoped to make a source of strength. When asked, in a poll taken during the final year of his administration, whether Bush could fairly call himself the education president based on his record in office, an overwhelming 81 percent of respondents said no—clear evidence that Bush had failed to win the public relations battle in education reform.[88]

During the 1992 presidential campaign and throughout the rest of the decade, Democrats would use the economic recession and the end of the Cold War to reemphasize their party's commitment to using the federal government to promote federal leadership on a number of pressing domestic issues, including education. The next stage in the construction of the new education policy regime would be heavily influenced by the Democrats' attempt to use the school reform issue strategically to reclaim the political center, much as Bush had tried, but ultimately failed, to do. But the rising profile of education and the continuing sense of crisis about student performance would push Democrats, as it had Republicans, to reconsider their longstanding opposition to a reform-oriented federal role in education. Under Bill Clinton, the Democrats would seize the initiative on school reform during the 1990s and revive the push for standards, accountability, and choice that Bush had begun but failed to consummate.

5. Laying the Foundation for a New Accountability Regime—Clinton, the 1992 Presidential Election, and Goals 2000 (1992–1994)

Bush's pledge to be an education president, the Charlottesville summit, and the debate over America 2000 significantly raised the profile of education as a national political issue. The fall of the Berlin Wall in 1989 and the end of the Cold War, meanwhile, had changed the dynamics of American politics—decreasing the importance of foreign policy issues and elevating the significance of domestic policy. The shifting political environment in the early 1990s produced new political pressures for Republicans and Democrats alike. Public opinion polls conducted in the early 1990s revealed that voters had grown tired of the ideological battles between antigovernment conservatives and big-government liberals that had dominated American politics in the 1980s.[1] In 1992 George H. W. Bush struggled to develop a domestic agenda without alienating the crucial conservative wing of the GOP. Bill Clinton, the 1992 Democratic presidential nominee, meanwhile, sought to distance himself from the more extreme liberal wing of his party and to appeal to moderate swing voters by advocating a centrist "third way" of governance. The education issue would figure prominently in both of these efforts and as a result assumed a high-profile role in the campaign.

THE 1992 PRESIDENTIAL ELECTION—THE EDUCATION PRESIDENT VERSUS THE EDUCATION GOVERNOR

The 1992 presidential election was the first election in more than forty years that was not dominated by the Cold War and foreign policy issues. The election took place in the context of an economic recession and large federal budget deficits, and concerns about unemployment, poverty, and health care topped the list of voter priorities. The Reagan revolution had succeeded in sowing great doubt about the efficacy of the liberal big government approach to solving social problems. But the public's increasing focus on domestic problems, along with the antigovernment rhetoric and decreased federal social spending of the Reagan and Bush years, had by 1992 left Republicans vulnerable on the issues of fairness and opportunity. Defending himself against charges that he had failed to deliver on his 1988 pledge to be an education president and that he did not have a domestic agenda, Bush focused on school reform during the 1992 campaign. Emphasizing educational improvement also enabled Bush to defer calls for more federal spending and activism on a broad array of social programs.

During the campaign and throughout the rest of the decade Clinton and the Democrats sought to capitalize on the widespread perception that Bush and the Republican Party were unconcerned about the plight of poor and middle-class Americans to promote a new vision of governmental activism. The focus on schools enabled Clinton to call for federal leadership and spending in a policy era where it had broad public support and was unlikely to engender welfare type criticisms. Clinton used education reform as a symbol of his efforts to move the Democratic Party to the center ideologically. As a result, both Clinton and Bush devoted a great deal of attention and rhetoric to the issue of school reform during the 1992 presidential campaign. Both candidates hailed school reform as a panacea for its ability to promote economic growth and competitiveness and to mitigate social problems such as welfare and crime. Bush and Clinton, however, struggled to craft federal school reform proposals that could appeal to swing voters without alienating key party constituencies.

The central dilemma for Bush in 1992 was that his administration had produced few domestic accomplishments to highlight during a campaign focused on domestic issues. The defeat of both of Bush's education reform packages in Congress put him in a difficult position during the campaign, as Democrats argued that Bush had done little to back up his pledge to be an education president. Bush was left to criticize Democrats in Congress for their obstructionism and to argue that Republicans were the only ones who would push for tough new reforms. Bush stated on the campaign trail that "many that control the educational establishment in Washington are in the grips of a very powerful union, the NEA . . . and it seems to be an arm of the opposition party. This NEA crowd is fighting any kind of change because they just like [the education system] the way it's been."[2] Bush and his spokespeople also argued that the president should be given credit for shifting the terms of the education debate. Alexander noted, for example, that "now you hear the country talking about a national examination system. Now you hear people talking about entirely new, break-the-mold American schools. That was not an agenda item a year ago. Now you hear a tremendous increase in the discussion over giving low- and moderate-income families more choice of schools."[3]

The Republican Party remained quite divided on education, however, and it was increasingly difficult for party leaders to publicly reconcile their different visions of the federal role in school reform. Bush and Republican moderates believed that standards and tests had the advantage of demonstrating a clear commitment to ensuring that all students were educated effectively, of holding the public education establishment's feet to the fire, and of offering a basis for increasing the academic rigor of K–12 curricula. But conservatives remained wary of national activism that might expand the federal role in education and threaten local control. Bush had come under fire from the right wing of the Republican Party for his abandonment of his "no new taxes" pledge and for his moderate positions on a variety of domestic policy issues. In his primary challenge, conservative Patrick Buchanan criticized Bush for his support of federal leadership in education and argued that the most effective way the federal government could help schools was to leave them alone. "American education," Buchanan argued in a campaign position paper, "is in a state of decline, largely the result of an ever-increasing education bureaucracy, and a lack of competition within the system. From affirmative action in hiring, to busing for racial balance and assaults on uniform, standard testing, too much ideologically motivated experimentation has been inflicted on public schools."[4]

As noted in the previous chapter, Bush responded to these criticisms by embracing private school vouchers and making the idea the center of his education agenda for the campaign. The hope was that his endorsement of vouchers would shore up his support from the right while also potentially increasing support among Catholics and racial minorities.[5] School choice also became a way for Bush to draw a wider philosophical contrast between his view of government and Clinton's.[6] Bush emphasized his position on school vouchers during his convention acceptance speech, where it was an important part of his "family values" theme:

> My opponent and I both want to change the way our kids learn. He wants to change our schools a little bit; I want to change them a lot. Take the issue of whether parents should be able to choose the best school for their kids. My opponent says that's okay as long as the school is run by the government. I say every parent and child should have a real choice of schools—public, private, or religious.

The Republican approach to education, he said, was illustrative of the party's "philosophy that puts faith in the individual, not the bureaucracy."[7]

The renewed emphasis on school choice was also reflected in the 1992 Republican Party platform, which called it "the most important education goal of all" and which, unlike the 1988 platform, explicitly called for private school vouchers. Elements of the moderate vision for education were also reflected in the party's 1992 platform, however. The platform declared support for standards by noting that "the critical public mission in education is to set tough, clear standards of achievement and ensure that those who educate our children are accountable for meeting them."[8] The platform thus reflected the ongoing tension between the moderate and conservative wings of the GOP and helped to muddle the party's message on education. Democrats would use public reservations about vouchers to portray Republican education proposals as radical and dangerous, and to contrast them with their own less controversial support for public school choice.[9]

Whereas Bush felt pressure from his right, Clinton had to contend with pressure from his party's left. A rift had developed within the Democratic Party between traditional liberals wedded to big government solutions to policy problems and a small but growing number of moderate New Democrats who wanted to push the party toward the political center and a more market-oriented philosophy. In response to a string of electoral defeats in the 1980s, moderate Democrats from the centrist Democratic Leadership Council (DLC) argued that the party needed to win back swing voters by shedding the party's tax-and-spend reputation. In 1989 the Progressive Policy Institute (PPI, the policy arm of the DLC) issued an important postmortem of the Dukakis campaign and the 1988 presidential election in which Elaine Kamarck and Bill Galston argued that the Democratic Party had come to be identified with a rigid "liberal fundamentalism" that had "lost touch with the American people," especially middle-class families.[10] In 1990, the DLC disseminated the "New Orleans Declaration: A Democratic Agenda for the 1990s," which specifically called for replacing the "politics of entitlement with a new politics of reciprocal responsibility." New Democrats believed that the party would not be competitive in presidential elections until it moderated its social and economic policies.

During the 1992 campaign, Clinton—a former DLC chair—successfully employed a rhetoric that emphasized expanded opportunity and shared responsibility.[11] Rather than defending the welfare state and the public school system against charges of ineffectiveness or irresponsibility, he accepted the need for reform but charged that the Republicans had not kept their promise to give all Americans the chance to succeed. Clinton argued that a skill- and knowledge-based economy required the Democratic Party to shift from a redistributive model toward one that fostered societal investment in workers. The Democrats' effort to reposition themselves and blunt Republican attacks on federal social welfare policies was evident in the party's 1992 platform, entitled the "New Covenant." The platform called for a "third way" that rejected "both the do-nothing government of the last 12 years and the big-government theory that says we can hamstring business and tax and spend our way to prosperity." It continued, "Rather than throwing money at obsolete programs, we will eliminate unnecessary layers of management [and] cut administrative costs."

Education investment and reform was a prominent part of the New Democratic agenda, and Clinton used his widely praised school reform efforts in Arkansas—and his detailed national education reform proposals—to demonstrate that he had experience in solving domestic problems and that his approach to doing so represented a break with liberal Democrats. This approach was evident in the 1992 Democratic platform's section on education, which stated that "governments must end the inequalities that create educational ghettos among school districts and provide equal educational opportunity for all" but also acknowledged that schools must be held accountable to "high standards of educational achievement." Though calling for greater federal investment in education, the platform noted that it is "not enough to spend more on our schools; we must insist on results."[12] Clinton's New Democratic opposition to traditional tax-and-spend liberalism was not very popular with the party's many tax-and-spend liberals, however, and this posed a major challenge for Clinton both during the campaign and while he was in office. As Will Marshall, the president of the PPI, noted,

> The strategic dilemma for Clinton on education in 1992 was a microcosm of the entire campaign—he was for free trade, welfare reform, and school reform, and these positions angered traditional Democratic groups like labor and advocates for the poor. But it was all part of Clinton's overarching strategy, which was to offer a New Democratic reform agenda that would tackle the country's policy problems and solve them and also deal with the Democratic Party's political problems. People didn't trust Democrats to fix broken public sector programs because of their alliances with powerful interest groups like the teachers unions. Clinton had to demonstrate that he was not like the old Democratic Party . . . and that he had the independence from the constituent groups in the party to do what needed to be done to fix the problems in welfare and education and other issues. So he was running as a reformer.[13]

Education thus became a centerpiece of Bill Clinton's 1992 presidential campaign and his New Democrat philosophy, and a key part of its electoral appeal. On the day in October 1991 when Clinton announced his candidacy in Little Rock, he promised that "in a Clinton administration, students and parents and teachers will get a real Education President."[14] Clinton linked Bush's record on schools with Reagan's economic program by arguing that "trickle-down education . . . won't help America any more than trickle-down economics helped us in the 1980s." One of the major issues of the campaign, Clinton said, should be "who can be the real education president and how America can be a country that puts education first again."[15]

Clinton's credibility as an education reformer—and as a New Democrat—was bolstered by his record of innovation in Arkansas. As governor, he secured passage of the country's first mandatory teacher competency test, student achievement testing, a statewide open enrollment (public choice) program, and annual report cards of school performance. Many of these reforms had been strongly opposed by the state's teachers unions, and Clinton highlighted their opposition to support his claim to be a more centrist Democrat who was willing to take on established liberal interests in the name of reform. Clinton remarked during the campaign that "education is the issue I know most and care most about," and one reporter noted that "Mr. Clinton is the first serious presidential contender whose national reputation rests substantially on his efforts in education reform, [and] he extols the virtues of school improvement with unique authority."

In the education governor's bid to be education president, Clinton was forced to contend with the tremendous power of the teachers unions in the national Democratic Party.[16] By 1992 the National Education Association had grown into the country's largest labor union, with 2.1 million members and an annual budget of $164 million, and it was widely regarded as one of the most influential forces in the campaign for the nomination. Approximately 500 NEA and AFT members served as delegates at the Democratic convention; this represented about 10 percent of the total delegate pool and was the largest block of delegates of any one profession. In 1992, both the NEA and the AFT endorsed Clinton by large margins, and NEA delegates gave Clinton the strongest support (88 percent) ever accorded to a presidential candidate.[17] The unions also devoted considerable material support to the Clinton campaign.[18] Clinton received the enthusiastic support of the NEA and AFT largely because of his opposition to private school choice and his support for increased federal education funding. The unions were passionately opposed to Clinton's call for enhanced public school choice and national standards and tests, however, and this opposition acted as a brake on Democratic school reform plans throughout the 1990s.[19]

Given the power of the unions and the traditional Democratic position on education, Clinton's acknowledgment that public schools needed major reform— and not simply additional money—was an important development in the campaign. According to PPI president Marshall,

> The New Democratic view was that there were systemic problems in the public education system that had to be tackled and that it didn't make sense to pour more money into a failing system. We believed that reforms—particularly of governance—had to be enacted first. The public school system was too often being run for the benefit of the adults in the system rather than the students. . . . We had to redefine the whole debate about what the federal goals in education should be—we needed to move beyond the traditional Democratic focus on access and resources.[20]

Clinton repeatedly declared during the 1992 campaign that "we need to overhaul America's public education system from top to bottom."[21] And he used his support for reform generally—and for standards, testing, and choice particularly—to bolster his claim to be an innovative New Democrat. As Clinton education adviser Andy Rotherham has observed, "Clinton's strong embrace of charter schools in

1992 was very important. The party did not go along with him on that, but he got the ball rolling by giving the idea bipartisan credibility and by proposing federal seed money. It helped Clinton to send the message that he was a different kind of Democrat on education and to contrast himself with liberals."[22] Education reform thus provided Clinton with what Paul Weinstein from the PPI calls a "sister soulja moment."[23] By embracing charter schools and public school choice, Clinton was able to demonstrate his independence from the teachers unions, which though they remained a key force in the Democratic Party were characterized by Republicans as an obstacle to genuine school reform. It also enabled him to be pro-reform and to co-opt the school choice idea from Republicans while portraying private school choice as radical and dangerous.

The Bush team had hoped that its support of vouchers would help it appear pro-reform on education and increase its support among voters (particularly minorities) for whom education was a top issue. But Clinton worked hard to portray private school choice as incompatible with efforts to improve public education. Democrats repeatedly argued that vouchers were not a reform but an exit option and would take money away from public schools. A poll taken late in the campaign—in October 1992—showed that Clinton was successful in convincing a majority of the public that vouchers were a bad idea. When asked if they supported giving parents a voucher to "use toward enrolling their child in a private school at public expense," respondents opposed the idea by almost a two-to-one margin.[24] The idea of public school choice—which Clinton championed as an alternative to private school vouchers—was viewed more favorably by citizens than were vouchers. When asked in October 1992 whether they favored proposals providing parents with choice among public and private schools or choice only among public schools, respondents favored the latter.[25]

Frank Newport, the editor in chief of the Gallup Poll, had noted at the outset of the 1992 campaign that if the Democrats wanted to "take on Bush in education the candidate has to show the public that the Presidency could make a difference, that Bush has failed as an education President, that it's important, and that they have a better plan."[26] Clinton appears to have achieved a great deal of success on all four counts during the 1992 election campaign and succeeded in winning the issue. Exit polls by the Voter News Service revealed that education voters (those who indicated that education was the issue mattering most to their vote) supported Clinton over Bush by a more than two-to-one margin (55 percent to 27 percent for whites, and 90 percent to 7 percent for blacks).[27] Clinton did equally well on the education issue among the general electorate. Though Bush was able to close the gap with Clinton on the issue somewhat over the final months of the campaign, polls indicated that Clinton was able to maintain more than a fifteen-point advantage on the education issue.[28] Education was not the top policy issue with voters in 1992, but it was one of the top five and was frequently cited as important to the economy, which was far and away the most important issue.

An important development during the 1992 campaign was the shift in rhetoric by both candidates regarding the proper purpose and scope of federal education policy. In previous elections, when education was discussed at all it was usually in the context of civil rights and improving opportunities for disadvantaged students such as minorities and the disabled. In 1992, however, Bush and Clinton (along with many of their primary opponents) emphasized that education reform was important not only to these groups and purposes but also for the economic growth and prosperity of the entire nation. Bush remarked that improving education "would render us much more competitive internationally, which gets you over into the economic side of things, and it will lift a lot of kids out of this impoverished state they're in and give them an opportunity at the American dream."[29] Clinton similarly commented that "in the 1990s, education is economic development. If we're going to compete, we need to overhaul America's education system from top to bottom."[30] The linking of education with individual and national economic competitiveness had the effect of significantly enhancing the political salience of school reform within the party's platforms and on the public agenda. As Mark Mellman, a Democratic consultant, noted, "people believe that if they were better educated, they would be making more money. And that if the nation as a whole were better educated, we'd be better-off economically. So education is not just a social issue anymore; education is a bedrock economic issue."[31]

Clinton's centrist New Democrat rhetoric in 1992 put the Republicans on the defensive by exposing the tension between the GOP's commitment to individual opportunity and its rejection of activist social policy. Seeking to honor both imperatives, Bush was forced to deny either the existence of social and economic inequities or that there was much government could or should do to help. In the face of public discontent stirred by a recession, this awkward stance left Bush seeming ineffectual and out of touch. During and after the 1992 election, the Republicans struggled to answer the challenge posed by the New Democrats without abandoning the party's historic principles. Republicans remained deeply divided on education, with conservatives in favor of eliminating the federal role in schools completely through the use of vouchers and block grants. Moderate Republicans, in contrast, believed that the federal government had an important role to play in school reform and endorsed national standards and increased accountability measures.

Clinton and the Democrats capitalized on the divisions within the GOP on education. They were quite successful in focusing the education debate during the campaign on spending and vouchers and in using those issues to claim that the candidates had very different visions for school reform and that Bush was a radical conservative. Although this was effective politically, it masked the considerable amount of agreement between Bush and Clinton on education. This agreement, in particular their support for national standards and tests, was a key development during the 1992 campaign. "What is astonishing," one reporter noted during the campaign, "is the degree to which the candidates' speech writers are working from the same notes [on education]. Both the self-proclaimed education president and the widely hailed education governor are challenging the longtime American tradition of local school control. Both are advocating reforms emphasizing national academic standards. . . . This uniformity of vision stands in stark contrast to highly partisan educational policy debates of the past."[32] Previous presidential election campaign debates over education had put Republican calls for privatization and deregulation against Democratic calls for increased federal spending and procedural mandates. In 1992, for the first time, the presidential nominees of both parties agreed on the need for both increased federal leadership in school reform and a new focus on standards, tests, and choice.

This convergence on education reflected the substantial momentum that had developed behind the idea of national education goals since the 1989 Charlottesville summit and increasing pressure to improve student performance. Neither conservative proposals for radical privatization nor liberal calls for increased funding of the status quo had been able to garner significant public support. Voters appeared to have tired of partisan ideological warfare and to want more pragmatic, centrist political leadership on education. A centrist, bipartisan coalition was thus beginning to emerge behind a new reform-oriented federal education policy regime centered on standards and tests. But considerable disagreement remained about the precise role that the federal government should play in designing and implementing them. Clinton vanquished his Republican opponent and won the White House on the strength of his New Democrat philosophy, but many liberals—particularly in Congress—continued to adhere to a very different view of government. And conservatives were increasingly identifying education as an important symbol in the fight against the expanding reach of the federal government. This was the challenging political context within which Clinton would have to pursue the enactment of his domestic agenda and his proposals to reshape federal education reform efforts.

GOALS 2000: LAYING THE PHILOSOPHICAL FOUNDATION
FOR A NEW REGIME IN EDUCATION

Clinton's victory in 1992 produced unified government, as Democrats maintained their majorities in the House and Senate. This unified party control, however, belied significantly different governing philosophies within the party. As a New

Democrat, Clinton pledged to deliver economic growth and improved social welfare by "reinventing" government with somewhat increased spending tied to increased efficiency and accountability in federal programs. However, the Democratic primaries had demonstrated that Clinton's call for restraint in government spending and regulation was not embraced by many within his own party. Most Democrats in Congress (and particularly those in the House leadership) remained "old Democrats" and were committed to the big government programs that had been created during the New Deal and the Great Society.[33]

Clinton's desire to reward the liberal groups that had supported him during the campaign also led him to appoint many liberals to his administration, and this ensured that the Democrats' intraparty disagreements would bedevil the executive branch as well. As Will Marshall has recalled,

> The big problem was that while Clinton was committed to New Democratic reforms, a lot of the people around him in the administration were not. He was surrounded by a lot of people who were . . . from the usual interest groups: Educrats filled the education positions [for example]. . . . There were a few key New Democrats, but the critical mass of advisers and administration officials which dominated were more traditional Democrats and were actively hostile to many New Dem reforms.[34]

After twelve years of Republican control in the White House, liberal Democrats were eager to expand old federal programs and create new ones. Conservative Republicans, meanwhile, continued to argue that federal social welfare programs were intrusive and ineffective and to push for their termination. The central dilemma of the Clinton administration thus became how to balance between the often incompatible demands of old and new Democrats while simultaneously dealing with the Republican opposition.

The public was generally supportive of Clinton's call for federal leadership in education reform. Strong majorities supported national education standards (70 percent), a national curriculum (69 percent), and national tests (77 percent).[35] Polls taken in January 1993 also showed that the public generally favored Clinton's views on education over those of Republicans in Congress by a wide margin, 66 percent to 20 percent.[36] But as the fight over America 2000 had revealed, many conservatives and liberals remained wary of national education reforms—conservatives because they believed such reforms would inevitably lead to federal control over schools, and liberals because they believed the problems facing schools were primarily financial rather than structural or pedagogical. The existence of Democratic majorities in the House and Senate ostensibly meant that Clinton could gain passage of his legislative agenda without Republican support, but sharp differences between liberal and moderate Democrats on education complicated the political picture.

The New Democratic vision for federal education reform was outlined in a 1992 book by the Progressive Policy Institute of the DLC that was seen as a blueprint for the administration. *Mandate for Change* emphasized that increased funding alone would not solve schools' problems and called for the president to "marshal public support for a radical redesign of U.S. education."[37] It claimed that conservatives had correctly focused on the problem of "public bureaucracies that exercise monopoly control over education" but had in vouchers picked the wrong solution. The authors urged Clinton to work to expand public school choice and the development of charter schools, noting that "the charter idea . . . can deliver the benefits of choice without bankrupting the public schools as a voucher system could." The DLC urged Clinton to claim the middle ground on education by proposing moderate but meaningful school reforms.

Many of the policy proposals of the middle ground, however, were opposed by liberal Democrats as well as by the NEA and much of the education establishment. Democrats had historically supported an expanded federal role in education but were divided over whether this role should continue to focus on resources, equity, and process or whether the federal government should leverage its influence to promote reform. Bill Galston, the member of Clinton's Domestic Policy Council in charge of education, noted,

> The Democratic position on education evolved relatively slowly. This was the source of considerable stresses and strains within the party during the early months of the Clinton administration because Clinton brought to the White House his experiences as a southern governor interested in education reform as part of a general process of economic and social development. If you are a southern governor, then you will have to convince a reluctant electorate to pony up for educational improvements, and you're not going to be able to do that unless you set up an accountability system that demonstrates quantitatively a return on investment. . . . That was the mentality that Clinton brought with him to the White House, but that wasn't the way that Democrats in Congress thought about the education issue. They were still thinking in 1970s terms about the use of federal funds and mandates to promote integration and equalization of resources. So they were not particularly preoccupied with standards and assessments—they viewed them as a diversion or worse: worse because many liberal Democrats feared that they could result in children being held responsible for the failures of their schools. There were titanic struggles in the early months of the Clinton administration about these two competing paradigms of what the federal role in education should be and more generally about what the right metric for measuring educational progress and achievement should be.[38]

This intraparty debate was further complicated by pressure from the powerful education establishment, whose demands for greater federal spending on education had been stymied during the Reagan-Bush years.

The NEA had for years aggressively fought against a wide variety of school reform proposals, including merit pay for teachers, teacher competency testing, standardized testing for students, and school choice (public and private). The opposition of the NEA—and many liberal Democrats—to meaningful education reform created a major challenge for Clinton. As Bush education secretary Lamar Alexander commented at the time, "it will be very hard for Bill Clinton to be a real education president with the NEA leaders draped around his neck. The Democratic constituency on education is the business-as-usual crowd—the crowd that has control, likes the schools the way they are and thinks a good education program is the maximum amount of money for the least amount of change."[39] Clinton, however, had implemented many school reforms in Arkansas, was on record during the campaign as wanting to initiate them at the national level, and saw them as central to his credibility as a New Democrat.

The controversy generated by the Clinton administration's early policy initiatives—including the defeat of his health care plan and the narrow passage of his budget—left the Clinton administration looking for a quick legislative victory in early 1994. It was then that Clinton turned to education and revived Bush's America 2000 proposal, making it the basis for his first major initiative on education.[40] Clinton and his advisers made the strategic decision to send his reform proposal (named Goals 2000) to Congress prior to consideration of the pending ESEA reauthorization so that it could serve as a blueprint to focus all federal education programs on national standards. As Clinton's education secretary, Richard Riley, noted, "we were determined that Goals 2000 become the prism through which all our new legislation and amendments to every other program in elementary and secondary education would be considered."[41]

Clinton had joined Bush in endorsing national academic standards during the 1989 Charlottesville summit and then in the 1992 campaign, and a centrist consensus of sorts had developed around the idea between moderates of both parties. Many conservatives and liberals remained adamantly opposed to the idea, however, and even among moderates there was tremendous disagreement over what the standards would contain, how they would be implemented, and the role that the federal government would play with regard to them. These were the same issues that had brought Bush's America 2000 plan under attack from both the right and the left. Everyone involved recognized that federal involvement with educational standards would mark the beginning of a new era in federal education policy.[42] In this context, the debate over Clinton's 1994 school reform plan took on added significance.

Clinton's Goals 2000 proposal called for the creation of voluntary national standards and assessments based on the six national education goals outlined in America 2000. States were charged with developing targets for the attainment of factual information and intellectual abilities that students should master at specified grade levels. Many observers were tempted to see Clinton's Goals 2000 plan as merely a repackaged and renamed version of America 2000—and indeed the bills' similarities were played up by the Clinton administration in seeking Republican support. But as Robert Schwartz and Marian Robinson have argued, despite the "surface similarities," "Goals 2000 represented a fundamentally different vision of education reform and of the federal role in stimulating and leading that reform."[43]

The most important distinction was the more robust federal role in standards development envisioned under Goals 2000. Though the states were free to devise their own standards, they were required to submit them to the U.S. Department of Education for approval before receiving Goals 2000 funds. In addition, Clinton's proposal called for the creation of a National Education Standards and Improvement Council (NESIC) and a National Skill Standards Board (NSSB) and for the strengthening of the National Education Goals Panel (NEGP) to assist and monitor state school reform efforts.[44] Another important difference between Goals 2000 and America 2000 centered on the different approach to school choice—Clinton's plan called for public rather than private school choice. The final difference between the Bush and Clinton reform bills concerned the weight given to inputs in the school improvement process. In a bow to Democrats in Congress, Clinton's proposal also called for the creation of an Opportunity to Learn Commission that would recommend the levels of funding necessary to achieve academic improvement.

If America 2000 and Goals 2000 differed in some important regards, however, they both had to navigate the same difficult political environment, one that featured strong congressional opposition on the left and right to an expanded reform-oriented federal role in education. Whereas some Republican moderates praised the emphasis placed on standards and accountability, conservatives vociferously objected to the Clinton plan because they said it would dramatically expand federal influence over schools. In an April 2 letter to Secretary Riley, the ranking Republican members of the House and Senate Education Committees outlined their opposition to national tests, having state standards reviewed by a federal agency, the inclusion of school delivery standards focused on inputs, and the creation of new federal education bureaucracies. Liberals, meanwhile, continued to focus on the issue of resources and to argue that the creation of standards and assessments to measure school outputs had to be contingent on efforts to improve and equalize school inputs. Specifically, liberal Democrats demanded that Clinton significantly boost federal spending on education and explicitly tie academic standards to opportunity-to-learn (OTL) standards.

America 2000 had been based on the premise that education reform was not contingent on greater resources for schools or enhanced federal funding. Bush

hoped to substitute tougher standards for additional resources, and to shift the focus of federal education policy from the inputs to the outputs of schools. But Democrats believed that schools—particularly those in high poverty areas—would not
be able to meet higher standards without additional funds. Their insistence during
the debate over America 2000 that school delivery standards be included along
with any academic standards had been a major reason for the bill's defeat. When
Clinton took office, liberal Democrats and the education establishment had high
expectations that he would significantly increase federal spending on education.
Limited by budget constraints and his desire to pass new reforms before allocating
increased resources, however, Clinton's Goals 2000 proposal only allocated $420
million for the program's first year. The combination of its limited funding and
its reform orientation led to a hostile reception for the initial draft of Goals 2000
among Democrats in Congress.

Secretary Riley met with Democratic members of the House Education Committee on March 23, 1994, to discuss the administration's proposal. The representatives criticized the bill for placing too much emphasis on academic standards and
assessment and not enough on school delivery standards and made clear that they
would not support the bill in its current form. As Riley himself would recollect,
"some House Democrats . . . saw the [Goals 2000] proposal to define goals, standards, and reform as substitutes for commitment, programs, and money."[45] He
told the committee members that while the administration hoped to budget more
money for education in the future, increasing funding alone would not improve
schools, and that the administration bill was important because it would reinvigo-
rate the federal role in education after twelve years of Republican inactivity. Riley
also argued that it was important for Clinton—and for the Democratic Party—to
seize the standards idea from Republicans.

Under pressure from union lobbyists, House Democrats continued to fight
for resources over reform. As Bill Galston later observed, "The NEA represented
a very traditional liberal emphasis on inputs . . . [but] my instructions from Clinton were to hold the line as far as I could with the NEA on his education reforms,
which brought us into conflict with members of Congress who were more responsive to the NEA and the other established education interest groups—that's what
the fight was all about."[46] Due to the hostile reaction by Democrats on Capitol
Hill, the Clinton administration was forced to postpone the introduction of the
Goals 2000 bill. A series of difficult and acrimonious negotiations between the
Clinton administration and House Democrats ultimately resulted in the removal
or weakening of many of the reforms contained in Clinton's original proposal.
Most important, the opposition to national testing—from both liberals and conservatives—led the administration to deemphasize it in its second draft, with the
proposed National Education Standards and Assessment Council renamed the

National Education Standards and *Improvement* Council and the independence of its membership curtailed. In addition, the administration placed greater emphasis on school delivery standards, which mollified some Democrats but made the bill even more objectionable to Republicans.

Once the bill was formally introduced, congressional debate quickly disintegrated into a partisan fight over resources, federal control, and school choice. Democrats secured approval—on party-line votes—of a number of amendments that reemphasized school inputs, including one that required states to take "corrective action" to meet school delivery standards in order to be eligible for federal money under Goals 2000. Republicans vehemently opposed these amendments during both subcommittee and committee debate on the grounds that they obscured the need for more substantive reform and dangerously expanded the federal role in schools. They continued to argue that the focus should be on results rather than resources and that the federal role should be confined to supporting states in the development and adoption of voluntary academic standards. Sen. Judd Gregg (R-NH), for example, warned that "although the title is innocuous, the administration's initiative is far-reaching. It is aimed at restructuring the way education is managed in America. . . . For the first time in the nation's history, the federal bureaucracy will define how education should be delivered on America's Main Streets. The traditional role of limiting federal direction in education to narrow areas, such as special education, will be abandoned."[47]

It was at this juncture that Clinton intervened forcefully and decisively in the debate. Clinton and his advisers recognized that making OTL standards mandatory would undermine the effort to shift the educational reform debate toward academic results and would generate such hostility from New Democrats and Republicans that it might sink the entire bill. Galston recollected that "at a couple of crucial moments, particularly during the struggles over Goals 2000, Clinton intervened very strongly and publicly on the side of the reform in a way that left no doubt in anybody's mind where his heart was."[48] In a public letter to House Democrats, he asked them not to support any effort to make federal funding contingent on OTL standards: "Amendments which require states, as a condition of federal support, to commit to specific corrective actions for schools that fail to meet these standards go too far. . . . The requirements will impede states' efforts to focus accountability on results. . . . I urge you not to support amendments that expand the definition or role of opportunity-to-learn standards."[49]

In response to Clinton's request and in order to gain Republican support for Goals 2000, Democrats ultimately agreed to water down the OTL provision and to include language designed to assuage fears that the program would lead to a dramatic increase in direct federal influence over state education policies.[50] Goals 2000 ultimately passed the House by a 306 to 121 vote, but only after the defeat of a substitute amendment (drafted by Republican Rep. Dick Armey of Texas) that would have eliminated all commissions, standards, and testing from the bill and would have redirected the funds toward public and private school choice programs, merit schools, and decentralized management.

Debate in the Senate over Goals 2000 lacked much of the partisan rancor that was present in the House, largely because Senate Democrats declined to add controversial language on opportunity-to-learn standards. After the defeat of a filibuster on school prayer by Sen. Jesse Helms (R-NC), the Senate passed the legislation 63 to 22. Goals 2000 was thus in the end approved in Congress by a fairly wide margin, which was somewhat surprising given the heated debate over the legislation and the earlier defeat of America 2000. A number of factors help to explain why Goals 2000 was passed despite strong misgivings from both conservatives and liberals. First, Congress had been largely relegated to a peripheral role in standards reform, and the legislation (as amended) offered the legislators a chance to regain a seat at the table in discussions that had been dominated by the president and governors. Second, Democrats had a majority and were under strong pressure to provide Clinton with a legislative victory on one of his signature domestic policy issues. Third, business leaders saw the bill as a crucial lever for workforce improvement and economic growth and pushed hard for passage. Fourth, many Republican moderates wanted to support standards-based reform because it had first been proposed by Bush and offered a means to make federal education policy more results-oriented. Support for the final legislation nonetheless had a decidedly partisan character, especially in the House, where Republicans voted 115–59 against the bill while Democrats supported it overwhelmingly by a vote of 246–6. Clinton signed the act into law on March 31, 1994.

The difficult political terrain, however, had forced Clinton to compromise with both Democrats and Republicans. The result was that while the final bill received the support of almost all of the major business and education groups and successfully navigated the treacherous congressional education waters, many of its proposed reforms were either eliminated or significantly watered-down. Perhaps most important, the law greatly circumscribed the federal role in creating standards or assessments or in holding states accountable for their education progress. The final legislation stated that national standards must be "sufficiently general" that they "will not restrict state and local control over curriculum and instruction methods . . . [and that states] can modify them to suit their own circumstances." The law also emphasized that the national standards were voluntary and that "states and communities can develop their own standards or modify and adopt those developed under national consensus." Federal funds were to flow to states and communities to "help them develop their own rigorous standards and implement their own programs of school reform." The act states clearly that "no state is required to have its standards or assessments certified or participate in Goals 2000 systemic improvement programs as a condition of participating in any federal education program."[51]

As enacted, therefore, Goals 2000 was a "least common denominator" kind of bill. Opposition from both the left and the right ultimately precluded the inclusion of any kind of meaningful accountability measure, and the law used carrots rather than sticks to push states to reform their schools. As a result, education adviser Andy Rotherham notes that "Goals 2000 was essentially a bribe to the states. Any reform that you want to accomplish in Washington has to be accompanied by some sugar, some money, to buy people off. Goals 2000 was a way to do that."[52] Education reformers hailed the law's focus on standards and school performance as an important step but recognized that the voluntary nature of the law limited its potential impact on state school reform efforts. Tom Loveless commented, for example, that "as befalls many great ideas, the codified reality [of Goals 2000] is distinguished more by pragmatic compromises than by soaring aspirations. . . . In accommodating [conservative and liberal] concerns Goals 2000 lost its focus. What we have now looks more like 2,000 educational goals."[53]

The Clinton administration had declared education to be, in Secretary Riley's words, "a local function, a state responsibility, and a national priority," and Goals 2000 reflected this complicated division of policymaking authority. The legislation contained a number of initiatives that were likely to increase federal influence over state and local school reform efforts while simultaneously increasingly the discretion and flexibility that states and localities had under existing federal education programs. As Riley described it, this reflected a "new partnership" between the federal government and the states on education, a partnership "premised on the idea of greater flexibility in exchange for increased accountability."[54] In contrast to other federal education legislation, the Department of Education did not issue rules to accompany Goals 2000. The legislation was also the first to give the department the authority to waive statutory or regulatory requirements in order to ensure flexibility and promote innovation in local reform efforts.[55]

Despite its flexibility and the lack of new mandates, however, Goals 2000 was widely recognized as a watershed moment in the history of American education. Secretary Riley noted that "for the first time in the nation's history, a statutory framework defines the federal role as one of supporting and facilitation to improve all schools for all children."[56] As Robert Schwartz and Marian Robinson have remarked, "Goals 2000 represented a very different federal strategy than ever seen before. . . . It was audacious not only in proposing to use federal funds to leverage whole system reforms at the state level, but also in creating new national structures to guide the states toward a national strategy."[57] Goals 2000 thus marked a fundamental break with the historical federal educational focus on promoting access and equity for disadvantaged groups and initiated a new era in which the federal government would emphasize academic improvement for all students. In the words of one education writer, "For the first time, the federal government will have substantial influence on what is taught, how it is taught, and how educational programs are evaluated."[58]

Prior to Goals 2000, there had been no single unifying purpose to federal education policy. Every group and educational problem had its own federal program that was animated by its own unique politics and policy framework. Goals 2000 attempted to unite these programs and to refocus them on academic standards and student performance. This philosophical shift for federal education policy was hailed by moderates from both parties as a pragmatic response to an underperforming public education system but was criticized by liberals who felt it was inadequately funded and targeted by conservatives who saw it as the first step toward a national curriculum. These concerns would resurface with renewed vigor during the debate over reauthorizing ESEA.

THE 1994 ESEA REAUTHORIZATION: LINKING FEDERAL EDUCATION FUNDS WITH REFORM

In late 1993, as Goals 2000 moved toward final passage, congressional committees began consideration of the reauthorization of the Elementary and Secondary Education Act (ESEA). As was noted earlier, participation in the Goals 2000 program was voluntary, and the only incentive for states to take part was to claim a share of the small pot of money that was specifically authorized with the bill's passing. ESEA, in contrast, was enormous in size and scope, as it housed the majority of federal education programs and allocated over $10 billion in funding. The Clinton administration's 1994 reauthorization proposal (entitled the Improving America's Schools Act, or IASA) called for tying federal aid for disadvantaged students (Title I), bilingual education, and many other programs to the standards developed under Goals 2000. Because all fifty states already accepted federal ESEA funds and because these funds (unlike the monies in Goals 2000) were sizable, these changes meant that the states would essentially be forced to adopt standards-based school reforms. Goals 2000 created a federal program to provide incentives for states to develop and implement standards-based reforms, and the administration's 1994 ESEA reauthorization proposal was designed to align existing federal education programs with state standards.

The original 1965 ESEA legislation had created a large number of targeted, categorical federal education programs to provide assistance to specifically identified groups and purposes. Subsequent reauthorizations of ESEA added additional groups and new programs that only exacerbated the disjointed nature of the original law. Federal programs continued to embody federal purposes, to operate separately from state and local programs, and to focus on compliance with federal rules and processes rather than on their contribution to student achievement. But by the 1990s there was a growing sentiment among Democrats and Republicans alike that ESEA was in dire need of reform. Clinton's education undersecretary, Mike Smith, noted that "as the 1994 reauthorization of ESEA drew near, it became increasingly clear that the federal programs were out of step with the growing reform movement in the states. They were focused on low-level skills and were fragmented. They did not support local and state reforms. And even on their own terms, they often were ineffective."[59] Many in Congress were receptive to the notion that federal education programs needed to be revamped and were supportive of federal efforts to encourage states to adopt *voluntary* standards and assessments. But Clinton's ESEA proposal generated a great deal of resistance from many members of Congress on both the left and the right because it was seen as essentially *mandating* standards and assessments.[60]

In a major shift, Clinton's ESEA proposal argued that disadvantaged students in Title I schools should now be expected to make progress toward the challenging content and performance standards and assessments that were applied to all of the other children in the state. Liberals and civil rights groups continued to be concerned that sufficient resources were not being allocated to help poor schools and disadvantaged students meet tough new standards and that a reduction in federal oversight and regulation would permit states to dilute their emphasis on traditionally underserved populations. As a result they fought Clinton's calls for increased flexibility and pushed for the inclusion of more specific requirements that the administration, as well as most Republicans, opposed. As Smith has noted,

> Some Democrats wanted to maintain this very rigorous set of timelines in ESEA, which really weren't realistic for states. We ended up in constant battle with liberal Democrats, especially the civil rights groups, over the business of implementing ESEA and the nature of the reforms. Our position was shaped by the fact that reform was being led by two small-state governors (Clinton and Riley) with pretty clear ideas about how states work and the desire to give them a lot of discretion. We wanted to keep the pressure on the states regarding education reform and to hold up examples of excellence and move people toward thoughtful reform and implementation, but we recognized these things take time.[61]

Moderate Republicans were generally supportive of the Clinton administration's efforts to introduce improvements and accountability into what they viewed as ineffective federal education programs. In a September 24, 1993, letter to Secretary Riley, Republican education leaders including Sen. Nancy Kassebaum (R-KS),

Sen. Jim Jeffords (R-VT), and Rep. Bill Goodling (R-PA) praised the administration's ESEA proposal. "It appears that we agree on many of the overall themes that will guide this reauthorization.... Many of these ideas—such as increased flexibility, program consolidations, and high achievement standards—have historically been supported by Republicans." The letter also warned, however, that their support for Clinton's education reform efforts would be jeopardized if Clinton did not resist liberal Democratic demands to place federal input mandates on states. "Republicans stand ready to work with you," it noted, "to oppose unfunded federal mandates and the creation of any program that attempts to impose Washington 'solutions' on such issues as funding sources and resource allocation decisions."[62] Conservative Republicans continued to object to expanded federal influence over schools, even in the pursuit of reforms such as standards and assessments that they supported in principle. In September "Dear colleague" letters, Dick Armey (R-TX) and John Boehner (R-OH) urged their Republican colleagues to vote against the legislation because it would lead to the federalization of education.[63]

Behind strong presidential lobbying that gained the support of most Democrats, the Improving America's Schools Act overcame conservative opposition to pass the House and Senate and headed to conference, where the issue of opportunity-to-learn standards once again threatened to derail the legislation. The bill approved by House Democrats, who were generally more liberal than their Senate counterparts, required states to develop and submit detailed OTL standards as a condition of receiving federal funds. The Senate version only recommended that states consider adopting such standards. In the major compromise of the conference negotiations, the House (under pressure from the Clinton administration) agreed to adopt the weaker Senate language, thus clearing the way for many Republican moderates to vote for the bill. The final conference report passed in the House by a vote of 262 to 132, with virtually all Democrats (230 out of 234) in support but most Republicans (128 out of 159) in opposition. The Senate vote on the conference report was 77 to 20, with all of the Democrats voting in favor and the Republicans split; twenty-one mostly moderate members joined Kassebaum and Jeffords, and twenty mostly conservative members voted against.

Despite the support of some Republican moderates, the debate over the IASA was widely regarded as the most partisan ESEA reauthorization since the act had been created in 1965. During the 1960s, 1970s, and 1980s the periodic reauthorizations of ESEA enjoyed broad bipartisan support, with between 72 percent and 99 percent of House and Senate Republicans voting in favor. In 1994, however, only 19 percent of House Republicans and 53 percent of Senate Republicans voted for the final ESEA bill.[64] The opposition to the IASA came largely from the same conservative Republicans who had opposed Goals 2000. And as Jack Jennings has noted, "The ESEA fight in the House and the nasty battle in the Senate over the Goals

2000 conference report were not isolated events; rather they were indications of broader trends showing increasing Republican opposition to federal aid to education."[65] This growing politicization of education in Washington occurred even as a consensus was building across the country among education reformers, governors, business leaders, and the public behind national standards and assessments.

In its final form (see Table 5.1), IASA was widely viewed as the most significant change to ESEA since 1965 because it restructured federal education programs to align with the new focus on academic improvement for all students that had been outlined in Goals 2000. Jay Diskey, a former Republican Education Department and congressional staffer, has observed that

> it was Goals 2000 and ESEA that kept standards-based education reforms alive. . . . The governors had started the discussion in a very bipartisan way in 1989, and then a Republican administration had stepped up for it in 1991, and then the Clinton administration had said "hey, we like standards reforms as well" and put it into federal law. There weren't a lot of mandates on it, but it was affirmation from the other side and showed that this was going to be something that states and school districts were going to have to pursue.[66]

The changes to ESEA required states to develop school improvement plans and challenging content standards in core academic subjects in order to receive federal funds. States were also required to develop assessments and to set benchmarks for the "adequate yearly progress" that a district's Chapter 1 students would have to make. Schools would have to publish disaggregated test results, and those that failed to meet state targets for two consecutive school years would be identified as needing improvement. States and districts were encouraged to take "corrective action" with failing schools, such as by withholding funds, reconstituting staff, instituting new governance, or transferring students. Following the template of Goals 2000, it also contained provisions for additional waiver authority to the Department of Education and granted states new flexibility in the administration of ESEA programs.[67] And finally, the legislation contained an important boost to public school choice by allowing school districts to use federal Title I funds to enable eligible students to transfer to another public school within that system and by providing a small amount ($15 million in the first year) of federal start-up funds for charter schools.[68]

In his comments at the signing of the Improving America's Schools Act on October 24, President Clinton remarked that the bill

> represents a fundamental change in the way the federal government looks at how we should do our job in helping you students achieve [education] goals. For 30 years, the federal government has shipped money to the states and the local school districts to try to help with problems that needed the money. But mostly, they

Table 5.1. Summary of the 1994 Improving America's Schools Act

Standards	In exchange for Title I grants, states must develop school-improvement plans that establish high content and performance standards in at least mathematics and reading or language arts. The plans may be based on those developed under Goals 2000 or another process already completed or under way. Standards must be established within a year of receiving a grant. State plans must also describe what constitutes "adequate yearly progress" of schools and districts.
Assessments	Assessments aligned with the content standards must be administered "at some time" between grades 3 and 5, again between grades 6 and 9, and again between grades 10 and 12. Performance on the assessments must be disaggregated within states, districts, and schools by gender, race, limited-English-proficient status, migrant status, disability, and economic status. States have one year after receiving their allocations for fiscal 1995 to develop standards and assessments. If they do not, they must adopt approved standards drafted by another state.
Opportunity to Learn	Each plan must include a description of how the state will help districts and schools "develop the capacity" to help children meet high standards and other factors a state deems appropriate. Those factors can include so-called opportunity-to-learn standards or strategies.
School Choice	Districts may use Title I money, in combination with state, local, and private money, to establish school-choice programs for Title I students. Such students could move between Title I schools upon the agreement of all schools involved. It also authorizes $15 million for aid to districts via states that want to establish charter schools.
Corrective Action	Schools that had been identified as needing improvement for the two consecutive years prior to enactment of the law must continue improvement activities. In addition, those Title I schools whose students do not make adequate progress as defined in the state plan for two consecutive years will be also designated for program improvement. Such schools must devote at least 10 percent of a single year's Title I funds to professional development over a two-year period. Districts are required to offer technical assistance to schools identified for program improvement, and they must take corrective action against a school if sufficient improvement does not occur within two years. Such action may include withholding funds, alternative governance, reconstituting the school staff, transferring students, or implementing state opportunity-to-learn standards or strategies adopted under Goals 2000.
Flexibility	Allows states and districts to consolidate administrative funds from such programs as Title I, Eisenhower mathematics and science, and bilingual education, with administrative funds under Goals 2000. Gives the Secretary of Education broad authority to waive certain regulations if he determines that this would improve instruction and student performance.

Source: Excerpted from "Summary of the Improving America's Schools Act," *Education Week,* November 9, 1994, http://www.edweek.org.

have done it in ways that prescribed in very detailed manner the rules and regulations your schools had to follow in applying for the money and in complying with it. . . . This bill changes all that. This bill says the national government will set the goals. We will help develop measurements to see whether [you are] meeting the goals. But you will get to determine how you're going to meet the goals.[69]

Much had been made during the congressional debate over Goals 2000 about the voluntary nature of the national standards and federal programs it established, but this changed with IASA. As Mike Smith, Clinton's education undersecretary, noted, the combination of "Goals 2000 and the 1994 ESEA changes imposed on the states a particular kind of reform—to play ball, states had to go along with standards-based reform."[70]

The IASA was widely seen as an important expansion and transformation of federal education policy, but views on its potential impact on schools varied widely. Patty Sullivan from the Council of Chief State School Officers observed that

the 1994 ESEA amendments represented the first time that the federal government got into the business with Title I of telling the states what they had to do. It was the first time that we had a mandate from the federal government that we had to have state-level assessments that were aligned to our content standards. At that point it was a pretty controversial issue since states were debating whether or not they wanted state-level standards or assessments, and many had decided that they didn't.[71]

Though many voted for the bill, liberals continued to have reservations about the ability of standards and assessments to improve poor schools in the absence of greater equity of resources. Conservatives believed the law would allow the federal government to dictate education policy to the states and ultimately end local control of schools. Gary Bauer, from the conservative Family Research Council, for example, said it would "centralize education decision making in Washington and seriously undermine parental authority."[72] Despite the Clinton administration's claims that the changes would increase the flexibility within ESEA programs, conservatives believed that they would force states to align their reforms with federal prescriptions. Bauer commented that "when the $11 billion ESEA reauthorization passed with a reform agenda almost identical to that of Goals 2000, the 'voluntary' nature of Goals 2000 became irrelevant. . . . In order to receive an ESEA grant, each state must submit a plan to the Secretary of Education. . . . This is not an invitation or a suggestion, as in Goals 2000. Backed by the influence of $11 billion, it becomes a mandate."[73]

If the 1994 reforms were criticized by liberals and conservatives for employing expanded federal power to promote school improvement and accountability, centrist reformers criticized it for not mandating tougher sanctions for states that did not meet the law's timetables for increased student achievement. The need to craft a legislative majority had ensured that the edge of Clinton's education reforms were softened as the legislation proceeded through Congress. As a result, the standards, assessment, and accountability provisions of the ESEA reauthorization ended up being fairly vague and unspecific and generally weaker than Clinton and many reformers would have liked. Amy Wilkins of the Education Trust, for example, noted that

> prior to the 1994 ESEA reauthorization, Title I was primarily a funding stream that had no expectations attached to it. They counted the number of poor children in your school and they sent you a check. There was no requirement from the feds that the kids actually learn anything. In the 1994 reauthorization, states were told to set up accountability systems and begin to hold . . . schools accountable for what these kids learn. But what, in fact, you found was that the states set up very flabby accountability systems—they weren't rigorous enough to make the schools move or to promote change in instructional practice or educational policy at the state level. . . . The federal government with the 1994 changes [signaled] impatience with the states by saying "We want you to have accountability systems" and also signaled a move to the standards movement, but this was resisted. The federal government was very polite—[it] said, "Here are the things we would LIKE you to do with this money"—but the states resisted, and really very little changed.[74]

Thus, if the ESEA reauthorization forced states to "play ball" on standards-based reform, it allowed them to write their own rules for how the game would be played. States thus were given the freedom to design their own standards, assessments, and accountability systems.

CONCLUSION

Clinton's rhetoric regarding the need for a strong federal role in education during the 1992 campaign and the legislative enactments of the first two years of his administration helped to further nationalize politics and policymaking in education. As one observer noted, "The Clinton administration education initiatives represent the most proactive federal policy agenda in 30 years."[75] In particular, his linking of education to economic growth established a strong and publicly accessible rationale for broader federal involvement in school reform efforts. Clinton's emphasis on the need for increased education reform, as opposed to merely increased spending, was also very important. His speeches and legislative proposals marked a clear break with the approach of Democrats in the past—and with the old liberal policy regime—which had framed the education debate in terms of promoting integration and equity through federal mandates and spending. By eschewing the traditional Democratic defense of the status quo in education and calling for a number of reforms such as standards and choice, Clinton also succeeded in identifying the Democratic Party as the party of school reform. Republicans, meanwhile, remained bitterly divided over how to respond to Clinton's activism in school reform and about the appropriate federal role in education more generally. This was clearly visible in the debates over Goals 2000 and the ESEA reauthorization, when a number of GOP moderates negotiated with the Clinton administration and ultimately supported the bills while their conservative colleagues simply opposed them outright as a dangerous expansion of federal influence or offered amendments on social and "culture war" issues that were unrelated to the core education questions.

Clinton capitalized on the increasing salience of the education issue with the public and Democratic control of Congress to gain passage of two major school reform bills—Goals 2000 and the Improving America's Schools Act—as well as a number of smaller bills, such as the Head Start reauthorization, the School to Work Opportunities Act (which created the country's first national system for moving high school students into the workplace), and the Safe Schools Act. As Jack Jennings has observed,

> After all the debate, the Democrats, including the most liberal ones, knew that politically they had to be with Clinton. And so they were willing to change their amendments to secure passage of the bill in the House and they were willing to make further changes to reach a conference agreement with the Senate. Despite concerns about the equity implications of standards reform and about the limited amount of funds being provided, House Democrats realized that there could be no gridlock over policy as there had been with Bush.[76]

Many school reformers (including Clinton himself) had called for the federal government to push states to adopt stronger standards, assessment, and choice provisions than those contained in these new laws. The power of liberal Democrats in Congress and of education groups such as the NEA, however, was sufficient to ensure that the toughest reform proposals were kept out of the final legislation and that the implementation of the new programs would be flexible. In the end, as Andy Rotherham has noted, "Clinton got as far as he could in 1994, but there was a lot of resistance. He had to rely on a strange alliance of moderate Republicans and Democrats to get the bills passed."[77] The continued opposition to a more rigorous federal role in promoting school reform would also limit the ability—or willingness—of the Clinton administration to actively implement even the weak enforcement provisions of the new laws. As Patty Sullivan recalled,

> The Department of Education under the Clinton administration . . . did not really push hard to enforce that law. . . . During the Clinton administration not a single

state lost funding because of a failure to comply with the law's requirements. The Clinton administration found very clever ways to find states in compliance because they wanted very much for states to be able to draw down their Goals 2000 money.[78]

Clinton's undersecretary for education, Mike Smith, agreed, noting that "the feds weren't going to take education money away from states, so there was no way that we could have applied strong sanctions, and nobody really wanted to in our administration."[79]

Though the new laws did not include many mandates for states, they nonetheless signified a sea change in federal education policy and comprised the first legislative component of a new policy regime. Goals 2000 codified the shift from the historical federal focus on ensuring equity for disadvantaged students and impoverished schools to a new commitment to improve the academic performance of all students and schools. Gordon Ambach, then the executive director of the Council of Chief State School Officers, observed,

> In the 1960s, when nearly all current federal elementary and secondary education programs were begun, the national assumption was that the performance of students not in poverty was adequate and, therefore, the major need was to raise the performance of poor children to that of their more affluent peers. In the 1990s the judgment [was] that the level of performance of even the affluent [was] not adequate for the challenges of the twenty-first century. . . . Goals 2000 addresses all schools and students.[80]

Clinton had repeatedly stated during the 1992 campaign that "in a Clinton administration, we will have no higher priority than the improvement of education for every child."[81] The new federal concern about *every* child was remarkable given the historic focus on only *disadvantaged* children. Since the creation of ESEA in 1965, the federal role in education had been narrowly crafted and largely concerned with process and inputs. The key element of the new federal focus on outputs—on student achievement—was the national standards outlined in Goals 2000 and then tied to ESEA in 1994.

In an unprecedented shift, henceforth the federal government would be committed to improving the quality of academic instruction in schools. Though George H. W. Bush had attempted to refocus the federal role on academic standards, he had been unable to secure the legislative victories necessary to codify the change. It had been left to Clinton to circumvent the opposition of both liberals and conservatives to an expanded, reform-oriented federal role in education. Will Marshall summed up the importance of Clinton's achievements with Goals 2000 and the 1994 ESEA reauthorization to federal education policy in this way:

> It produced a very important and large legacy—Clinton and the Democrats helped bring the country behind a new education agenda based on choice, high standards,

and accountability for results rather than the old debate over more spending or vouchers. Validating choice for Democrats was a huge accomplishment; he gave active encouragement to charter school movement in this country and added to the momentum of standards reform and accountability in states. The 1994 reforms, even though they were relatively weak and toothless, helped establish the right principles and goals and paved the way for a more radical breakthrough later on in the No Child Left Behind law. . . . Clinton really helped bring about a major change in the federal role in education—it becomes focused on academic quality and performance—that is an enormous breakthrough and a radical change. . . . I think the New Democrats deserve a lot of credit for that even though I don't think Clinton got that far.[82]

Many of the reform ideas that would later form the core of the 2002 No Child Left Behind Act—such as standards, assessments, adequate yearly progress, school report cards, and corrective action—found their first expression in the 1994 ESEA reauthorization. But in the early 1990s the lingering conservative opposition to a strong federal role in education and the continuing liberal reservations about testing and accountability meant that Goals 2000 and the ESEA reauthorization contained little in the way of mandatory reforms for the states. The shift in ends and means of the federal role in elementary and secondary education was of great import, but tougher reforms paired with federal sanctions would have to wait.

Another important element of the debate over Goals 2000 and the 1994 ESEA reauthorization was the growing split between moderate and conservative Republicans on education. Whereas conservatives for the most part voted against the Clinton education reform legislation, many moderate Republicans supported it. In part this reflected a more pragmatic and less ideological approach to federal policies and programs among moderates, but it also was due to increasing support for standards-based reform among the nation's Republican governors and business leaders and organizations such as the Chamber of Commerce, the National Alliance of Business, and the Business Roundtable, which often allied with the Republican Party. Business groups had been heavily involved in the state education reform efforts that had sprung up in the wake of *A Nation at Risk* and had come to embrace the necessity of national education standards and tests to improve student achievement and better prepare them for the workplace. But business support for national leadership in school reform was at odds with conservative Republicans' fears of increased federal control over schools. As one observer noted,

Together, the business community and social conservatives helped elect Ronald Reagan and George Bush President. Their continued alliance is considered an essential element in Republican visions of retaking the White House and gaining ground on Capital Hill and in state politics. In many ways, however, the groups are now working at odds. Nowhere are the fault lines more evident than on the issue of how schools should change. . . . Business officials have been watching closely as grassroots activists, many with religious ties and strong concerns for traditional moral values, have gained public support by opposing outcomes-based reforms— reforms for which business leaders have in many instances been among the most prominent proponents.[83]

During and after the 1992 election, the Republicans struggled to answer the challenge posed by the New Democrats without abandoning the party's historic free-market and small-government principles. Republicans were divided on how best to respond to Democrats' education initiatives, with some calling for more aggressively advocating market reforms, such as public school choice, charter schooling, and school vouchers, and others endorsing curricular and governance reforms such as national standards and stronger accountability measures. Many Republicans continued to fear, as they had with America 2000, however, that national standards and accountability would only increase federal influence and red tape in schools. As a result, as Mike Smith has observed, "Conservatives in the Republican Party focused on opposing the federal role in education—they didn't really have thoughtful ideas about the federal role in reform. But moderate Republicans were often very much with us [the Clinton administration] on a number of issues."[84]

The problem with the standards-based approach for Republicans was that it represented the first step on a slippery slope toward nationalizing curricula and schooling. This was the concern that had sunk Bush's America 2000 plan, and it would cause the Republicans, in the end, to shy away from any national system of accountability during most of the 1990s. In fact, congressional Republicans would attack Clinton's Goals 2000 plan for its proposal that the federal government encourage the development of national standards and play an active role in coordinating and supporting state testing. Most Republicans were content to argue that though schools faced serious problems, they could and should address them on their own without the help—or meddling—of the federal government. Unwilling to debate Democrats on the details of a federal role that they opposed on principle, conservatives expended most of their energies on education on issues that had little to do with improving schools' academic performance. Many of their criticisms of Goals 2000 and the 1994 ESEA reauthorization, for example, revolved around the wider debate over family values and the culture wars. Conservatives argued that Goals 2000 promoted an abortion rights and sex education agenda, would teach children to embrace homosexuality and be promiscuous, and would allow the federal government to remove children from "at risk" families. As a result, the GOP did not offer a comprehensive alternative vision for federal education policy in the mid-1990s, and this furthered the growing public perception that the party was anti-education.

The passage of Goals 2000 and the 1994 ESEA reauthorization reflected (and furthered) Clinton's efforts to move the Democratic Party to the center on education and was to have lasting significance. As former House Democratic education staffer Jennings has noted,

> Clinton thought that there ought to be higher standards and public school choice in education and that the federal government had a role to play. He was at variance with the more liberal Democrats in Congress on this. These folks had voted against Bush's America 2000 plan, but Clinton gradually convinced Democrats to accept that standards-based reform was a legitimate reform. It was an effort to move Democrats to the middle on education by talking about raising standards and not just about equity concerns.[85]

As Democrats began to assume a more centrist, reform-oriented position, however, political developments were pushing the Republican Party position on federal education policy further to the right.

Republicans made historic gains in the 1994 midterm elections and captured control of both the House and Senate by riding the backlash against Clinton's ambitious health care proposal, which brought back memories of Democratic big government. Under the leadership of conservative Newt Gingrich (R-GA), Republicans in Congress declared a new "Contract with America" and launched an ambitious effort to roll back the federal government and abolish several cabinet agencies. Vitriolic conservative opposition to the recently expanded federal role in education was a prominent item on their agenda, and as a result school reform would remain a very visible and controversial issue throughout the remainder of the 1990s. A crucial part of Goals 2000—and the one which was meant to provide the means to spur states to adopt tough new standards—was the provision that gave NESIC the power to "certify" state standards. As such, it was also the provision that was subjected to the most political controversy and would become a prime target for elimination.

Another major area of contention during the rest of the decade would be the level of federal funding for education. Clinton called for greatly increased federal spending during the 1992 campaign, but the economic recession, expanding entitlement programs, large budget deficits, and the spending caps put in place by Graham-Rudman prevented him from delivering during 1993 and early 1994. By mid-1994 an economic recovery was well under way, and the administration was prepared to propose significantly expanded funding for education. Republican control of Congress, however, dramatically altered the political equation in Washington. The new conservative-led Republican Congress would fight the attempts by Clinton and Democrats in Congress to secure large increases in federal education spending and to create an assortment of new federal education programs.

Extending Reagan's argument that government was the problem rather than the solution, Republicans also would try to reduce federal involvement in education by cutting federal spending, by converting it into block grants or vouchers, and by eliminating the Department of Education entirely. Clinton had succeeded in laying the legislative foundation for a reoriented federal role in education based on standards, choice, and accountability, but the emerging new policy regime remained under attack from the left and right.

6. Showdown—The Conservative Assault on the Federal Role in Education (1994–1996)

The overwhelming victory of Republicans in the 1994 midterm elections fundamentally changed the political environment at the national level. The Republican victory was widely viewed as a rejection of Clinton's big government proposals in areas such as health care. The GOP's gains in 1994 were largely attributed to the bold political leadership of Newt Gingrich (R-GA) and the extensive mobilization of the religious right. As a result, when Republicans took over control of Congress in 1995, the party's leadership was committed to enacting the conservative policy agenda outlined in its Contract with America, calling for cutting taxes and eliminating government programs and agencies. Clinton acknowledged the new political climate when he declared shortly after the election that the "era of big government is over" even as he portrayed himself as the defender of an active, smaller, and more effective government.

Republicans handed Clinton a significant political opportunity, however, when they mistook popular rejection of big government for a rejection of government in general and tried to eliminate many popular federal programs and agencies. These proposals were generally seen as extreme by the public, particularly when Clinton's veto of them resulted in a widely publicized government shutdown. Democrats were able to depict the GOP as unconcerned about the problems facing middle- and lower-class Americans and, in particular, as hostile to education and other services for families and children. Though Republicans would succeed in repealing some of what they saw as the more intrusive provisions of federal education laws, their proposals to eliminate the Department of Education and to convert federal education funding into vouchers or block grants were ultimately defeated by a coalition of Democrats and moderate Republicans.

Education became a dominant issue in the 1996 presidential election, which was widely viewed as a referendum on Clinton's vision of expanded federal leadership of school reform. The Republican nominee, Robert Dole, adopted the antigovernment rhetoric and policy positions of the Contract with America. Clinton once again portrayed himself as a New Democrat and coopted the rhetoric of limited government, simultaneously arguing that government had an obligation to assist the disadvantaged, families, and children. Clinton championed federal activism, particularly on education, but did so with small, targeted "micro-initiatives" in pursuit of opportunity rather than redistribution. With conservatives unwilling to support federal activism in education, Dole had to counter Democratic appeals primarily by arguing that federal involvement was counterproductive. He attacked the teachers unions as emblems of the Democratic attachment to big government and bureaucracy, arguing (like Bush before him) that school vouchers could provide a coherent response to concerns about educational quality. But Clinton successfully portrayed conservative efforts to roll back federal spending and support for vouchers as an attack on public education. Voters saw Clinton and the Democrats as better able to deal with the education issue by a wide margin; this increasingly important "education gap" led to a fundamental reassessment of the Republican Party's position on federal education policy in the late 1990s.

THE 1994 MIDTERM ELECTIONS AND THE REPUBLICAN PUSH TO END GOALS 2000 AND ELIMINATE THE DEPARTMENT OF EDUCATION

In their historic victory in the 1994 midterm elections, which many at the time called an electoral realignment, Republicans were able to gain control of both chambers of Congress for the first time in forty years. Education played a prominent role in the unusually unified Republican campaign message, which included a call for the elimination of Goals 2000 and the federal Department of Education and the restoration of local control over schools. The Christian Coalition also made education a focus of its 1994 voter mobilization and education drives, with opposition to federal influence and outcomes-based education and support for school prayer and school vouchers at the top of their agenda.[1] These education positions appear to have motivated a high turnout among voters in the GOP's conservative base.

The conservative proposals to decrease federal spending and activism in education, however, continued to be viewed unfavorably by most voters, with 81 percent in an election-night poll opposed to any decrease in federal aid to education.[2] Other surveys conducted in the weeks before the election revealed that the public continued to view the Democratic Party more favorably than the Republican Party on the education issue by a large margin.[3] Of particular import was the approximately twenty-point Democratic advantage on the issue among the demographic groups with large numbers of swing voters: independents, moderates, women, and Latinos.[4] How then were Republicans able to win control of Congress while "losing" the education issue? Election-night polls demonstrated that the issues of health care and crime were viewed as much more important than education; these issues took center stage in most congressional campaigns.[5]

Many Republican commentators nonetheless urged the new GOP congressional leadership to make education a priority and to focus on rolling back the education initiatives enacted during the first two years of the Clinton administration. In a December 1994 report, for example, the Heritage Foundation urged Republicans to initiate a major overhaul of federal education programs, calling for the repeal of IDEA, most of Goals 2000 (including the National Education Standards and Improvement Council), and many of the major provisions of ESEA. It also advocated the elimination of the federal Department of Education within five years and the passage of a parent and student empowerment act that would provide federal grants to fund state school-choice experiments. The report stated that "the dramatic shift in power both in Congress and in the states gives conservatives an unprecedented opportunity to undo many of the harmful education programs of the last 30 years. To the extent that government should be involved in education, it is a matter for local and state government, not the federal government."[6] Many conservative pundits announced their opposition not just to federal education programs but to the idea of national academic standards as well.

In a December 1994 article in the *National Review*, former Republican education secretaries Lamar Alexander and William Bennett joined with Sen. Daniel Coats (R-IN) in adding their support to Heritage's recommendations. They blasted Goals 2000 and the 1994 ESEA reauthorization, declaring that they were "bad for children, for education, and for American federalism. . . . They set back the cause of serious school reform, waste billions of dollars, and erode local control of American schools." Clinton, they charged, had hijacked the standards movement begun by President Bush and "transformed a nationwide reform effort into a federal program" that resurrected a discredited emphasis on school inputs and immobilized genuine school reform efforts like charters and choice. "It is time," they argued,

> for the federal government virtually to withdraw from elementary and secondary education and relinquish the authority it has seized in this domain. Dozens of federal programs ought to vanish. The resources they now consume should be made available—perhaps through a federal tax cut or an expanded version of chapter two [the block grant program of ESEA]—to states and localities to do with as they judge best. . . . Insofar as any education functions stay in Washington, their guiding principles should be choice, deregulation, innovation, accountability, and serious assessment keyed to real standards in core subjects.[7]

While chiding Republicans for failing to stop or significantly modify Goals 2000 and ESEA, Alexander, Bennett, and Coats encouraged them to seize the opportunity to radically reduce and reform the federal role in education and to return power to parents and to state and local governments.

Gingrich and the Republican leadership of the 104th Congress worked hard to enact much of this agenda. In May 1995, the House and Senate budget committees released resolutions to balance the federal budget, in part through significant cuts in education spending. The House resolution called for a $12.4 billion cut in spending on education, training, and employment, the elimination of 150 of the 240 Department of Education programs, and the abolition of the department itself within a year. Senate Republicans proposed a somewhat smaller $10 billion cut in education-related programs. The senators called for the elimination of thirty small education programs but for preserving the rest (and the department) at reduced levels of funding. Democrats strongly opposed the Republican proposals, and the votes on the budget resolutions were predictably along party lines. In November 1995, House Republicans advanced proposals to eliminate the Department of Education and to create a private school voucher program for the District of Columbia, but these were defeated when a number of GOP moderates joined with Democrats to oppose them. In introducing these proposals, Republicans argued that they were against federal control of education, not education per se. They emphasized that federal programs had failed to benefit schools and that money was not the essential ingredient of education reform. Lindsey Graham's (R-SC) remarks were typical of the conservative criticisms of federal education policy that appeared at the time:

> The Department of Education has failed miserably to improve education in our country. What's more, it has become an intrusive and meddlesome force in the education of our youth. It's time to eliminate the Department of Education and return control to the states, localities, school boards, parents, and teachers. . . . It is the general belief of many Democrats that increased spending will solve many of the nation's social problems including America's education woes. Statistics prove that, where education is concerned, that is not the case.[8]

The Goals 2000 program also became a major focal point of the debate over federal education policy when Republicans in Congress pressed for its elimination.[9] Despite the support of moderate Republicans, business leaders, and a majority of the public, conservatives had long held serious reservations about the idea of national standards, which they viewed as a threat to local control of schools. Conservatives claimed that Goals 2000 threatened to "federalize education policy," encourage "homogenized content standards," and enable the federal government to "influence every public school student and every public school."[10] Former Republican education secretary Lamar Alexander warned that though Goals 2000 was cloaked in the garb of aiding state reform, he "would treat it the same way you would treat a fox dressed as a duck at a duck family reunion."[11] House Republicans voted to eliminate funding for Goals 2000 in both 1995 and 1996, but the threat of a presidential veto and compromises with the Senate ultimately restored funds for the program.

The Republican-controlled Congress did succeed in passing a number of significant amendments to Goals 2000 in 1996 that were intended to eliminate what they saw as the most intrusive provisions of the act. First, the NESIC—the National Education Standards and Improvement Council—was repealed. The council had been established to create model national academic standards and to "certify" state academic standards. It had become a lightning rod for fears about the expansion of federal influence over the standards-setting process; many conservatives saw it as a precursor to a national school board. Finn commented that "it symbolizes everything that's wrong with Clintonism in education: namely, Washington knows best."[12] The release of highly controversial history standards around this time brought the national standards movement under fire. Recognizing the strong political opposition to the NESIC and inclined to give the states the lead in setting standards, the Clinton administration did not fight to preserve the council.

A second change to Goals 2000 was the repeal of the federal authority to establish opportunity-to-learn standards and the requirement that states identify the "standards or strategies" for ensuring that schools have sufficient resources to promote student learning. A third change removed the specific requirements governing the composition of the state and local planning panels; this was left completely to the discretion of governors and state education agencies. A fourth major change to Goals 2000 was the addition of language clarifying that Goals 2000 could not be construed to require any school, state, or local education agency, as a requirement of receiving program funds, to provide outcome-based education, school-based health clinics, or social services. Fifth, conservative Rep. Ernest Istook (R-OK) added an amendment that permitted states to use their Goals 2000 funds solely to purchase technology instead of to fund the development of standards and assessments as was originally intended. Istook even wrote a personal letter to all fifty governors encouraging them to use federal funds for computers rather than on developing standards and tests. Sixth, the Ed-Flex program was expanded to allow six additional states waivers from some federal regulations. Seventh and finally, the 1996 amendments removed the requirement that each state submit a detailed plan outlining its intended education reforms in order to be eligible for continued funding from the Goals 2000 program. Instead, states could merely submit to the secretary of education assurances that a plan for meeting the requirements of Goals 2000 and improving students' performance had been developed.

These changes significantly altered Goals 2000 by removing federal oversight and accountability from the standards-setting process, instead allowing states to use federal school improvement monies for whatever purposes they wanted and to vouch for their own progress in increasing student performance. Goals 2000 was essentially transformed into a block grant (which is what many Republicans had argued for all along). As Clinton education adviser Bill Galston observed,

> The Republicans were quite successful in their effort to roll back the federal role in education. They forced the administration to accept very significant rollbacks in Goals 2000; many journalists and other observers viewed the legislation as having been gutted by the 1995–96 changes, or at least defanged. The formalization of the federal role over content standards . . . never came into being. . . . This represented a frontal attack by Republicans on the most formal institutionalized mechanism for some national-level deliberation about state content standards. . . . [Little] was left of Goals 2000 after the 1995 changes. . . . [It] became an alternative funding stream loosely dedicated to processes of education reform.[13]

The Republican effort to repeal or weaken Goals 2000 received the support of some liberal Democrats who remained wary of tough federal standards or accountability measures, particularly when not supported by considerable new federal resources. The 1995–1996 debate over the Goals 2000 amendments was thus an interesting example of how conservative opposition to federally mandated education reforms and liberal opposition to education reforms with real consequences produced a strange alliance against meaningful federal school reform efforts during the 1990s.

It appears, however, that Gingrich and his fellow conservatives misjudged the nature and extent of their political mandate in 1994 and as a result overreached with their antigovernment zeal. This was true generally, but it was perhaps most striking in the area of education. As noted previously, public opinion polls clearly demonstrated that citizens continued to support an active federal role in education. A poll taken two months after the November 1994 election found that 70 percent of respondents believed that the Department of Education was "very necessary."[14] Public support for the department continued to remain strong even after Republicans advanced their legislative proposals for its elimination.[15]

Support for federal spending on education also remained high, and Republican proposals to reduce it were viewed very negatively by the public. A March 1995 poll, for example, found that 79 percent of respondents felt that Republican proposals to cut the Department of Education's budget were a step in the wrong direction, with 68 percent holding that view "strongly." Only 15 percent of those surveyed felt the Republican proposals were a step in the right direction.[16] Despite the frequent criticisms of federal education programs by conservative politicians and interest groups during the 1980s and 1990s, public support for an active and well-funded federal role remained strong. Large majorities of citizens, in fact, wanted federal spending on education to *increase* and believed that doing so should take priority over almost all other federal program areas.[17] Significantly, the public supported funding for education even while it endorsed Republican proposals for fiscal restraint more generally. A 1995 *Washington Post*/ABC News poll, for example, found that though eight out of ten people surveyed favored a balanced budget amendment, two out of three would not support such an amendment if it meant that education (or social security) spending would be slashed. These polls were a clear indication that Republican attempts to convince the public that federal influence and spending on schools were harmful and/or unnecessary had failed, and that future attacks on the federal role in education could be politically harmful to the party.

The major problem that Republicans faced concerning education was that their efforts during this period focused on attacking existing federal programs rather than offering specific proposals to improve schools. As Mike Smith noted, the "1995 and 1996 amendments to Goals 2000 were really a part of the Republican opposition to a federal role in education, not so much about a different vision of what the federal role should be."[18] The GOP's abstract philosophical arguments concerning school reform were hard to sell to the public in the presence of tangible Democratic proposals for school improvement. As Galston noted, "Republicans weren't able to make more progress with their assault of the federal role in education because they didn't have much credibility with the public on the issue—they were not seen as defenders of public education. Calls for the [department's] abolition . . . could easily be heard by the public as a retrenchment of the national commitment to and federal role in education, and this was opposed by public."[19] Clinton and Democrats in Congress repeatedly hammered Republicans for being anti-education and for failing to fund essential programs for schools and children.

THE DEMOCRATIC COUNTERATTACK ON EDUCATION

In the aftermath of the Republican gains in the 1994 elections, Democrats scrambled to identify the source of the apparent public backlash against the Democratic Party and the means by which they could respond. The election was widely interpreted as a wake-up call for President Clinton and a repudiation of his (and the Democratic Congress's) big government proposals during the 1993–1994 period. Democrats commissioned focus groups and polls that revealed that although Republicans had successfully tapped into a general antigovernment sentiment among the public, public support for particular government programs, such as those in education, the environment, and Medicare and Medicaid, remained strong.

Democrats saw an opportunity to portray themselves as the defenders of these popular programs against the extremist budget cutting and devolution proposals of Republicans. New Democrats urged Clinton to use the remainder of his term to return to the centrist proposals that had been so popular during his 1992 presidential campaign. While many liberal Democrats remained committed to a more activist brand of government interventionism, moderate Democrats cautioned that the public had rejected this approach in the midterm elections and that the party would seriously harm its prospects in the 1996 elections unless it changed course.

Fred Siegal and Will Marshall observed in an influential article in the *New Democrat* in September 1995, for example, that "the defeat of President Clinton's comprehensive health care reforms marked the end of a half-century effort to create a full-blown American version of the European welfare state." They warned that "where liberals see a compassionate if ungainly state, much of the public sees a bloated and imperious federal government, mired in bureaucratic dysfunction, responsive not to the wider concerns of the middle class, but to a proxy public of organized interests and transfer-seeking groups that feed on the body politic." Siegal and Marshall called on Democrats to focus on "restoring opportunity for the many by confronting the privileged defenders of the old economic order" and emphasized the key role that education reform must play in this effort.

> Entrenched interests, however, fiercely resist these essential changes . . . [as] teachers and administrators block attempts to replace a standardized, centralized public education system with a more competitive and decentralized model that expands choice and provides accountability. . . . For Democrats, the path back to power lies not in recreating the failures of the European welfare state but in finding new ways to make the party's traditional values of limited government and responsible individualism workable again.[20]

The centrist Democratic Leadership Council called for a "progressive alternative" to the Contract with America that would transfer power from the national government to states and localities but also use expanded reform-oriented federal leadership and investment to solve pressing social problems.

The broad and growing political appeal of the education issue led Clinton and the Democrats to choose it as the focal point of their response to the Contract with America and the conservative assault on federal government activism. As Ed Kealy, executive director of the Committee for Education Funding, noted, "Democrats recognized how vulnerable Republicans would be politically on the issue if they were identified with cutting aid for poor kids."[21] In 1995, Democrats proposed that more than $18 billion in additional funds be directed toward existing education and training programs, with school-to-work, Head Start, Goals 2000, and charter school grants singled out for the largest increases.[22] While politicians and scholars debated the importance of spending to educational achievement, Democratic and Republican pollsters alike agreed that the public viewed support for education largely in terms of funding. Mark Mellman, a Democratic pollster, remarked that "it has been very clear and very consistent that there's strong public support for education and strong antipathy for anyone who wants to cut education. [Education] is sort of vague at the federal level, but it's a for-it or against-it kind of thing. And if you're against it, you're in trouble."[23] Clinton's substantial record of activism on education, combined with public opposition to Republican cutbacks, made it an issue on which he could paint a stark contrast and one that worked in his favor with voters.

In recognition of the new political environment, however, Clinton did not propose any major new federal education programs during 1995. Instead, he called for increases in funding for existing programs and reforms that polls indicated were quite popular. Speeches by Clinton and other administration officials sought to depict Republicans as running, in Vice President Al Gore's words, "the most anti-education Congress in the history of this country" while reminding voters of the legislative accomplishments in education during Clinton's first two years in office.[24] Rhetorically, the administration continued to stress the importance of education reform to individual economic opportunity and to national economic growth. It also portrayed the debate between the Democratic and Republican parties as one of financial capital versus human capital, and government abandonment versus government reinvention.

Clinton's speech to the California Democratic Party in April 1995 was typical of these efforts as he seized on the education issue to contrast his vision for the country with Republicans'. He portrayed Republican proposals to cut federal spending on education and other popular programs as extreme and out of touch with mainstream America and painted himself as the defender of education and an advocate for children.

> "The [Republican] House . . . bill had terrible cuts in it. They cut education. They cut child nutrition. They cut the environment [and] housing [and] gutted the national service program. A lot of it was politics and ideology. It was extremist. . . . The Senate Republicans were even embarrassed by some of the things [the House] did and they put some back in."[25]

Claiming that his approach was pragmatic and centrist and avoided the pitfalls of both conservatives and liberals, Clinton insisted on restoring some of the cuts.

> You know they [Republicans] used to attack us and say, "oh, the Democrats are indiscriminate. They just want to spend money on everything." Well that's not true anymore. We cut 3,000 programs. I asked the Congress to cut 400 more and consolidate them. I don't want to spend more money on everything. I want to spend

more money on the right things. They want to spend less money on everything. Neither extreme is right. The right thing to do is to say education is the fault line in the modern world; if you want the American dream, if you want the middle class to grow, if you want us to go up and down together, we had better get every last person in this country a decent education. And we had better not walk away from it.[26]

Clinton decided to make a very public stand on the 1995 Republican rescissions bill, which called for large additional cuts in federal programs.

Clinton had threatened to veto the bill if it cut education spending significantly or attempted to undo his education reforms such as Goals 2000. When it ended up doing both, he declared it would do irreparable harm to children and quickly vetoed the bill in June 1995. The budget stalemate between Clinton and Republicans in Congress led to a high-profile shutdown of the federal government. In a televised address shortly after the veto, Clinton introduced his own plan to balance the budget, which called for 20 percent across-the-board reductions in discretionary federal spending in all areas except defense and education. The address marked the beginning of a Clinton counteroffensive against the Republican Congress and, in some ways, the beginning of his 1996 reelection bid. Clinton declared education to be his first priority, and in other speeches throughout 1995 and 1996 he and members of his administration continued to highlight the issue and to use it to portray the Republican Congress as extreme and irresponsible.

In remarks to the NEA in July 1995, for example, Clinton acknowledged the need to balance the budget but argued that education funding should be preserved. "You and I know," he said, that "it would be self-defeating to cut our investments in education. Cutting education today would be like cutting defense budgets at the height of the Cold War. Our national security depends upon our ability to educate better, not just to spend more money but to reach more people, to perform at a higher level, to get real results." Clinton emphasized that the Republican budget would cut education by $36 billion whereas his plan would balance the budget in a slightly longer period of time but would increase spending on education by $40 billion. "We do have a responsibility to balance the budget," he noted, but "we've also got a responsibility to invest in our children and our future. We cannot restore the economy, we cannot rebuild the middle class, we can't recapture middle-class dreams or restore middle-class values if we walk away from our common responsibilities, the education of our people."[27]

At the suggestion of political strategist Dick Morris, Clinton sought to triangulate between liberal Democrats and conservative Republicans in Congress by advocating an active but limited government. The key message was built around what became known as "M2E2": "balancing the budget in a way that protects our values and defends Medicare, Medicaid, education, and the environment." As Richard Stengel and Eric Pooley noted, "Clinton had arrived at a golden synthesis, bridging the traditional Democratic notion of protecting entitlements with the New Democratic position of fiscal responsibility."[28] This strategy was unveiled in Clinton's nationally televised January 1996 State of the Union speech when he embraced Republican rhetoric about limited government while calling for targeted federal activism in a number of areas. "The era of big government is over," Clinton stated, "but we cannot go back to the time when our citizens were left to fend for themselves."[29] This approach enabled Clinton to oppose both irresponsible government and irresponsible cuts in government. The speech emphasized the need to increase educational opportunities for Americans through a combination of reforms such as Goals 2000 and additional funding for school technology and college scholarships.

The Democratic defense of the federal role in education during the 104th Congress was greatly assisted by a number of moderate Republicans who fought to preserve the Department of Education and federal programs and spending more generally.[30] These moderates warned that efforts to kill Goals 2000 would create the perception that the Republican Party was unconcerned about the problems facing America's schools. Diane Ravitch, a former Reagan administration education official, for example, cautioned that "a vote to repeal [Goals 2000] undoubtedly would be countered by a veto. Even if successful, repeal would send an unfortunate message that the new Congress is against academic standards."[31] Chester Finn, a leading Republican thinker on education, also counseled against trying to eliminate the Department of Education. Critical of many parts of Clinton's 1994 reforms, he argued that the federal government had an important (if limited) role to play in school reform. Finn warned that "the conservatives' reform agenda [in education] is bold, comprehensive, and in most respects promising. But it isn't perfect. Its shortcomings arise from illusions and half-truths to which conservatives are vulnerable, like a driver so anxious about the truck on the road ahead that he doesn't see the car in the blind spot alongside."[32] He cautioned that Republican proposals to institute vouchers and to eliminate federal education programs and the Department of Education would not solve the problems facing American schools. GOP opposition to national standards and assessments was also misguided, he warned, as it would prevent the collection of data essential for holding schools and teachers accountable for academic results.

Moderate Republicans in Congress had observed the Gingrich revolution and the rise of the religious right's influence over the party with great trepidation on both political and policy grounds. They were concerned that the party's association with the more extreme positions of the religious right would harm the image of the Republican Party and its prospects in the 1996 presidential election. The increasing influence of Christian conservatives within the Republican Party led moderate Republicans such as Sens. Arlen Specter (R-PA) and John Danforth

(R-MO) to publicly worry about the party's ability to attract moderate voters. Danforth, for example, observed in 1994 that "a party which is relentlessly conservative, sharp-edged and sharp-elbowed is not a very attractive party and is not going to succeed."[33] Specter, meanwhile, established the Republican Majority Coalition and the Big Tent PAC to warn against the excesses of the religious right and to promote moderate Republican candidates and issues. Although the most contentious and visible fight between Christian conservatives and moderate Republicans was over abortion, they also held widely divergent positions on federal domestic policy issues, especially education policy.

A group called the Republican Main Street Coalition was formed in the mid-1990s to organize Republican moderates to fight conservative proposals in education and on other issues. Jason Foster, the policy director for the group, noted that "on education, we opposed attempts to eliminate the Department of Education—we believed that there should be a strong federal component to education policy. As the general population in America started to emphasize that education was their number-one concern, eliminating the Department or the federal role was also very unpopular."[34] Led by Sens. James Jeffords (R-VT), Nancy Kassebaum (R-KS), and Specter and by Reps. Bill Goodling (R-PA) and Dale Kildee (R-MI), Republican moderates in Congress worked to soften the education proposals put forward by the conservative GOP leadership. They used their committee and subcommittee leadership positions to fight the conservative Republican leadership's attempts to create a federal voucher program, slash federal education spending or convert it into block grants, and eliminate the Department of Education.

From his influential position as chairman of the Senate Subcommittee on Education, Arts, and Humanities, Jeffords argued that federal spending on education should be increased rather than decreased. "I want to emphasize at this time," he said in April 1995, "when we're trying to cut the deficit down, that it is counterproductive to cut education."[35] Because Republicans held only fifty-four seats in the Senate and thus fell short of the necessary sixty for cloture, Democrats and moderate Republicans like Jeffords were able to force Senate Republican leaders to compromise on many of the more extreme education measures passed in the House. The congressional deliberations over funding for Clinton's Goals 2000 program epitomized this dynamic. The House voted in 1995 to eliminate the program, but the Senate, led by Democrats and moderate Republicans, insisted on providing $350 million in funding, which though significantly less than the $750 million requested by the president, enabled the program—and the new federal role in promoting standards—to continue.

Throughout this period the business community also continued to actively support Goals 2000, national standards, and federal education reform leadership.[36] A number of influential groups, including the Business Roundtable, the

U.S. Chamber of Commerce, the National Alliance of Business, and the National Association of Manufacturers, created the Business Coalition for Education Reform and lobbied Congress to continue to leverage federal programs and money to push states to improve their schools. As Jack Jennings has noted, "The business community . . . opposed the new shift of the [Republican] party away from federal aid to education and from the new purpose of encouraging states and local school districts to raise their education standards. Their support was crucial for moderate Republicans in Congress who agreed with them and disagreed with their party's abandonment of the national commitment to aid public schools and students."[37] The National Governors Association also reaffirmed its support during the summer of 1996 for Goals 2000 and the new standards-based approach that Clinton had implemented. The business community and the governors urged that federal programs be modified rather than repealed and were an important pro-reform force throughout the 1990s.

By late 1995 the united front that the Republican Party displayed during and immediately after the 1994 elections was splintering, and the antigovernment zeal of Gingrich and his conservative supporters was increasingly being challenged by moderates within the party. As one observer noted in November 1995, "two things are [now] clear. First, the libertarian component was an important aspect of the Contract and the Republican victory but not the only one. And second, the Contract represented a temporary truce between often warring conservative factions who came together in opposition to facets of New Deal/Great Society liberalism . . . but were and remain divided over what should replace liberalism."[38] The opposition of moderate Republicans to many conservative education proposals also helped Clinton and the Democrats make the case that the positions of the congressional GOP leadership (including Senate majority leader and future presidential candidate Robert Dole) were ideologically charged and extremist.

As important as the legislative and budgetary defeats on education were for conservatives, their failure to convince the public of the need for the changes was even more significant. As Jim Hirni of the Heritage Foundation would later observe, "the conservatives clearly lost the message war on education."[39] Republican arguments on education during the 1980s and the first half of the 1990s had centered on federalism and governance issues. Amid escalating concern over the performance of the public education system, however, parents and citizens were more interested in hearing about specific proposals to improve schools. Jay Diskey, the communications director for the House Education and Workforce Committee at the time, noted that

Republican positions on education were really hard things to sell—because they had more to do with theory and governance. Not too many soccer moms out there really understand block grants—it's a Washington term. If you go out there and ask soccer moms (or dads) whether they would rather have block grants or school computers, they're going to say school computers. Republican proposals were remarkably hard to push, and it led by the late 1990s to a Republican Party that wanted to be very engaged in education but was still having trouble doing it because of these debates over governance and federalism. We weren't providing the types of things that Clinton and the Democrats were pushing, like reading programs and education technology. As a result, the Democrats were able to command the education issue from 1994 right up to the 2000 election.[40]

Polls showed that despite Republicans' concerted efforts on education after the 1994 election, the public continued to view Clinton's school proposals much more favorably.[41]

The principled opposition of Republicans to federal spending and mandates in education came across to voters as a lack of concern for the widely reported problems of the country's public schools. GOP proposals for vouchers and block grants were effectively portrayed by Democrats as an attack on democratic control of public schools and on the idea of public education itself. Will Marshall from the Progressive Policy Institute, for example, explained the failure of Republican efforts to roll back federal influence in education in the following way:

> Most Americans are pro public education, and Republicans expressed hostility towards it. Most Americans are not free-market libertarians and believe that we need public education if you want to make equal opportunity a reality. Republicans oversold vouchers as a panacea, and it didn't seem very plausible to people. The Republicans tended to attack—they demonized teachers. We [New Democrats] have criticized teachers but we have done it in a substantive and empirically grounded and respectful way while the Republicans did it dripping with disdain. Democrats have always had great credibility on the issue of education while Republicans have not.[42]

As the 1996 elections approached, Republicans in Congress grew increasingly concerned that their unpopular positions on education could hurt them at the ballot box and essentially abandoned their assault on the federal role in schools. Most visibly, they gave up their efforts to cut federal education spending and instead embraced large increases. Majority Leader Trent Lott (R-MS) introduced an amendment to add $2.3 billion to the Department of Education, including an extra $1.5 billion for K–12 programs. Republican leaders acknowledged at the time that the change of heart was an effort to reverse public perceptions that the Republican Party didn't care about education. As Sen. Specter observed, "we cut too much, [and] we're going to put a fair amount back in."[43] At the same time, more than fifty Republicans in the House signed a letter of support calling for an increase of $2–3 billion on education. In a public statement endorsing the effort, Rep. Jim Leach

(R-IA) declared that "any political party that takes on education and the teaching profession does it at the risk of being called shortsighted."[44]

In the final analysis, the conservative effort to roll back the federal role in education during the 104th Congress had been an abysmal failure—both in policy and political terms. The effort not only failed to appreciably decrease the size or scope of the federal role in education but also had generated a public backlash against Republicans. As Chester Finn acknowledged,

> After the 1994 election Republicans promised that the Education Department would be eliminated, the federal role downsized, Goals 2000 repealed, and control restored to parents and communities, but essentially nothing has actually been done. Though some obnoxious features were finally trimmed from Goals 2000 (with Administration acquiescence), it and the Department remain vigorous. Nothing has been block-granted, nothing voucherized, nor anything of significance scrapped. The Democrats deftly depicted Republicans as "anti-education" rather than "anti-federal control" [and] the GOP did a woeful job of making its own case.[45]

Republicans failed to lessen the federal government's role in education because they were unable to change public perceptions of the federal role as positive and necessary and because of bad timing—public concerns about schools were peaking at the very moment that the GOP was calling for the national government to leave the issue to the states. A Republican president (Bush) had initiated the federal push for standards and accountability, and it proved impossible for conservatives to put that genie back in the bottle.

THE 1996 PRESIDENTIAL ELECTION: A REFERENDUM ON FEDERAL EDUCATION POLICY

The widely publicized debates over Goals 2000 in 1994 and the high-profile budget battles fought between Clinton and the Republican Congress in 1995 and 1996 dramatically increased the salience of education as a national issue in the 1996 presidential election. Vince Breglio, a Republican pollster, for example, noted in June 1996 that "education has come from some kind of sleepy, second tier issue . . . to what I would call a first-things-first position. Education has truly risen in many people's minds to the top of the agenda."[46] Polls showed that education was the issue voters most wanted candidates to talk about in 1996, that the public saw it as one of the most important issues in the campaign, and that it would play an important role in how they voted.[47] Even more than in 1992, education was seen as crucially important not just for its own sake but also for its connection to wider debates about economic opportunity and social issues.[48] The issue became the core of Clinton's effort to appeal to moderate middle-class swing voters in 1996, particularly women with children—the so-called soccer moms who were identified as being the crucial swing demographic. As a result, whereas education had been *a* central issue in Clinton's 1992 campaign, it would be *the* central issue in his 1996 bid.

The salience of the education issue among voters—and especially conservative voters—was not lost on Republican strategists either, and as a result school reform assumed a prominent place in the campaigns of GOP presidential primary candidates. Clinton made his proposals for increased federal activism on education a focus of his campaign, but Republican presidential candidates—despite the earlier shift in the GOP congressional position—largely embraced the antifederal role position. Clinton contrasted his record of investment and reform for schools with Republican opposition to federal spending, programs, and even to the Department of Education itself. He proposed a number of small, poll-tested new federal programs during the campaign, including programs for school construction and renovation, class size reduction, a new reading corps, connecting classrooms to the Internet, and school uniforms. As Vic Klatt, a former Republican congressional education staffer, observed,

> Clinton was always triangulating between Democratic and Republican positions with his education policy proposals. He supported accountability and choice but also jumped on the bandwagon for more money and other initiatives for purely political purposes, like the 100,000 new teachers proposal that was designed to please teachers unions. . . . They also knew that it was an idea that polled well and connected with parents and teachers, and it was a big winner for them. It put us [Republicans] in an awkward position to oppose it. School construction was another issue like this—there was no way the federal government could pay for all the necessary school construction, but it polled through the roof and interest groups loved it and it was a win-win for them.[49]

At the same time, however, Clinton was careful to avoid the appearance of favoring "big government," a perception that voters had rebelled against in the 1994 midterm elections. He sought to reestablish his New Democrat credentials by talking about the 1994 education reforms and frequently employing the popular buzzwords of "flexibility" and "local control" even as he argued that the federal government had an important role to play in education.

It was a difficult balancing act for Clinton, but one that even Republicans acknowledged he was able to pull off. As Chester Finn observed grudgingly, "Clinton's playing the education-reform fiddle like a Stradivarius, while Bob Dole, the 104th Congress, and the GOP in general have been unable to make any music on what some surveys say is the top issue on voters' minds."[50] Education enabled Democrats to champion federal activism, as long as they used a rhetoric of equal opportunity and investment rather than of redistribution. This allowed centrists to cater to the party's base while crafting an appeal more amenable to suburbanites and southerners. Clinton proposed new investments and programs in education but also emphasized the need to demand more from teachers and schools and to hold them accountable for results by replacing those who do not improve.

At their convention in Chicago, Democrats emphasized education in speech after speech, contrasting their support for teachers and public schools with Republican proposals to cut spending and to give aid to private schools through vouchers. In his keynote speech, Sen. Evan Bayh (D-IN) emphasized, for example, that "no issue more clearly defines the differences between the two major parties and their nominees than education." The party's platform declared,

> Today's Democratic Party knows that education is the key to opportunity. In the new global economy it is more important than ever before. Today, education is the fault line that separates those who will prosper from those who will not. President Clinton and the Democrats have spared no effort over the last four years to improve the quality of American education and expand the opportunity for all Americans to get the education they need to succeed. Every step of the way we have been opposed by Republicans intent on cutting education. Now they want to cut education from Head Start through college scholarships. . . . Today's Democratic Party will stand firmly against the Republican assault on education.[51]

Clinton used his convention address to declare: "I want Americans to build a bridge to the twenty-first century in which we expand opportunity through education."

Though Clinton ran in 1996 as a centrist New Democrat, GOP strategists convinced Dole to run a conservative campaign. This decision was due to the powerful influence of conservatives within the GOP primary electorate and the belief that Bush had lost the general election in 1992 not because he had moved too far to the right, as some suggested, but because he had not moved *far enough* to the right. This reflected the belief of many Republicans that the party's victories in the 1994 midterm elections were the result of a fundamental conservative shift in the electorate. Dole's platform of tax cuts and small government, however, made it difficult for him to offer federal leadership in solving public policy problems generally or to be proactive on the education issue, even had he been willing or able to do so. But while Clinton had been an "education governor," Dole had spent little time on the issue during his legislative career, and it was not one that he was very comfortable talking about or could claim a record on. Dole was thus at a distinct disadvantage in trying to counter Clinton and the Democrats on education. For these reasons, even though Republicans in Congress had begun to abandon their opposition to federal activism in education by 1996, Dole chose to embrace the conservative agenda on school reform during the campaign.

There continued to be strong opposition to federal activism in education among conservatives and members of the religious right, which had become increasingly powerful within the Republican Party. Religious conservatives had demonstrated their power to make or break a candidate's pursuit of the party's nomination through their influence in the 1992 primaries and at the convention. This power also extended to the general election, as a 1992 exit poll of Republican voters found that 17 percent of those who voted, and almost 30 percent of those who voted for Bush, described themselves as born-again or fundamentalist Christians.[52] Conservative influence within the Republican Party had been expanded in 1994 when the Christian Coalition joined forces with Christian leaders Pat Robertson and Jerry Falwell to register new conservative voters, distribute voter guides on behalf of conservative candidates and issues, and raise and distribute campaign contributions to conservative candidates. These efforts were seen as having played a decisive role in the Republican midterm victories in 1994 and had given religious conservatives extensive influence over the GOP agenda.

The Christian Coalition made abolishing the federal Department of Education a plank of its "Contract with the American Family" in 1996, and all of the Republican primary candidates endorsed the idea. Despite abundant evidence that the conservative assault on the federal role in education during 1995 and 1996 had been unpopular with the general public (and especially with moderate voters), this position was made a prominent part of the 1996 Republican presidential and congressional campaigns. The Republican presidential primary candidates were united in their criticism of public schools and teachers unions and in their opposition to a federal role in education. All nine supported the elimination of the department, prayer in public schools, and school vouchers. Phil Gramm's statement during the primaries that "I don't want to be an education president, I want to be an education parent"[53] was typical of the tenor of Republican comments about education. Though polls showed that the general public was greatly concerned about the poor academic performance of public school students, Republican candidates devoted more rhetoric to the need to inculcate moral values in the young than to improving their academic performance.

This approach to education was popular with the more conservative Republican primary voters, but it was much less effective in the general election. Dole was unable to offer specific proposals for solving the nation's educational problems because he argued that doing so was a local responsibility. This perspective was embodied in the GOP's 1996 platform and convention, which placed little emphasis on the issue of education. The platform stated,

> Our formula is as simple as it is sweeping: the federal government has no constitutional authority to be involved in school curricula. . . . That is why we will abolish

the Department of Education, end federal meddling in our schools, and promote family choice at all levels of learning. We therefore call for the prompt repeal of the Goals 2000 program and the School to Work Act . . . and we further urge that federal attempts to impose outcome- or performance-based education on local schools be ended.[54]

As this platform excerpt demonstrates, the Republican message on education in 1996 was largely one of opposition—opposition to current federal policies, programs, and influence. This stood in marked contrast to Bush's endorsement during the 1992 campaign of an active reform-oriented federal role in education focused on national academic standards. The best thing that the federal government could do in education, Dole now made clear, was to leave it alone.

This had the effect, however, of leading many voters to think that the Republican Party had no positive agenda on education. A school superintendent who attended a Republican candidates' forum remarked, for example: "They haven't given any concrete or factual information about how to fix the problems they seem to identify. They seem to be cutting things and don't have an answer as to how to carry out an improvement program."[55] Republican pollster David Winston agreed, noting in retrospect that

Republicans knew that people didn't like Washington bureaucracy and thought that the attempt to eliminate the Department of Education would go over well with public. But education is a very different topic for most Americans. . . . People see education as the future for their kids. The key thing people wanted to know was "What are you going to do to improve children's education?" but there was no connection between that solution—getting rid of [the department]—and improving one child's score. Instead it was viewed as a conservative ideological construct that smaller government and local control is better—which may in fact be true, but you need to describe why local control is better, and we didn't do this very well. In 1995 and 1996 Republicans fought an ideological battle on education without showing why this mattered.[56]

While Clinton talked frequently about education during the general election and put forward a laundry list of specific federal programs and reforms, Dole devoted much less attention to the issue and offered only a call for decentralization and local control.

To the degree that the Republican Party advocated educational initiatives in 1996, they largely centered on issues of morality and vouchers rather than school improvement per se. The party platform devoted as much emphasis to addressing the moral problems of public schools as their academic ones, with its call for abstinence education, voluntary school prayer, and reinforcing the teaching of American heritage. Republicans highlighted their call for private school vouchers in response to criticisms that they did not have any constructive proposals for reforming education. While voucher reforms enjoyed significant support among minority and urban voters, however, the general public remained skeptical and tended to view them more as an exit option from public schools rather than a means for improving them. If there was a case to be made that vouchers could exert a competitive effect on public schools to force them to improve, Dole did not effectively make it. A poll taken after the first presidential debate—in which vouchers were discussed—found that viewers favored Clinton's position on private school choice over Dole's by almost a two-to-one margin (58 percent to 31 percent).[57] As Jennifer Marshall of the conservative group Empower America noted, "Conservatives were happy with Dole's proposals for choice and for moving more power to the state and local level but did not think he was the best messenger. He did not give a good explanation of the proposals or a good defense of why these were winning ideas and ones that most Americans support when they are adequately explained."[58]

Dole did not emphasize education in his campaign until August, which many Republicans thought was much too late for such an important issue. In a series of speeches and forums in five cities, Dole sought to counter Democratic proposals on education by arguing that federal involvement was counterproductive and attacked the teachers unions as emblems of the Democratic attachment to big government and bureaucracy. Polls indicated, however, that the public saw the unions more as a positive than a negative force in education.[59] Clinton also deftly portrayed Dole's attacks on unions as an attack on teachers, who continued to enjoy strong public support in their local communities. Kay Lybeck, president of the Arizona Education Association, noted that Dole's remarks infuriated parents and Republican union members. "It's going to mobilize our members, and I think it's going to mobilize parents. . . . [Teachers] are the union. We're the same people. There's no difference in our minds or in the minds of our constituents."[60]

The Clinton campaign hammered at Dole for his support for vouchers, his opposition to the Department of Education, and his votes against federal education spending and reforms such as Goals 2000 and the 1994 ESEA amendments. The Clinton campaign also worked diligently to associate Dole with the conservative congressional leadership of the preceding two years and to portray him as out of touch with the average American voter. This effectively fueled voters' fears that Dole's positions on education were too extreme and that they would deny opportunities to children. When Clinton was heckled by Dole supporters during an October speech in Columbus, Ohio, for example, Clinton responded by saying, "I would be screaming too if I wanted a country that took Head Start and Big Bird away from 5-year-olds, school lunches away from 10-year-olds, summer jobs away from 15-year-olds, and college loans away from 20-year-olds."[61]

In the end, Clinton defeated Dole and won reelection by a wide margin. Though a number of factors clearly contributed to this result, there was general agreement among the media and campaign staff from both parties that education had been a critical issue during the 1996 presidential election and that Clinton had won the issue decisively. Polls showed that Clinton again massively outpaced his Republican opponent on the education question, leading Dole 64 percent to 31 percent when the public was asked who would do a better job on the issue.[62] The education gap between the parties had existed for many years but assumed greater importance as the issue itself took on increased salience among voters. Reflecting the heightened profile of education, for example, 86 percent of Americans indicated in 1996 that the candidates' education policies were extremely important or very important in determining their presidential vote.[63] Because Clinton had made his record and proposals on education a centerpiece of his campaign, many took his victory as a public endorsement of an active federal role in education. Secretary Riley, for example, would later offer the following assessment:

> In contrast to the ultraconservative ideologues, we offered the American people specific proposals to improve reading, to reduce class size, to modernize schools, to improve teaching, to connect classrooms to the internet, to increase learning time through after-school opportunities, and to get parents and communities more involved in education. Looking back, the outcome of this philosophical battle over the national role was a defining moment for American education. President Clinton's victory in the 1996 election established, once and for all, that the American people expected and demanded an ongoing national role in improving education.[64]

If Democrats viewed the election results as a mandate for a continuation of their efforts to reshape and expand the federal role in school reform, Republicans generally saw them as a repudiation of their emphasis on privatization and decentralization. Dole's defeat by a wide margin in the 1996 presidential election caused a good deal of soul-searching within the Republican Party. The public's perception of the party as antigovernment and extremist was widely blamed for Clinton's easy reelection, and the party's position on education was seen as having been particularly damaging. As Bob Sweet, senior Republican staff member on the House Committee on Education and the Workforce, observed,

> There were two years of Gingrich/conservative efforts to sell a conservative vision for education and then Dole ran on the conservative education agenda and lost, and that sent a message. . . . The public saw Republicans as anti-education even as education was becoming a more important national political issue, and things changed from that point on. The public equated the decline of the quality of public education with lack of federal funding of education because it was successfully portrayed this way by Democrats.[65]

In a poll of registered voters conducted shortly before the election, for example, respondents indicated that Dole's support for eliminating the Department of Education was the number-one issue that made them wary of voting for him.[66]

CONCLUSION

The expansion of the federal role in education that had been pushed through Congress during the first two years of the Clinton administration came under determined attack once the Republican Party won control of Congress in 1995. The GOP gains in the 1994 elections were widely attributed to the activism of right-wing and religious organizations and the political leadership of conservatives such as Newt Gingrich. As a result, the agenda of the Republican Congress in 1995–1996 embraced conservative antigovernment rhetoric and policy aims. The GOP advanced proposals to eliminate the Department of Education, to cut federal education spending, and to convert what funds remained into private school vouchers and block grants. These proposals made progress in the House but were ultimately defeated by a coalition of Democrats and Republican moderates in the Senate backed by the threat of presidential vetoes. The steadfast support of the business community and the National Governors Association for federal leadership on education reform was also an important influence during this period. Though unsuccessful in fundamentally redirecting federal education policy, conservatives were successful in significantly undermining federal influence over state reform efforts. The elimination of the National Education Standards and Improvement Council, the weakening of the National Education Goals Panel, and the increased flexibility given to states in the use of federal funds prevented the federal government from prodding states toward compliance with the standards and performance goals outlined in Goals 2000.

In addition to the intense policy fights in Congress, this period also saw a very public battle over ideas, as liberals, conservatives, and moderates advocated three very different visions for education reform. Republicans devoted considerable time and energy to convincing the public that federal involvement in education was harmful, that funding was not the key element in improving schools, and that vouchers were not a radical idea. They largely failed on all three counts. The conservative position on education, though popular with the Republican Party's base, remained extremely unpopular with the general public and particularly with moderate swing voters. In explaining why this was the case, Empower America's Jennifer Marshall has acknowledged that

Conservatism often comes across as being against things, as negative. . . . When I hear about getting rid of the Department of Education, what I'm thinking is that means greater control to the people who really matter in a child's life. But that's not what the man on the street hears—he hears you're cutting services, you're downsizing, you're hurting my local school. . . . The way it was communicated, it came across very negatively, a slash-and-burn kind of message—Republicans very quickly realized that this was how it was being perceived.[67]

Clinton and the Democrats, meanwhile, were very successful during the early and mid-1990s in focusing national attention on the problems in America's schools, in arguing that school improvement should be a federal priority, and in positioning the Democratic Party as the party of education spending and reform. Polls showed that the public rejected Republican proposals to cut spending for the Department of Education and to eliminate the department altogether by wide margins, and these proposals permitted Democrats to depict the Republicans as hostile to education. The extent of public displeasure with the conservative agenda on education was revealed forcefully in the 1996 presidential election, when voters favored Clinton over Dole on the issue by more than a two-to-one margin.

Dole's defeat in 1996—after having embraced a conservative platform—contributed to a growing recognition among Republicans that the party's stance on education and other key issues had been politically costly and that it needed to develop a more appealing domestic philosophy and policy agenda to compete with Clinton's popular "Third Way." By opposing both redistribution and federal programs to equalize opportunity during the 1990s, Republicans were portrayed effectively by Democrats as mean-spirited, and this public perception was widely seen as playing a major role in their electoral defeats in the 1992 and 1996 presidential elections. The stage was thus set for a reconsideration of the longstanding Republican opposition to energetic national leadership in education reform during the late 1990s.[68] The 1994 GOP midterm victories, continuing Republican control of Congress, and the conservative attacks on the federal role in education, meanwhile, helped Clinton in his efforts to move the Democratic Party to the center on education and other social issues. Between 1994 and 1996 education became a decisive electoral issue, and the liberal focus on regulation and resources and the conservative focus on privatization and decentralization were discredited. This confluence of political developments ended the debate over whether there should be a federal role in education and created an opening—a "policy window" in John Kingdon's terms—for bipartisan discussions about a centrist compromise that would establish a new reform-oriented federal education policy regime.

7. Stalemate—The Republican Retreat on Education and the Search for a New Consensus (1996–2000)

The 1996 election was a decisive moment in the contemporary politics of school reform. Education became widely recognized as a national electoral issue—one that was able to sway votes, particularly those of key swing voters such as women. Following Clinton's victory over Bob Dole, Republicans recognized that they could no longer afford to be seen as anti-education and that they would therefore have to soften their opposition to federal involvement in schools. As a result, from 1997 to 2000 the debate at the national level was no longer about whether there should be a federal role in education, but about what the nature of that role should be.

More specifically, the education policy discussions at the national level during this period centered on how much flexibility to give states in the use of federal funds and how much accountability to demand regarding their schools' performance. Led by Clinton and a growing number of New Democrats in Congress, the Democratic Party began to advance a more reform-oriented view of the federal role. This shift reflected a growing awareness among Democrats—including many liberals who had long supported the equity regime—that more spending alone would not improve schools, as well as political pressure to respond to new, more comprehensive Republican reform proposals. The movement of both parties toward the middle on education would provide the basis for the development of a new bipartisan consensus on school reform. This emerging consensus ultimately became the foundation of a new policy regime built on using the federal government to promote school improvement and increased student achievement through choice, standards, assessments, accountability, and additional spending.

REPUBLICANS EMBRACE FEDERAL ACTIVISM AND SPENDING

Dole's defeat by a wide margin in the 1996 presidential election caused a good deal of soul-searching within the Republican Party, particularly since it came on the heels of the "conservative revolution" of 1994. The public's perception of the party as antigovernment and extremist was widely blamed for Clinton's easy reelection, and the party's position on education was seen as having been particularly damaging. Democrats had long "owned" the education issue, but this had not been of great political consequence to the Republican Party when the issue had relatively low salience with the public. By 1996, however, school reform had completed its steady climb to the top of the public agenda, and the Democratic advantage on education had assumed great national political significance. The issue resonated strongly among voters generally, but was found to be particularly important to women and the "soccer moms" who had been identified as a crucial swing voting bloc.

At a meeting of Republican Party leaders after the election, closing the gender gap was emphasized as essential to the political future of the Republican Party. Exit polls and postelection surveys commissioned by the Republican National Committee (RNC) found that Dole had beaten Clinton among men (49 percent to 39 percent), but Clinton's decisive 59 percent to 35 percent advantage among women had played a major role in his victory. Furthermore, the education issue was found to be "a key component" of the gender gap. Whereas 24 percent of men viewed "improving education" as the top priority in choosing candidates and 44 percent viewed education as "extremely important," the percentages for women were 29 percent and 52 percent, respectively.[1] Ann Stone of Republicans for Choice added that "education has a great impact with female voters and is one of the critical things in order for Republicans to close the gender gap."[2]

Republicans at the meeting criticized the party for doing a poor job of explaining its governing principles and allowing its positions on policies such as education to be mischaracterized by Democrats. Texas governor—and future president— George W. Bush remarked that "the Republican Party must put a compassionate face on a conservative philosophy. . . . The message to women . . . is we care about people. . . . There is no question that from a political perspective, he [Clinton] stole the education issue and it affected the women's vote. . . . Republicans must say that we are for education."[3] Sen. Spencer Abraham (R-MI) added that "instead of talking about abolishing the Department of Education, we should be talking about sending more money back to mothers and fathers. Closing the Department of Education translated into [a message of] less benefits for your children." Haley Barbour, the RNC chairman, echoed this sentiment and urged the party to recast its position on education in a way that would be more appealing to women and families. "This election should be a reminder to us," he said, "that it's crucial that the public see our positive ideas, what we would do and are doing to solve the problems that affect voters' families."[4]

A subsequent analysis of the 1996 election by Republican leaders in *Policy Review* echoed these sentiments. Florida governor Jeb Bush argued that "the election of 1996 should remind conservatives that American voters generally care less about ideological labels and the impassioned pursuit of principle than about 'getting the job done.' . . . On election day, the American people chose a president who worked hard to show he was looking out for their loved ones and pocketbooks, too. Although conservatives may have had better ideas, Clinton had compassion."[5] Lamar Alexander added that "we conservatives . . . must learn to say what we are for in plain words. . . . Eliminating the U.S. Department of Education and encouraging home schooling alone do not answer the education question for 90 percent of American families. We must paint a vivid picture of how we will help create the best schools in the world."[6]

Moderate Republican governors and member of Congress had long urged GOP leadership to abandon strong ideological stands in favor of more pragmatic (and politically popular) positions on domestic policy issues such as education. In the wake of the 1996 election, they again called on the party to do a better job of explaining what it was for in education instead of allowing itself to be defined by what it was against. Working through the Republican Main Street Coalition, these moderates seized the opportunity to launch a concerted effort to reposition the party on education. Rep. Michael Castle's (R-DE) 1997 *Roll Call* op-ed piece entitled "Republicans Really Are a Pro-Education Party" was typical of this endeavor. Castle acknowledged that the GOP had failed to present the public with a positive program for education reform at the national level. "Most of the proposals," he noted, "began with the words 'abolish,' 'eliminate,' or 'cut.' Thus Americans were left with the impression that Republicans wanted to eliminate the federal role in education . . . [and] that Republicans did not think that education was important.[7] Castle argued that the focus on eliminating the Department of Education and reducing funding for education programs was misguided because "the federal role is necessarily limited but important" and "there are legitimate roles for the federal government."[8] These roles, he indicated, included educating poor and disadvantaged children through Title I and providing a "national vision," fortified by voluntary national standards and tests, to guide state education reform efforts.

Responding to these pressures, as well as to the business community's support for national standards and tests, Republican leaders in Congress continued to soften their opposition to federal leadership in education. As David Winston, a Republican pollster and strategist, noted,

> The clear and decisive defeat of Dole in 1996 and the starkness of the numbers on education began to force Republicans to significantly reassess what we were saying on education. Dennis Hastert, JC Watts, and John Boehner really shifted the Republican message in the late 1990s—they made it clear that Republicans would never use the "let's get rid of the DOE" argument again. Rather than debating what programs to fund, the argument was that funding could only do so much, and the

emphasis turned to pushing standards and accountability. The public view of Re
publicans on education began to . . . become more favorable, and polls showed that
the public increasingly saw standards and accountability as more important than
funding in education, even though funding was still viewed as important. That was
a structural shift in the way people viewed the education issue.[9]

Instead of proposing the elimination of the Department of Education or funding cuts, Republicans now supported increases in funding and some new federal
programs but called for giving most federal money to the states in block grants,
which would have the effect of reducing federal control. And whereas Republicans
had long focused on vouchers, they now spoke more broadly about public and
private school choice.

Clinton, meanwhile, saw his reelection as a clear mandate to push for additional federal education programs, increased spending, and tougher reforms. He
also apparently viewed the issue as a key component of his presidential legacy.[10]
Indeed, though education had figured prominently in his public speeches during
his first term, the frequency and expansiveness of his education oratory increased
significantly during his second term. In his second inaugural address, for example,
Clinton stated that "in this new land, education will be every citizen's most prized
possession. Our schools will have the highest standards in the world, igniting the
spark of possibility in the eyes of every girl and every boy. And the doors of higher
education will be open to all. The knowledge and power of the information age
will be within reach not just of the few but of every classroom, every library, and
every child."[11] Less than two weeks later, in his State of the Union address, Clinton
issued what he termed "A Call to Action for American Education" and declared
that "my number-one priority for the next four years is to ensure that all Americans have the best education in the world."[12] He outlined a $51 billion "crusade" to
revitalize American education that included tougher academic standards, an army
of reading tutors, tax breaks for college tuition, and new funds for classroom technology and school modernization and construction.

Clinton continued to view education as an issue that could reap him and his
party large political rewards. His education rhetoric and proposals were frequently
cited as a central component of his New Democrat centrism, as they embraced
ideas from both the right and the left. Character education, school discipline, and
choice and competition were popular with conservatives, whereas expanded federal funding for existing programs as well as new ones, such as school construction, were popular with liberals. Clinton's continued emphasis on—and financial
support for—charter schools was important because it enabled Clinton and the
Democratic Party to be pro-choice in education and to counter Republican calls
for voucher programs while avoiding alienating the teachers unions. In addition,
Clinton reiterated his more controversial call for national standards in education

and again pushed for voluntary national tests—a proposal that had been dropped during his first term after encountering significant opposition from both the left and right. He promised to veto any spending bill that prohibited new national tests, created school vouchers, or converted federal education spending into block grants.

Desperate to avoid the blame for another government shutdown and to close the education gap with voters, GOP leaders restored many of their cuts from domestic programs and provided for full or almost full funding for many of Clinton's priorities in education, such as the national service program, Goals 2000, Title I, and student loans. As Ed Kealy, president of the Committee for Education Funding, has observed,

> By 1996, the Republicans were really feeling burned by the negative image that Gingrich and the conservatives got them into by cutting education. They wanted to get that monkey off of their backs—they wanted to change the picture, change the story. So there began to be this period of competition between the Democrats and the White House and the Republican congressional leadership about who could be more in favor of education funding increases, and this lasted for the rest of the Clinton administration and even into the [George W.] Bush administration.[13]

As a result, GOP Congressmen who had recently voted to eliminate the Department of Education or drastically cut its funding began to push for additional federal resources and programs for schools.

Republicans clearly made a strategic decision to use their support for increased spending on education to develop a more favorable public perception of the party on the issue. As a result, federal education policymaking became increasingly bipartisan, and Democrats and Republicans engaged in a bidding war of sorts to demonstrate their commitment to education through increased federal spending. The May 1997 budget agreement between Clinton and Republicans in Congress, for example, provided for an additional $7 billion in education spending for the following year—the largest increase in three decades and significantly more than President Clinton had initially requested. The Republican-controlled Congress also ultimately enacted many of the education proposals that Clinton laid out in his 1997 State of the Union speech, including substantially increased federal funding for a youth literacy program, teacher certification, charter schools, and school technology.[14]

The about-face on education spending by Republicans in Congress angered many religious and states' rights conservatives who continued to oppose a strong federal presence in schools. The focus on inputs also upset reform-minded conservatives who believed that federal influence should be directed at school outputs. Krista Kafer, an education policy analyst at the Heritage Foundation and a former congressional staffer, observed,

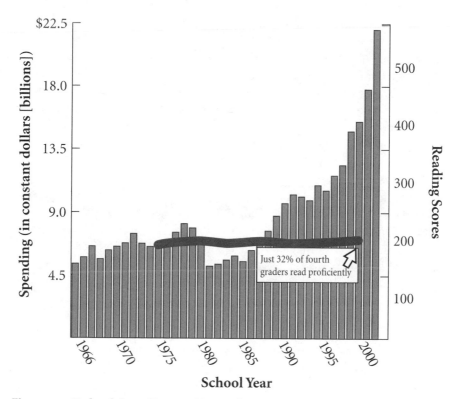

Figure 7.1. Federal Spending on K–12 Education (Elementary and Secondary Education Act), 1966–2001

Source: U.S. Department of Education Budget Service and *NAEP 1999 Trends in Academic Progress.*

The Republican shift on education began during the later part of the Clinton administration when they abandoned the effort to abolish the DOE. They gave up their negative message publicly and started talking about a positive message of accountability and local control and spending money on what works. . . . Public opinion really drove the Republican shift. Some politicians who know in their heart that school vouchers are right still won't support them because they fear public opinion. That's why politicians stopped talking about abolishing the Department of Education and supported throwing more money at education. All of the polling coming back to Republicans was supportive of testing and accountability—they did what was good for them.[15]

Once the GOP abandoned its opposition to an active federal role in education, the debate in Washington shifted to how to make it more effective.

Both Republicans and Democrats increasingly embraced using the national government to promote standards and accountability in school reform, but they continued to disagree over the precise federal role in actually setting standards or holding states accountable. As Chester Finn noted, "if national testing goes down in flames it will be because of people on the left who hate the word 'testing' and people on the right who hate the word 'national.'"[16] Clinton responded to these concerns by making the tests in his proposal voluntary and relatively short, and focusing them on only two core subjects (math and reading) in two pivotal grades (fourth and eighth). Negotiations over the precise shape of the new testing and accountability measures dominated debate over federal education policy during Clinton's second term.

Conservatives warned that national tests would lead to federal coercion and manipulation in education. Lynne Cheney, for example, wrote in the *Wall Street Journal* that "Clinton's reading and math tests are merely the first step on a path toward central control of all aspects of education."[17] Liberal Democrats, meanwhile, remained concerned that tough national standards and tests would unfairly judge and stigmatize disadvantaged students and their teachers and could be used to penalize them or to mobilize support for more radical reforms. Opposition to Clinton's testing plan thus produced a strange—and rare—alliance between liberal Democrats and conservative Republicans. The Family Research Council, the Eagle Forum, and the Christian Coalition were joined in their fight against the tests by the NEA and the Congressional Hispanic and Black Caucuses.

On September 11, 1997, the Senate voted 88 to 12 to allow the development of national tests to go forward but shifted control of them from the Department of Education to an independent board. A week later, however, more than seventy House Democrats joined Republicans in a 295–125 vote to prohibit the use of federal funds for national tests. Clinton threatened to veto the bill unless the tests were allowed to go forward, after which a compromise was reached that allowed preliminary development of national tests to continue but at a slower pace than Clinton wanted. The compromise stipulated that explicit congressional approval was required for the national tests to be deployed and that such permission would not be given until after 2000. A similar deal on funding for national tests was struck the following year. The compromises meant that though the movement toward national tests would continue, it would do so slowly, and Clinton's hope to have national tests in place during his presidency would be thwarted.

EMERGING PRESSURE FOR PERFORMANCE-BASED ACCOUNTABILITY

In his January 27, 1998, State of the Union address, Clinton praised Congress for enacting many of his education proposals and announced several additional education initiatives, the centerpiece of which was what he called "the first ever national effort to reduce class size in the early grades." He proposed that federal funds be allocated to help schools hire 100,000 new teachers to reduce class size in the first, second, and third grades to an average of eighteen students per class. Clinton also requested funding for an expanded after-school program and a reform project for urban schools, and reiterated his earlier call for federal funds for school construction. Finally, Clinton called for an end to "social promotion" in schools—the practice of passing a student from grade to grade even though he or she hasn't mastered the material. These proposals were typical of the targeted "micro-initiatives" put forward during the 1996 presidential campaign and in the second Clinton administration—relatively small but popular programs that addressed tangible public concerns at a relatively low cost but that involved the federal government in areas of education policy where it had previously had no role.

The reaction to Clinton's call for federal funding for 100,000 new teachers was indicative of how the politics of education was changing. Many Democrats and some Republicans were pleased with the class-size reduction proposal, but a number of reform-minded centrists from both parties questioned its focus on inputs and its likely efficacy. An unusual coalition that included the Heritage Foundation, the Progressive Policy Institute, and the Brookings Institution, for example, joined together to criticize the program in a letter to members of Congress. "The U.S. does not have a serious aggregate teacher-quantity problem today," they argued, "but rather, a problem of quality (many teachers don't know their subject well) and distribution (few of the best teach the neediest kids)."[18]

These groups and many moderate education reformers criticized the proposal for moving away from the centrist bipartisan consensus on the importance of focusing on the outputs rather than the inputs of schooling. The editors of the *New Democrat* called on their party to become the "party of education results, rather than simply the party of education investment." They recommended a "simple rule for Democrats: never, ever talk about more spending for schools without talking about accountability for schools."[19] The ability of groups from the left and the right to unite in opposition to this proposal demonstrated the extent to which the politics of education reform had undergone a major transformation in recent years. Although there was an increasing base of bipartisan support for federal education reform efforts, there was a concomitant desire that these reforms focus on standards and accountability.

Republicans in Congress, however, continued to argue that if schools were going to be held accountable for their performance, they had to be freed from federal regulations and mandates. In a nationally televised speech the day after Clinton's address, Senate majority leader Trent Lott (R-MS) posited that federal education programs did not give school districts enough flexibility. "Washington today has more than 750 education programs in 39 different bureaucracies. That just doesn't make sense."[20] Reflecting Republicans' desire to appear pro-education, however, Lott did not argue that most federal programs should be eliminated or federal spending for them reduced, but instead that that they should focus on reform and that fewer strings should be attached to federal monies. To that end, he proposed an expanded federal block grant to states along with tax-free savings accounts for private school tuition, school voucher demonstration projects, and increased federal special education spending.

Republicans used their control of the House and Senate education committees to continue to draw attention to the ineffectiveness of existing federal programs and spending in improving educational opportunity for poor and minority students. The widely publicized "Crossroads" report, released in July 1998, for example, argued that the expanded federal role in schools encompassed more than 760 separate education programs and $100 billion in annual spending but had created a system "fraught with failure and bureaucracy." "America's educational system," the report declared, "is at a crossroads. . . . Current indicators paint a disappointing picture overall of the preparedness of today's students to continue our nation's economic strength." Its authors found "little evidence proving the effectiveness of federal programs" and called for reforms centered on "flexibility, choice, charters, scholarships, and getting dollars to the classroom."[21] The report, along with others issued by academic researchers and think tanks, highlighted the extent to which federal education policy had failed to improve schools or educational opportunity and put additional pressure on Democrats to abandon the old equity regime.

Public opinion polls conducted during the 1998 congressional election campaigns, meanwhile, reinforced the electoral importance of education and the fact that Republicans had not yet rehabilitated their image on the issue. The polls showed that education remained the number-one concern on the public agenda, that opposition to federal education programs was still unpopular, and that the issue continued to play a major role in the gender gap between the parties. One poll asked nationally registered women voters the following question: "Would you be more or less likely to vote for a Member of Congress who supported eliminating the Department of Education and cutting national funding for public schools because this is a state and local issue?" Seventy-two percent of the respondents said that these positions would make them less likely to vote for such candidates (with 59 percent "much less likely" to do so), while only 22 percent were more likely (and only 11 percent "much more likely") to do so.[22] Republican education committee staffer Bob Sweet observed that these poll numbers were not lost on GOP members of Congress:

> Republicans were painted by the Democrats between 1994 and 1996 as anti-education . . . and you found that many of the people who were strongly conservative

advocates of abolishing the department turned tail and ran. . . . They were subject
to losing their congressional seats if they didn't change their ways, because their
constituents in their own communities wouldn't support them even though they
would support them on other issues that were more conservative.[23]

And so in 1997 congressional Republicans switched gears—instead of opposing
federal activism in education, they embraced it. The following year Republican
governors and members of Congress launched a coordinated effort to emphasize
that the GOP had a clear vision for education reform, one that contained a constructive role for the federal government in promoting school improvement and
accountability.

THE FAILED ESEA REAUTHORIZATION OF 1999:
STRAIGHT A'S, THREE R'S, AND THE DEVELOPMENT
OF THE GRAND BARGAIN

The periodic reauthorization of ESEA came due in 1999, which provided a natural
forum for a debate over the competing visions of federal education reform and the
national government's role in standards and accountability. Positions on the ESEA
reauthorization generally broke down into three camps: conservative Republicans
wanted to give states broad discretion, give parents broad choice, and eliminate as
much federal red tape as possible; liberal Democrats fought for additional federal
funding and programs and for a more prescriptive federal role in specifying procedural safeguards and resource targeting for disadvantaged groups; and Clinton
and moderates from both parties sought additional funding and flexibility in tandem with testing and measures that would hold states accountable for academic
results. Bipartisan discussions were organized by Sens. Slade Gorton (R-WA) and
Joseph Lieberman (D-CT) in 1998 and included representatives of the Heritage
Foundation, the Thomas Fordham Foundation, the Progressive Policy Institute,
the Education Trust, and the Education Leaders Council. Together they spoke to
the increasingly strong sense that a centrist compromise on the pending ESEA reauthorization was within reach.[24]

The core elements of the emerging consensus on federal education policy were
visible in the similarities between the different ESEA reauthorization proposals
debated in Congress in 1999 and 2000. Clinton's "Educational Excellence for All
Children" plan sought to build on the standards and accountability framework
that had been outlined—but never fully fleshed out—in Goals 2000. In his February 2000 State of the Union speech, Clinton called for a "twenty-first–century revolution in education" and emphasized the need for greater spending on education

along with higher expectations and accountability for results. "For seven years," Clinton said, "we have worked hard to improve our schools, with opportunity and responsibility: investing more, but demanding more in return. . . . It's time to support what works and stop supporting what doesn't. As we demand more than ever from our schools, we should invest more than ever in our schools. Let's double our investment to help states and districts turn around their worst-performing schools—or shut them down."[25] Clinton had largely succeeded in making academic standards the centerpiece of federal education reform efforts but now had to convince reluctant liberals and conservatives to embrace federal accountability for schools' progress toward meeting the standards.

As was the case with his earlier education initiatives, however, Clinton sought to navigate the difficult political terrain surrounding education by emphasizing both inputs and outputs and by expanding some existing programs even as he reduced or reformed others. His proposal called for additional federal funds for Head Start, after-school and summer school programs, classroom technology, character education, class-size reduction, and school construction and modernization. The final budget that Clinton presented to Congress contained dramatically increased federal spending on elementary and secondary education. It requested $40.1 billion in discretionary funding for the Department of Education, which was roughly $4.5 billion, or 12.6 percent, more than the previous year, and which would have been the largest increase in the department's history. But Clinton also called for a number of substantive reforms in federal policy, such as increased flexibility from federal regulations, an end to social promotion, a requirement that schools release report cards on the performance of their students and be held accountable for results, and a "new teacher quality initiative" to recruit, train, and test new teachers.

Susan Collins (R-ME) delivered the GOP response to Clinton's address and emphasized that "education is at the top of the Republican agenda." She outlined a "four-point plan for educational excellence" centered on increasing federal funding for elementary and secondary education, returning more control over how federal funds are used to local decision-makers in exchange for improved results, strengthening teaching excellence, and continuing support for access to higher education. These themes comprised the heart of the Republican alternative to the Clinton education reform plan, the "Academic Achievement for All Act." The Republican response to Clinton's speech and the Straight A's proposal (as it became known) were striking for their embrace of federal activism in education—albeit with fewer strings attached—and for the similarities between the Democratic and Republican proposals. A mere three years after the GOP had made abolishing the Department of Education a part of its national platform, Collins bragged about how "Republicans boosted education spending by $500 million more than the president's budget."[26] Clinton and the Republicans both called for increased

federal spending on education, for new federal programs to promote teacher re
cruitment and professional development, for greater flexibility, and for greater accountability for results.

The Republican Party's Straight A's proposal marked an important milestone
in the history of federal education policy as it represented the first comprehensive
GOP plan to use the federal government to bring about school improvement. The
plan sought to build on the flexibility given to states and school districts as part of
the Ed-Flex bill by giving them even greater discretion in how to use federal education funds in exchange for certain accountability guarantees. Sponsored by Sen.
Judd Gregg (R-NH), it called for a fifteen-state pilot program that would convert
the funding from fourteen federal education programs into block grants for states.
In exchange for the increased flexibility over how to spend the federal money, the
states would have to publicly report on student achievement annually and agree to
meet certain performance targets. As Chester Finn and Michael Petrilli observed
at the time, Straight A's

> is not a traditional block grant proposal, which confers freedom over the money
> but demands nothing in return. Instead, Straight A's recalls the arms-control
> maxim: trust but verify. It hinges on the one form of education accountability that
> really matters: whether kids end up learning more. If they do, the state (or district)
> gets to keep its freedom and earns a bonus. If they don't, it's back to the regulatory
> woodshed for the unsuccessful jurisdiction.[27]

The Straight A's plan seemed to reflect a recognition by Republicans that federal
spending and influence in education were here to stay and that they should be
harnessed in pursuit of school and teacher accountability. Straight A's essentially
offered Democrats a deal—Republicans would agree to a federal role in holding
states accountable for results if Democrats would agree to eliminate (or at least
dramatically reduce) the federal role in determining how schools operate.

Most of the major conservative groups in education—such as the Heritage
Foundation, the Cato Institute, Empower America, the Family Research Council, the Eagle Forum, the Christian Coalition, and the Education Leaders Council—lined up behind the Straight A's proposal. They were part of a coalition of
thirty groups called EXPECT (Excellence for Parents, Children, and Teachers)
that started in 1999 and worked throughout the ESEA reauthorization to advance
Straight A's. As Jennifer Marshall, education policy analyst for Empower America
and a participant in the coalition, recalled,

> Conservatives rallied around the Straight A's proposal. Never before had a Repub-
> lican Congress overseen an ESEA reauthorization—we saw this as our opportunity
> to have reform-minded groups rally around a central reform proposal to take the
> opportunity to really change the direction of ESEA. After thirty years, ESEA had

failed to achieve its objective of eliminating the achievement gap between disadvantaged students and their peers. We thought that rather than do the same old thing, which was adding new programs and funding, we needed to fundamentally restructure the way that programs ran. We all agreed on Straight A's and hoped for a formula of "flexibility plus accountability equals results."[28]

Centrist Democratic senators Joe Lieberman (D-CT) and Evan Bayh (D-IN) introduced their own reform plan, entitled the "Public Education Reinvestment, Reinvention, and Responsibility Act," in November 1999. Dubbed "The Three R's," their proposal was based on ideas developed by the Democratic Leadership Council with input from the White House, and it represented an attempt to find middle ground between Democrats and Republicans on ESEA reform. Lieberman stated upon introducing the plan that previous education reform proposals present "a false choice between a Democratic agenda of more spending and programs and a Republican agenda of more block grants and vouchers."[29] Three R's called for a dramatic increase in federal spending on education, with a $25 billion boost (over five years) in the Department of Education's discretionary budget for programs for disadvantaged children; an increase in spending on Title I by 50 percent, to $12 billion; $3 billion for teacher quality programs; and $1 billion for English acquisition programs. It also proposed the consolidation of hundreds of existing federal education programs into five broad grants to the states and an increase in state flexibility in how federal funds could be used. Perhaps most significant, the Lieberman-Bayh plan called for states to be monitored on their progress toward state achievement goals and to be rewarded or penalized accordingly. The Department of Education for the first time would be allowed to withhold funds from schools that failed to meet student performance targets.

The Three R's proposal was based on the belief that state and local governments have more direct influence over school improvement efforts but also that the federal government could play an important role in providing leadership and funding for reform. As Lieberman remarked upon the introduction of his plan, "Our approach is humble enough to recognize there are no easy answers to expanding opportunity, and that most of them won't be found here in Washington. But it is ambitious enough to try to harness our unique ability to set the national agenda and recast the federal government as an active catalyst for success, instead of a passive enabler of failure."[30] Taken as a whole, the Three R's plan went farther than Clinton's plan in restructuring federal education programs but did not go as far as many Republicans had proposed. The plan's call for large spending increases and its avoidance of vouchers generated significant support among Democrats, despite concerns among more liberal members about the strong accountability measures and the elimination of many targeted programs. The focus on accountability, public school choice, and flexibility, meanwhile, drew praise from many

Republicans, with Nina Rees of the Heritage Foundation remarking that "it consolidates, it streamlines, it focuses education policy on academic achievement, and from that aspect, we think it's a great idea."[31]

Although the most dramatic and visible change of heart on federal education policy during the 1990s occurred among Republicans, liberal Democrats also were beginning to alter their longstanding positions in ways that were equally important to the evolution of the federal role in school reform. Liberal Democrats always had opposed standards-based education reform and federal accountability measures on the grounds that they ignored the problem of inadequate and unequal resources and created unreachable targets for students in failing schools. Significantly increased per-pupil spending, however, had failed to generate significant school improvement in the country's worst schools—those concentrated in urban areas and disproportionately populated by minority students. As Patty Sullivan of the Council of Chief State School Officers has noted,

> There was growing impatience on the part of some liberal Democrats that poor kids were not getting a good education and that if the public school system was left untended, if pressure wasn't put on the schools to change, the public system would produce too much evidence that we needed a voucher system, and that would ultimately destroy the public school system. There was a lot of data coming out on Title I that showed no improvement in schools . . . and it was getting harder to argue that we should keep spending money on something that we knew wasn't working. There was also a lot of data coming [from] civil rights groups that made the case that we needed accountability to force change at the school building level.[32]

In late 1999, for example, the Citizens' Commission on Civil Rights issued a strongly worded report entitled "Title I in Midstream: The Fight to Improve Schools for Poor Kids" that criticized the Clinton administration for failing to enforce the standards provisions of the 1994 ESEA amendments vigorously enough. The commission's director, William Taylor, argued in the report that "the standards-based reforms that were adopted by Congress in 1994 can be made to work . . . [but] the policies and enforcement practices of the Department of Education have . . . in some cases thwarted the promise of the new law with respect to our poorest children."[33] Frustration with the lack of improvement in urban schools also led to increasing grassroots support among minorities in the United States for school vouchers.[34]

As a result, by the end of the 1990s, some civil rights groups and influential liberal Democrats began, after many years of resistance, to support tougher standards and tests and to demand that the federal government hold states accountable for improving student achievement. Political pressure on the left and right was thus pushing both political parties toward the center on education reform and toward a new accountability regime. As Christine Wolfe, director of policy for the undersecretary of the Department of Education in the George W. Bush administration, observed,

> In the late 1990s Democrats such as George Miller began to push to have flexibility tied more closely to accountability—so that only states that were in compliance with the 1994 law and were making progress toward Title I assessment goals would be eligible for Ed-Flex or Straight A's, for example. . . . A consensus developed around accountability—there was a certain point at which everyone was trying to out-accountability everyone else. Republicans liked the idea of accountability—but accountability for results, not for process. And they wanted accountability to be accompanied by an appropriate relaxation of federal requirements. As massive infusions of money began to be pumped into federal education programs, there was a sense that Republicans should not only start taking credit for that but also develop a positive message about equity and make sure that these programs work.[35]

Another important development in the politics of education during this period was the deepening concern about public schools among the public at large (see Figure 7.2). The historically strong support for teachers and their unions began to wane due to growing frustration with the poor quality of many schools and the unions' vocal opposition to popular education reforms. A 1998 *Wall Street Journal*/NBC News poll, for example, found that 41 percent of the public believed that the unions were a part of the problem in public education.[36] This view—combined with the continuing public perception that public schools were performing poorly and needed to be reformed—was creating pressure on the unions and their Democratic allies to focus more on school outputs and to compromise on reforms such as choice, standards, and accountability.[37]

The unions continued to be a powerful political force within the Democratic Party, but with education ensconced at the top of the public agenda, Democrats were under pressure from voters to improve schools. As Sen. Bob Torricelli (D-NJ), a cochair of the Democratic Senatorial Campaign Committee, noted in 1998, "among the public there is a rejection of the [education] system as now designed." He warned that while "the movement for reform may be understood last by those in the classroom . . . [teachers unions] could find themselves out of the process. All of us are not going to wait."[38] Torricelli was one of eight Democratic senators to support a 1998 proposal for tax-free educational savings accounts that could be used for students in public or private schools. The political pressures on Democrats and Republicans concerning education were thus creating the conditions under which a bipartisan compromise on a major overhaul of federal education policy would be possible.

In the end, however, despite these developments none of the three competing education reform plans debated during 1999–2000 was adopted, and Congress

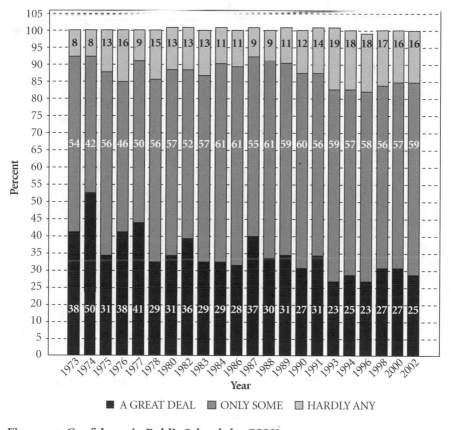

Figure 7.2. Confidence in Public Schools by GSS Year, 1973–2002
Source: Analysis conducted by author using General Social Survey Cumulative Datafile, 1972–2002, National Opinion Research Center.

failed to reauthorize ESEA on schedule for the first time since its passage in 1965.[39] The 2000 election cast a long shadow over these deliberations as both Democrats and Republicans were confident that their party would fare well at the polls and that they would be able to return to ESEA under more favorable political conditions. Feeling the sting of several failed education struggles with President Clinton, Republicans in Congress were inclined to postpone the reauthorization until after the election in the hope that a Republican president would share their educational vision to a much greater extent. Democrats, meanwhile, believed that they could regain control of Congress and use it to advance increased federal spending and influence over education reform.

The reauthorization debate had revealed that after twenty years of partisan rancor over education, a considerable degree of consensus had developed between

Democrats and Republicans on how to improve schools. As Republican education committee staffer Bob Sweet has observed, "the Straight A's and Three R's
plans in the late 1990s represented a closing of the gap between the old Republican
position of abolishing the Department of Education and the old Democratic position, which was to fund everything they could. Basically the ultraconservatives
and the ultraliberals lost their battles, and [a] sort of a middle path . . . was created."[40] The Lieberman-Bayh plan had attracted significant support from centrists
in both parties for what some called "the grand bargain"—significantly increased
federal funding and flexibility in education in exchange for greater accountability for academic improvement. These proposals for reforming federal education
policy would be carried into the 2000 presidential election as Democratic nominee Al Gore and Republican nominee George W. Bush endorsed many of their
provisions.

CONCLUSION

President Clinton and the Democrats had won a decisive victory in the rhetorical war over education by convincing citizens of the need for expanded federal
spending and leadership. As a result, in the late 1990s, Republicans dropped their
proposals to eliminate the Department of Education and to cut federal education
spending, and put forward their own vision for federal educational leadership. In
an effort to appear more pro-education to voters, Republicans agreed to fund most
of Clinton's educational priorities for elementary and secondary education, and
they added additional money to support their own priorities in education. The
result was that the Republican-controlled Congress appropriated more money for
education than Clinton even requested, and the 1996–2000 period witnessed the
most dramatic increases in federal K–12 education spending since the 1960s.[41] The
increased spending went to support existing federal education programs but also
to fund a wide variety of new initiatives that brought the national government into
many areas of school policy where it had never before ventured.

Republican activism on education during the late 1990s represented a major
political and policy challenge for Democrats, who were forced to respond to an
alternative comprehensive national reform plan for the first time. The Democrats'
response to this challenge was shaped by (1) a growing recognition that money was
a necessary but not sufficient condition for improving educational opportunity,
and (2) increasing pressure from minority groups and voters generally for more
meaningful reform. These factors, along with Clinton's leadership and his centrist
New Democratic philosophy, led the Democratic Party during the 1990s to move
away from its traditional focus on inputs and equity and to embrace standards, ac-

countability, and (public) choice. As a result, the positions of both the Democratic and Republican parties moved toward the center on education over the course of the decade as support grew for tying expanded federal investment in education to state accountability for their school improvement efforts. In a question and answer session with education reporters in April 2000, for example, Clinton emphasized that "the fundamental lesson of the last seven years, it seems to me, is that education investment without accountability can be a real waste of money. But accountability without investment can be a real waste of effort. Neither will work without the other. If we want our students to learn more we should do both."[42] The efforts to secure passage of a national test and tough accountability measures at the national level were defeated during the 1990s, but their adoption at the state level helped to build momentum for these reforms among educational reformers and the public at large.[43]

The policy changes and political developments in education during the 1990s helped to lay the ideational foundation for a new accountability-based policy paradigm and shifted the alignment of the political parties on education, but a new policy regime had yet to be institutionalized. Both the liberal and conservative approaches to federal education policy had been discredited, and there was a growing consensus around a grand bargain of greater federal investment in education in exchange for increased flexibility and accountability. As House Education Committee staffer Alex Nock has observed, "By the time No Child Left Behind was debated in Congress, standards-based reform had been around at the national level for 7–8 years and at the state level for well over a decade. It really wasn't controversial anymore for the federal government to be asking states to set standards and assess children."[44] The increasing salience of education in national politics and the pragmatic convergence of the parties on the nature of the federal role led both major party nominees to make education the central issue in their 2000 presidential election campaigns and to offer remarkably similar education platforms. This, in turn, would set the stage for a bipartisan compromise to reauthorize and reform ESEA along the lines of the grand bargain after the election.

8. Maneuver—George W. Bush, the 2000 Election, and the New Politics of Education

The 2000 presidential election would be remarkable from the perspective of education in several ways. Education was, for the first time, the dominant issue of a presidential campaign, with voters ranking it as their most important priority. The candidates responded by developing detailed education reform plans and by emphasizing education in their campaigns to an unprecedented degree. And in a dramatic shift from the presidential elections of the 1980s and 1990s, the Republican candidate, George W. Bush, agreed with the Democratic candidate, Al Gore, on preserving and even expanding the federal role in education. As one observer noted early in the campaign, "the contrast with recent political history is impossible to miss. No one is arguing over whether the federal government has any business sticking its nose into local schools. The argument is over how best and how far to stick it in. The candidates are scrambling to achieve national leverage over the traditionally local issue of education."[1] Both candidates also agreed that the focus of education should be on improving school performance for all students. Bush's activism on education during the election would enable him to neutralize the longstanding Democratic advantage on the issue—but committed him to an active education agenda as president. His success also pushed Gore, and later Democrats in Congress, to embrace a more reform-oriented stance on national school policy. These developments helped to pave the way for a bipartisan compromise on ESEA and the consummation of a new federal education policy regime.

EDUCATION, PUBLIC OPINION, AND THE 2000 ELECTION

To understand the central role education played in the 2000 presidential campaign, the election must first be framed in its wider political context. At the outset of the campaign incumbent Democratic vice president Al Gore was widely expected to defeat the Republican challenger, Texas governor George W. Bush. Gore was able to claim membership in an administration that had presided over an extended period of economic growth and peace and whose president, Bill Clinton, continued to enjoy high public approval ratings heading into the campaign despite his widely

146

publicized marital infidelities. A survey of the political landscape in 1999 revealed that the highest priorities for voters were generally domestic issues such as education, social security, the environment, and health care—all issues that Democrats were typically viewed more favorably on than Republicans. Despite Gore's apparent early advantage, the remarkably close election finish spoke to the dominant feature of the campaign: the rough parity between the Republican and Democratic parties in the electorate and the subsequent need for both candidates to appeal to independent (and generally moderate) swing voters. As many observers were to note, the 2000 election became a race to the center by both candidates—and education was to become the central issue in their centrist campaigns.

In the 1992 and 1996 elections Clinton had successfully captured this center by distancing himself from both conservative Republicans and the liberal wing of the Democratic Party. This "triangulation" enabled Clinton to promote a "third way" to solving public policy problems and to campaign as a moderate "New Democrat." In 2000, both Gore and Bush would seek to take a page from Clinton's centrist handbook. Clinton's strong approval ratings and the strength of the economy gave Gore an incentive to align his candidacy with the administration and to pledge to continue its policies in education and other areas. Despite Gore's experimentation with populist-oriented rhetoric in 2000, he generally stuck to Clinton's centrist policy agenda, which combined the traditional Democratic call for enhancing opportunity for citizens with the New Democrat demand for citizen and governmental responsibility. As Clinton had done in 1992 and 1996, Gore would seek to use the issue of education reform—with both new investments and new accountability reforms—to establish his centrist credentials and to tap into Americans' longstanding support for "equal opportunity" by repackaging government activism as an effort to ensure that all Americans have the opportunity to succeed. By making education one of the central themes of his campaign, Gore also sought to capitalize on the salience of the issue with voters, the widespread support for increased spending on schools, and the traditional Democratic advantage on the issue among voters.

To meet Gore's New Democrat challenge and redress the Republicans' recent disadvantage on domestic issues, Bush felt compelled to develop a new, more moderate approach to social policy and to reforming public education. Bush and his campaign staff were convinced that the Republican defeats in the 1992 and 1996 presidential elections necessitated a new kind of campaign for the 2000 election. There remained significant disagreement between moderates and conservatives within the Republican Party, however, about the proper role of the federal government in promoting social welfare and bringing about educational improvement. During the campaign Bush would seek to distance himself from the extreme (and unpopular) wing of his party—the conservative congressional Republican leadership epitomized by Dick Armey and Trent Lott. Bush sought to elucidate a new centrist political doctrine—what he called "compassionate conservatism"—to contrast his philosophy and policy positions with conservative Republicans and with his Democratic opponent. Education was quickly identified by the Bush campaign as the best issue around which to enact this strategy. By emphasizing his commitment to education reform, Bush could establish his credentials as a more moderate and compassionate conservative and try to appeal to portions of the electorate (women, minorities, and moderates) that the GOP had lost in recent presidential elections.

The nation's substantial projected budget surpluses made it easier for both candidates to advocate new domestic spending in a variety of areas, including education. The surplus negated the need for deficit reduction or spending cuts—major issues in previous elections—and encouraged both candidates to propose increases in many existing federal programs as well as a number of new ones. If the elections of 1992 and 1996 had seen a shift from foreign policy concerns to domestic issues, the 2000 election marked the first time that substantial new resources were available for federal responses to these problems. The surplus enabled Gore to propose a major new federal investment in education without being criticized for increasing the national debt. And though Bush would propose using part of the surplus to fund a large tax cut, the surplus also made it easier for him to propose (and for his fellows Republicans to accept) a number of modest new spending proposals, including several for education.

Both candidates were encouraged to devote considerable attention to federal school policy during the campaign because public opinion polls showed that education was at the top of voters' agendas in 1999 and 2000 (see Table 8.1).[2] A January 2000 poll, for example, reported that 86 percent of respondents indicated that the issue of K–12 public education was either extremely important or very important in determining how they would vote in the presidential election.[3] By August 2000 this number had climbed to 91 percent.[4] Another poll revealed that 63 percent of people thought that the issue of education was more important to their vote for president than it had been in recent presidential elections.[5] As a result of the clear and substantial voter interest in education, both the Bush and Gore campaigns made the issue a centerpiece of their campaigns—the first major policy speech by each candidate, for example, was on education.[6]

Education was increasingly seen by the public as crucial to economic advancement in a skills-based economy. At the same time, perceptions of the quality of American public education were generally poor. When asked to evaluate the condition of K–12 public education during the campaign, 54 percent of poll respondents felt it was worse than when they were students.[7] Asked how satisfied they were with the quality of K–12 education in the United States, 61 percent were somewhat or completely dissatisfied.[8] Voters were conflicted on the issue of edu-

Table 8.1. Public Perceptions of the Nation's Most Important Problem, 1960–2004

Year	Candidates	Issue Rated Most Important by Voters	Relative Ranking of Education	Standardized Rank of Education
1960	Kennedy-Nixon	Foreign relations	14th of 20 issues	Lower 33 percent
1964	Johnson-Goldwater	Civil rights	24th of 24 issues	Last
1968	Humphrey-Nixon	Vietnam	17th of 17 issues	Last
1972	McGovern-Nixon	Vietnam	26th of 26 issues	Last
1976	Carter-Ford	Inflation	Not listed in 27 issues	Last
1980	Carter-Reagan	Inflation	23d of 41 issues	Middle 33 percent
1984	Mondale-Reagan	Recession	17th of 51 issues	Upper 33 percent
1988	Dukakis-Bush	Drugs	8th of 26 issues	Upper 33 percent
1992	Clinton-Bush	Economy	5th of 24 issues	Upper 33 percent
1996	Clinton-Dole	Economy	2d of 31 issues	Top 10 percent
2000	Gore-Bush	Education	1st of 11 issues	First
2004	Kerry-Bush	Iraq	5th of 46 issues	Top 10 percent

Note: Respondents were asked some variant of "What do you think is the most important problem facing this country today?" All surveys were conducted within two months of the presidential election, except for 1988 (July) and 2000 (June).

Source: Roper Center for Public Opinion Online, http://web.lexis-nexis.com/universe/form/academic/ s_roper.html.

cational federalism, with most supporting increased federal leadership in promoting school reform but also wanting flexibility for states to set their own policies.[9] When asked about the appropriate role for the federal government in education, 46 percent felt that the federal government should be more involved in education, 29 percent thought it should be less involved, and 22 percent thought that federal involvement should remain about the same.[10] Another poll demonstrated, however, that only 23 percent favored directing federal education money to specific program activities whereas 71 percent felt that states should be given flexibility in determining how to spend federal education money.[11]

Although there was some ambivalence among the electorate as to the specific federal education policies that should be pursued, there was a broad consensus on the need for federal leadership to promote reform supported by increased federal funding. When asked to identify the most important thing a president could do to improve education, voters' top answer was to increase government funding.[12] In addition, almost 70 percent of Americans supported having all students in the country meet a single set of national academic standards.[13] Exit polls showed that voters expressed a strong preference for public (as opposed to private) education, with 78 percent indicating that when public schools are failing, the government's priority should be to fix the problems rather than give parents vouchers to pay for private schools.[14]

Table 8.2. Public Perceptions of Parties' Credibility on Education Issue, 1979–2004

Year	Democrats (%)	Republicans (%)	Advantage
1979	25	16	Democrats +9
1984	37	19	Democrats +18
1988	55	22	Democrats +33
1992	42	17	Democrats +25
1996	59	30	Democrats +29
2000	44	41	Democrats +3
2004	42	35	Democrats +7

Note: Question wording was similar but varied slightly from year to year. The basic question was "Regardless of how you are likely to vote, do you think the Republican party or the Democratic party will do a better job of improving education in America?"
Source: Various polls, Roper Center for Public Opinion Online, http://web.lexis-nexis.com/universe/form/academic/s_roper.html. Accessed June 25, 2001, and March 31, 2005.

Americans seemed less clear, however, on how new spending should be utilized or the direction federal reforms should take. One observer summed up the national mood on education and its influence on the election in this way: "We are witnessing not just a move to the center [on education] by both parties, but the creation of a new center. Americans of all stripes are convinced that education is central to our personal and national success; they are convinced that Uncle Sam has an important role to play, in partnership with states and localities. At the same time, they do not want too heavy a hand on the education reins."[15] There was thus significant public pressure on the presidential candidates to articulate an energetic (but not heavy-handed) role for the federal government in education reform. As a result, as Melissa Marschall and Robert McKee note in their analysis of the 2000 election, "both candidates [would come to embrace] a set of education reforms—accountability, standards, funding, and teacher training and recruitment—that appeared to target the median voter."[16]

The importance of education as an issue in the election would seem to have presented an advantage for Gore. As noted earlier, the Democratic Party had for many years been viewed by voters as more capable of handling the education issue (see Table 8.2). Early in the campaign, however, it was apparent that Bush's experience with education reform in Texas and his support for an active federal role gave him an opportunity to make inroads on the issue. Both Bush and Gore faced challenges as well as opportunities in advocating an active federal role in education reform. Gore's dilemma centered on the desire of many liberal Democrats (and many key Democratic constituencies) to pump more federal money into education without attaching any strong accountability measures. Given the general public's strong sense that public education had serious problems and that previous federal education spending had not been used effectively, such an approach was problematic. Bush, meanwhile, had to contend with conservative Republicans who had long opposed a strong federal role in education. It was clear to Bush and his campaign staff that the earlier Republican emphasis on vouchers and the elimination of the Department of Education was unpopular with voters and, if continued, would likely be used (as it had in the past) to claim that Republicans did not care about education. Both candidates thus had incentives to embrace an active federal role in education but also to advocate significant reforms to make that role more effective.

BUSH, EDUCATION, AND COMPASSIONATE CONSERVATISM

The electoral and policy defeats of the Republican Party in the 1990s created an opening for a new kind of Republican candidate and a new Republican position on education in the 2000 presidential election. Republicans were eager to regain the nation's highest office, and many in the party came to believe that this would only be possible if the party united behind a Washington outsider with moderate views (or at least a strong appeal with moderate voters). As a result, Governor Bush (the son of former president George H. W. Bush) was identified early in the 2000 election campaign as the party's most promising candidate and was ultimately nominated despite a primary challenge by Arizona senator John McCain.

Bush and his advisers believed that running a traditional conservative campaign in the 2000 general election was likely to have the same result as the 1996 election—defeat. As James Ceaser and Andrew Busch have noted, "Bush entered the race accepting that the campaign would be fought in large part on terrain traditionally chosen by Democrats, because these issues were the ones of greatest concern to Americans. Bush's aim was to win on some of these issues with Republican counter-proposals, or if not to win, then at least to cut down dramatically on the margins by which Republicans had been losing on these issues in the recent past."[17] Bush proclaimed throughout the campaign that he was a different kind of conservative—what he called a "compassionate conservative," using a phrase coined by Marvin Olasky in *The Tragedy of American Compassion* (1990) and *Compassionate Conservatism* (2000). This philosophy enabled him to stake out a more activist role for the federal government than had been advocated by traditional Republican candidates and leaders. As Ceaser and Busch have written, compassionate conservatism was designed to "show that [Bush] was 'a new kind of Republican' and to put symbolic distance between himself and the congressional wing of the

Republican Party, which, at least in the public mind, was identified overwhelmingly with a negative or 'less government' approach."[18] Bush's articulation of this new philosophy was to have important implications for the outcome of the election, the future direction of his party, and the federal role in education policy.

In a widely circulated speech in Indianapolis on July 22, 1999, Bush began to describe the tenets of his new brand of government activism and pointedly criticized conservatives who denied the positive role the federal government could play in addressing social problems. He dismissed those with "a destructive mindset: the idea that if government would only get out of the way, all our problems would be solved. . . . An approach with no higher goal, no nobler purpose than 'leave us alone.'" Bush distinguished his philosophy from modern liberalism by noting that "this will not be the failed compassion of towering, distant bureaucracies. On the contrary . . . it will be government that both knows its limits and shows its heart."[19] Bush's compassionate conservatism represented a clear break (rhetorically at least) with the limited-government philosophy of conservatives such as Ronald Reagan. Though it was initially unclear what particular policies would be implemented under a compassionate conservative administration, the potential electoral appeal of the philosophy itself was obvious.[20] Bush did not invent compassionate conservatism but was the first national Republican candidate to embrace it and to sell it to others in his party as a politically necessary change.[21] Recognizing both the increased salience of education in the electorate and the potential to use the issue as a symbol of compassionate conservatism, Bush would make education reform the centerpiece of his campaign.

As a governor, Bush had been one of the first Republicans to recognize that the party's position on education was problematic politically and to push for a change. As noted in the previous chapter, Bush had begun talking about the importance of education to the Republican Party's national electoral strategy as early as 1996. He saw it as the key issue for addressing the "gender gap" in the electorate—the tendency of women to vote disproportionately for the Democratic candidate in presidential elections—that had contributed significantly to Bob Dole's 1996 defeat. In 2000, Bush and his advisers were determined to position themselves more effectively on education in the campaign. As Bush adviser Sandy Kress has noted,

> There is no question that education was central to Bush's 2000 campaign strategy, to his compassionate conservative philosophy—it was a big issue to him and to the campaign. It was a big part of defining to the country who he was and what he thought was important. . . . The Bush approach to education was a more popular and more generally supportable position than some of the earlier Republican positions in the past. The president was trying to define . . . a new way of looking at some of these issues that was conservative and yet results-oriented and [that cared] about people and children.[22]

Though Bush had been reluctant to embrace a major role for federal leadership in education reform while governor, his presidential campaign developed a detailed reform plan centered on making the states accountable to the federal government for the performance of their schools. Bush and his advisers concluded that opposition to federal spending and leadership on education had become politically unsustainable and that the party had little choice but to embrace the federal role and to try to shape it toward productive ends. Most Republicans were willing to go along with Bush's support for a more active federal role in education because he convinced them that it was central to the party's efforts to win back the White House. As Gore education adviser Bill Galston has observed,

> The longer a party has been out of power, the hungrier it is. Bush succeeded in persuading the Republican Party that if it wanted to have a chance of capturing a national presidential majority it would have to at least speak to some of the domestic issues where Republicans had historically been at a disadvantage. . . . Bush persuaded the party that its best shot was to go with a different kind of Republican, someone who was seen as an innovator, a real player in domestic policy and someone who could break the Democratic stranglehold on education and social policy issues. . . . If Bob Dole had tried to do the same thing in 1996 . . . the results would not have been as good because Republicans were angry in 1996; but [in 2000] they were hungry.[23]

In addition, as was noted in the previous chapter, Republican leadership in Congress had already begun to reposition the party on education in the late 1990s.

Bush emphasized his commitment to education by talking about the issue more than any other, by putting forward a detailed education reform plan, and by visiting more than 100 schools in the first fourteen months of the campaign.[24] To bolster his claim to be a serious education candidate, Bush's campaign also emphasized his experience with education reform in Texas and touted what it claimed was significant improvement in student performance during his administration. As governor, Bush had championed the state's stringent accountability plan as a means to ensure that all children—especially Hispanic and black children and those in urban areas—were receiving an adequate education.[25] In Texas, the credibility he earned with his staunch support of accountability and his successful effort to reach out to minority communities had permitted Bush to advocate school choice, oppose significant increases in educational expenditures, and criticize the public school establishment. Whereas other Republicans had appeared anti-education when they took similar stands, Bush's credible commitment to educating all students had permitted him to argue that he was pro-education even when he opposed funding measures or criticized the existing public school system.

While the extent of the "Texas miracle" in education was hotly debated by the Gore campaign and in the media, Bush was able to claim that he had substantial

experience in dealing with education reform and that this experience would enhance his effectiveness as an education president. As Sandy Kress has observed,
"Bush invested a great deal of time, energy, and personal commitment to education reform during his time as governor in Texas. . . . He felt strongly about the
right policies, and he became very committed to them. . . . Bush's speeches on education during the campaign demonstrated this—there hasn't ever been that kind
of serious attention to education issues by anybody running for president, Republican or Democrat."[26] Bush's track record and comfort level with education was in
marked contrast to the previous two Republican nominees (his father and Dole),
who had little experience with school reform. Thus one commentator noted that
"for the first time in decades, the Republican candidate knows more about the
education issue than his opponent does, has been more directly involved with proposing and implementing education reforms, and is more comfortable expressing
deep-felt views on what the next administration should do to improve the nation's
schools."[27]

The education plan that Bush unveiled during the 2000 campaign contained
a number of reforms that he had utilized in Texas, such as choice, standards, testing, and accountability. Bush's plan also, however, embraced the importance of
federal leadership and federal spending to state education reform efforts, a position that broke with Republican orthodoxy. Though significantly smaller than
Gore's proposal, Bush's call to increase federal education spending by $13.4 billion
over five years was remarkable given the historical opposition of his party to the
federal role in education. The official Bush campaign summary of his education
policy stated that "Governor Bush will reform the nation's public schools. . . . He
will close the achievement gap, set high standards, promote character education,
and ensure school safety. States will be offered freedom from federal regulation,
but will be held accountable for results. Performance will be measured annually,
and parents will be empowered with information and choices."[28] In recasting the
Republican position on education and emphasizing the important role of federal
reform efforts, Bush was attempting to improve his party's image on the issue and
use it as a symbol of his wider compassion. DLC president Al From noted at the
time that "what Bush is doing is contesting Democratic turf on education in ways
that Republicans in Congress and Dole never did."[29]

As they assembled their education plan for the campaign, Bush and his staff
borrowed ideas from the same policy organization that Clinton had relied upon—
the New Democrat Progressive Policy Institute. Co-opting the moderate ideas developed by centrist members of the opposing party was a very effective way to
claim the middle ground on education. Much as Clinton had done with the issue
of welfare in the 1992 election, Bush shrewdly chose to transform his party's position on an issue that had been an Achilles heel (and one of the opposing party's

strongest issues) in recent elections. As noted in the previous chapter, the PPI had released a comprehensive federal education reform plan in April 1999 that called for federal education spending to be consolidated into five broad categories and for states to be given new flexibility in meeting federal mandates as long as they met certain achievement goals. School districts that consistently failed to meet these goals would have their federal aid cut under what was called "performance-based funding." The education plan released by the Bush campaign in fall 1999 bore a striking resemblance to the PPI plan and contained most of its key elements. The plans were so similar that PPI president Will Marshall stated during the campaign that "I can't criticize [the Bush] plan because it's ours."[30] This was a brilliant tactical move by the Bush campaign. Not only were they able to bolster their credibility on education by putting forward a comprehensive education reform plan before Gore had done so, but by co-opting the leading centrist reform ideas on education they forced Gore either to say "me too" or try to differentiate his plan by moving to the left.

Not surprisingly, however, though Bush's adoption of many centrist education proposals was an effective play for the median voter, it did not go over well with many conservative Republicans. Patrick Buchanan, who mounted a third-party bid against Bush, criticized Bush's stance extensively and called for the elimination of the federal role in education.[31] Disagreements within the Republican Party on the federal role in education were also on display at the party convention during the contentious deliberations about the education plank of the party's 2000 national platform. Republican convention delegates needed no persuading of the increasing importance of education as a political issue—a survey of the delegates revealed that whereas only 2 percent of the 1996 delegates had ranked the issue as the top priority in their states, 26 percent did so in 2000.[32] Many of the delegates were less convinced of the need for *federal* leadership in educational reform, however, and Bush's desire to moderate the platform's traditional hostility to the federal role in education encountered a great deal of resistance. The call to abolish the Department of Education was so ingrained with many Republicans, for example, that it took Bush's personal intervention with the platform committee to ensure that such a proposal was not included in the 2000 platform (as it had been in 1996).

In the end, the GOP platform emphasized many traditional Republican education positions—choice, competition, accountability, local control, home schooling, and values. It declared,

> We recognize that under the American constitutional system, education is a state, local, and family responsibility, not a federal obligation. Since over 90 percent of public school funding is state and local, not federal, it is obvious that state and local governments must assume most of the responsibility to improve the schools,

and the role of the federal government must be progressively limited as we return control of parents, teachers, and local school boards.[33]

The Bush campaign's desire for the platform to embrace a more active federal role was not met, but it did succeed in moderating the tone of the plank. Nina Rees, an education analyst for the Heritage Foundation and a member of the platform committee, noted at the time that "Republicans had a vigorous debate about the proper role of the federal government in education. . . . It's a pretty big accomplishment to take that language out on abolishing the Department of Education."[34] Aware that vouchers were extremely popular with the conservative wing of the Republican Party but opposed by key moderate swing voters, Bush tiptoed carefully around the issue during the campaign. During the primaries, where conservative Republicans were disproportionately influential, Bush emphasized his voucher proposal and downplayed his plans to increase the spending and influence of the federal government in education. During the general election campaign, however, Bush emphasized the latter and deemphasized the former, generally avoiding the word *voucher* in favor of the more ambiguous and politically palatable phrase *choice*.

The Bush campaign's stance on education during the election represented a significant break with the position adopted by Dole in the 1996 election and with the positions that many conservative Republicans continued to hold. Bush acted from a recognition that, as one observer put it, "traditional Republican education rhetoric ('money doesn't make a difference') is a thundering nonstarter. For better or worse, the federal role in education is here to stay."[35] In fact, Bush called for increasing federal spending on education and for giving the federal government an important role in promoting academic standards and in ensuring accountability for student performance in public schools. As Jay Diskey, former spokesman for the Republicans on the House Education Committee, remarked,

> It was important that many of Bush's ideas on education were things that Democrats often talked about—like programs to help kids in the early grades learn to read. He did not go on the campaign trail and talk about block grants or doing away with the Department of Education. Instead he talked about inputs, tangible benefits, and programs, and those were the type of things that made people think he cared about education. He had a clear, concrete, and detailed plan for how to improve schools and avoided the unpopular things that congressional Republicans had talked about in the mid-1990s.[36]

Another observer noted that

> George W. Bush has ripped a page from Bill Clinton's "triangulation" handbook. Bush has made federal education policy the centerpiece of his campaign, at once distancing himself from Republicans' calls for a smaller federal role and co-opting

Democrats' case for more cash. . . . He is calling for a stronger federal role in setting classroom performance standards (long anathema to conservatives), but with tough penalties for schools that fail to meet those standards (which liberals resist).[37]

During the 2000 campaign, Bush would cite his attention to education to blunt claims that Republicans were not concerned about the plight of the poor. Republican pollster David Winston observed that "education was essential to Bush's image as a compassionate conservative. Bush felt most comfortable talking about the issue of education—if you watch the debates you can see that he was a natural on the issue—he was very good on it. Compassionate conservativism was talking about children and how to make a better future for them, and education was central to this."[38] Bush would effectively resurrect the Reagan argument that the Republicans wanted to help the disadvantaged and that the best way to do so was to provide opportunities. However, whereas Reagan had claimed that expanding opportunity required getting government out of the way, Bush argued that it required government intervention to ensure that the liberal education and social welfare establishment was being held accountable for serving disadvantaged children and citizens in need.

The Bush appeal served to put the onus for social problems on ineffective public agencies and employees—in the case of schooling, on school districts and teachers—and enabled him to end the longstanding Republican deficit on education by achieving near-parity with his Democratic opponent on the question of educational leadership (see Table 8.3). Bush and his advisers essentially used education against Gore in 2000 in the way that Clinton had used issues such as crime and welfare against Republicans in the past—to neutralize his opponents' advantage by embracing the importance of the issue and proposing centrist solutions similar to those advanced by the other party. As Jack Jennings, president of the Center on Education Policy, has observed,

> Bush understood that he had to sound more in favor of improving education . . . so he drew upon what he was familiar with in Texas (standards-based reform), what his father had proposed, what Clinton had set the federal government on the road to doing, and what the business community wanted, and he proposed NCLB and tried to move the Republicans to the middle on the issue. . . . Bush knew he had to pick one or two high-visibility issues where he sounded like he was a moderate and where he would bring about improvement on an issue which people cared about. . . . He took what had been a negative record and turned it into a positive political position.[39]

Bush's moderate stance on education during the campaign thus was intended not only to eliminate the education gap between the parties but also to induce a more favorable perception of his general ideological orientation among moderate voters.

Table 8.3. Public Perceptions of Presidential Candidates' Credibility on Education, 1984–2004

Year	Democrat (%)	Republican (%)	Advantage
1984	42 (Mondale)	39 (Reagan)	Democrat +3
1988	51 (Dukakis)	34 (Bush)	Democrat +17
1992	47 (Clinton)	24 (Bush)	Democrat +23
1996	64 (Clinton)	31 (Dole)	Democrat +33
2000	44 (Gore)	42 (Bush)	Democrat +2
2004	41 (Kerry)	41 (Bush)	Even

Note: Question wording varied slightly, but respondents were asked a variation of "Which candidate do you think would do a better job on education?" In 1992, Ross Perot was listed as a third choice for respondents, thus lowering the totals for each of the major party candidates.

Source: Roper Center for Public Opinion Online, http://web.lexis-nexis.com/universe/form/academic/s_roper.html.

GORE AND THE DEMOCRATIC DILEMMA ON EDUCATION

Bush's aggressive foray into education presented a serious challenge for Democrats and Al Gore's campaign. There was still widespread support within the Democratic Party for increased federal funding and new federal programs in education. By 2000, however, there was a sense among voters as well as poor and minority advocacy groups that the public school system was failing and that sweeping reforms were needed. Though most Americans continued to have mixed feelings about vouchers, support for them was growing in certain quarters, particularly among low-income and minority voters—two crucial Democratic constituencies. Even many of the public education system's strongest advocates were arguing that it had to be fundamentally reformed if it was to survive. These views, along with the Republican call for new accountability measures and private school choice, put pressure on Gore to advocate substantive reforms along with increased spending. As Amy Wilkins from the Education Trust has noted,

> Bush with education was like Nixon going to China. . . . For Democrats it challenged them on what they thought had always been a safe issue for them. . . . The traditional Republican argument on education had been that it was a local issue and that there shouldn't be a federal role. So the Democrats could sit there and say that they were the party of education because they were in favor of a federal role, but they didn't have to think very hard about what that role should be to improve schools. When Bush [adopted] the education issue in 2000 he forced Democrats to really think about education in a different way.[40]

As had been the case during the late 1990s, Republican activism on education thus bolstered the case of the New Democrats and helped prod the Democratic

Party to adopt a more robust reform agenda in education. Like Bush, however, Gore would struggle to define a stance on education that would allow him to appeal to moderate swing voters while maintaining the support of his party base.

The Democratic Party and its teachers union allies had vigorously opposed private school choice during the 1980s and 1990s and had long argued that the key to reforming public schools was additional resources. But a number of polls and media accounts documented the growing receptiveness of African-Americans to school voucher proposals. A 1999 survey by the Joint Center for Political and Economic Studies on education, for example, found that blacks rated their local public schools much more negatively than did whites and saw them as getting worse. The survey also found that three out of five blacks (60 percent) supported school vouchers. Black support of vouchers had increased substantially from the previous year and was significantly greater than white support.[41] Liberal activists feared that in the absence of educational improvement, school vouchers would emerge as a wedge issue within the black community and could ultimately lead to the movement of substantial numbers of black and Latino voters to the Republican Party. NAACP president Julian Bond, for example, acknowledged that the voucher question "will create real schisms in the black community. . . . In local or municipal elections, where the clever politician can inject vouchers, this is a wedge. . . . I'm sure that these schisms will widen, and if someone is clever enough to exploit them, it will disrupt black politics and urban politics as we have come to know them."[42] Democratic strategists thus viewed the growing support for vouchers within the black community with great trepidation.

Aware of these developments, Bush made a very public effort to cast education reform and choice as a civil rights issue and to court the black and Latino vote during the campaign. It was not a coincidence, for example, that Bush first introduced his voucher plan in a campaign speech to Latinos in Los Angeles. Later, in his acceptance speech at the convention, Bush stated that "on education . . . too many American children are segregated into schools without standards [and] shuffled from grade to grade because of their age, regardless of their knowledge. This is discrimination, pure and simple—the bigotry of low expectations. And our nation should treat it like any other form of discrimination . . . we should end it."[43] This kind of Republican education rhetoric and the concomitant appeals to minority voters put Gore and the Democratic Party in a bind. Christopher Edley Jr., a former Clinton aide and Gore adviser, noted during the campaign that Bush's voucher plan was "a brilliant tactical move because it positions voucher supporters as the allies of children in desperate straits. You've got desperate kids and their families. One side is offering vouchers as an escape, and the other side is offering three-year plans. That's not much of a contest." Edley added that the Democratic Party would pay a steep price unless it developed a comprehensive education reform proposal to counter the call for vouchers. If it failed to do so, he warned, "you're not going to see mass defections by the Democratic base, but there'll be erosion at the margin, and there are certainly a number of swing voters to whom education is important."[44]

In 2000, Gore thus felt pressure from important Democratic groups and from voters generally to continue the push for standards and accountability that Clinton had begun. Gore was caught, however, between the diametrically opposed demands of two key Democratic constituencies on education—teachers and minorities. The teachers unions were by far the Democratic Party's biggest national donor bloc—the NEA, AFT, and other teacher unions contributed $6.7 million between 1991 and 1999 alone.[45] The teachers unions' large membership base had also long provided an important source of volunteers and votes for Democratic candidates. The unions clearly found Gore's proposals for greatly increased federal spending on education and raising teachers' salaries appealing, and he received the endorsement of the NEA and the AFT in 2000. The NEA, however, remained staunchly opposed to strong choice or accountability reforms, which made it difficult for Gore to aggressively counter Bush's education proposals and address the widespread dissatisfaction with the performance of the public school system.

In the end, these competing political pressures led Gore to respond to Bush's appeals to minorities and to education voters generally by proposing significantly more spending than Bush, and calling for limited public school choice and charter schools. Gore called for an additional $115 billion for schools over ten years to recruit more teachers, increase teacher salaries, reduce class and school size, and provide universal preschool. As Clinton had done in the 1992 and 1996 elections, Gore tried to use his support for higher levels of educational spending to attack Bush's commitment to schooling. However, Bush's strong stance on accountability and his experience with education in Texas, coupled with a small number of targeted spending proposals, permitted him to parry Gore's attacks by painting Gore as a captive of the public school establishment. This response helped Bush to tap into quiescent concerns that Democrats were using "investment" and "opportunity" as excuses to tax and spend. As Will Marshall from PPI noted,

> The way Gore handled education played into Bush's hand, because he tended to sound like a traditional Democrat and emphasized more spending. Gore sounded like he was defending the current system while Bush came across as a reformer, "a reformer with results" as he called it. Bush attacked Gore as being a champion of big bureaucratic government, but Gore played into his hands by seeming to defend big public sector programs and to mute his reform ideas. Gore had some important and good reform ideas (like expanding charters), but there was a difference between Gore's policies and Gore's message. On the campaign trail, Gore didn't put education reform front and center the way that he should have. And that allowed

Bush to make headway and to do what Republicans don't usually do, which was to be competitive on education.[46]

Throughout the campaign Bush blamed the country's "education recession" on Gore and Clinton and their unwillingness to hold teachers and schools accountable for high standards. Gore responded by blasting Bush and Republicans for their unwillingness to give schools the resources they needed, stating that "investment without accountability is a waste of money [but] accountability without investment is doomed to fail."[47]

Gore's plan contained a number of accountability proposals that were similar to those contained in the Bush plan. His proposal required, for example, that states and districts take action to turn around poor-performing schools. Schools that failed to improve after two years would be shut down and reopened as charter schools or "reconstituted" schools with new staff and leadership. But Bill Galston, Gore's education adviser, agreed with Marshall that the elements of accountability and reform in Gore's education proposals were drowned out by the emphasis on spending increases and Bush's activity on the issue:

> Gore's policy proposals represented a continuation of the Clinton agenda on education in many respects, but there were some important departures as well. There was a much greater awareness of the problem of failing schools, and the Gore campaign developed a very elaborate mechanism to give states incentives to intervene in failing schools. The Gore position and timetable were quite similar to [Bush's] . . . but to some extent these proposals got buried in the larger, more laundry-list–style education program that the campaign put out. Gore also focused on a number of other issues, and the issue of education didn't get the prominence in his campaign that it did in Bush's.[48]

Though Gore would face some disagreement within his party on education, for the most part his education proposals were generally consistent with those of his Democratic predecessor. Gore tried to balance support for more education spending with support for more reform, and support for federal leadership with respect for local control of education. Gore stated that "one of the most important responsibilities we face is that of educating our people. I believe that education must remain a state and local responsibility, with those closest to our children making daily decisions, but I also know that education must be a national priority, with bold national leadership and ample national investment."[49] The result of this balancing act was that Gore continued the longstanding Democratic push for an expanded federal role in education policy. But he was also forced to advocate standards, testing, and accountability reforms that (when combined with Bush's move to the middle on education) closed what had been a yawning gap between the parties on the federal role in education policy.

CONCLUSION

In response to the rise of education on the national agenda, both candidates in 2000 scrambled to craft new positions for their campaigns that would be politically viable with both their party's core constituencies and the wider electorate. Bush and Gore both ran as "education candidates," and in the quest to appeal to the all-important moderate swing voter, each put forward a centrist education reform plan that contained elements long resisted by more extreme members of their respective parties. Though there were several important differences, their plans were remarkably similar in a number of key respects. Both advocated a stronger federal role in education and school improvement through higher academic standards, increased federal funding, expanded support for charter schools, and tests to allow the federal government to hold schools accountable for student achievement. Gore advocated greater increases in spending than Bush, who in turn proposed a more comprehensive and rigorous accountability system than Gore. Given the wide chasm between the two major party candidates on education in the past, however, these differences were less remarkable than the many areas of agreement.

Education had an unusual prominence in the 2000 presidential campaign—several studies have demonstrated that education was one of the most frequently discussed issues by both candidates. Gerald Pomper, for example, found that the Gore campaign designated eight campaign days as "education/family policy days" (second only to the category of taxes and the budget) and that Bush designated ten such days—the most for any issue—during the campaign.[50] Marschall and McKee analyzed the press releases from each of the campaigns and found that 38 percent of Bush's releases devoted substantial attention to education, more than any other issue. Gore, meanwhile, focused on education in 50 percent of his press releases—a higher percentage than Bush but slightly less than the amount of attention Gore devoted to taxes.[51] Such attention to education reform was typical for a Democratic presidential candidate but remarkable for a Republican and gave Bush greater credibility on the issue than previous nominees from his party had enjoyed.

In the end Bush was able to eke out a narrow victory in the Electoral College, despite losing the popular vote. Although Bush's victory cannot be attributed to a single issue or factor, it is clear that his effort to recast the Republican Party's conservative image and to address the party's historic disadvantage on the education issue was largely successful and played an important role in the election. Exit polls conducted by the Voter News Service revealed that Bush performed much better among education voters in 2000 than Dole had done in 1996. In 1996, 78 percent of education voters supported Clinton and only 16 percent supported Dole. But among the 15 percent of voters who identified education as their top concern in 2000, 52 percent voted for Gore and 44 percent voted for Bush.[52] Republican pollster David Winston noted that this

> was a huge shift and is why Bush is president. Education was THE deciding issue in 2000. The groups that were most interested in education were the key swing voters—independents, Catholics, married women with children. It was an issue that you clearly saw a dramatic shift on. The economy was not a big issue in 2000 and so for swing voters, education was a critical issue for them. Going from minus 62 to minus 8 [on education] and you barely win the election, you have to assume that's the gap that closed.[53]

It is also likely that Bush's more moderate stance on education contributed to a more favorable view of his overall ideological orientation, particularly among two key demographic groups—parents and suburban voters. Bush won a majority of these groups' votes in 2000 (they had favored Clinton over Dole in 1996).[54]

Winston suggests that Bush was able to do so well on education and so much better than previous Republicans for three reasons:

> First, the education system was not performing at the level that people wanted—there was dissatisfaction with it. Second, standards and accountability (as opposed to funding alone) were emerging as important ideas, as a more important force in improving education, even without Republicans pushing it. In addition, Bush talked about education a lot. Republicans for some reason had long felt uncomfortable talking about education and therefore had never talked about it: if you don't talk about it, you can't do well on the issue. Bush felt very comfortable talking about education . . . and got a very positive response. . . . He told parents what specific things he was going to do to improve children's education—teacher training, technology, etc.—not about how local control instead of federal control might improve education. It was a very different sound—[Bush was] talking to people at a very different level—a benefit and value level.[55]

Bush responded to the increased salience of school reform and the unpopularity of the GOP's education proposals during the 1990s by embracing an active federal role in education and increased federal spending. His ability to contest what had traditionally been a solid Democratic issue, meanwhile, forced Gore to call for more rigorous accountability and (public) choice reforms than he might otherwise have supported.

The treatment of education in the 2000 election had several consequences for the federal role in education policy. The election continued—and expanded—the trend of nationalizing the rhetoric and politics of education reform. Despite lingering conservative opposition to federal "interference" in education, the endorsement of an active and even expanded federal role in education policy by a Republican

presidential nominee was a significant milestone in the history of federal education policy and fundamentally altered the politics of education at the national
level. The detailed policy proposals and frequent public statements by both candidates on education further legitimized federal leadership in this area. The extensive rhetoric about education during the election also created the expectation
among voters and the media that there would be strong and sustained national
leadership in education reform.

Gore and Bush embraced a remarkably ambitious scope for the federal role
in education reform. They repeatedly argued that the federal government had a
responsibility to ensure a quality education not just for the disadvantaged groups
(racial minorities, disabled children) that the federal government had long assisted, but for *all* students. Gore, for example, remarked during his nomination
acceptance speech that "education may be a local responsibility, but I believe it has
to be our number one priority. We can't stop until every school in America is a
good place to get a good education."[56] The broad scope of Bush's vision of federal
responsibility in education, meanwhile, was visible in the title of his education
plan: "No Child Left Behind." Both Bush and Gore proposed to require states (as
a condition of receiving federal education funds) to produce annual report cards
detailing the performance of every one of their schools. The result was a remarkable degree of convergence on the issue of education during the campaign as both
candidates called for a substantial federal role in education reform and increased
spending but also standards, accountability, and choice. This convergence set the
stage for a historic compromise between the parties on the pending ESEA reauthorization following the election and for the establishment of a new federal education policy regime.

9. Convergence—The No Child Left Behind Act and the New Federal Education Policy Regime (2001–2005)

The widely publicized debates about school reform in Congress and during the 2000 presidential election campaign built up a significant amount of momentum behind restructuring federal education policy. As Chester Finn, Bruno Manno, and Diane Ravitch observed shortly after the election, "For the first time in memory, both major parties and both sets of candidates agree that the federal government has important contributions to make in reforming America's schools. . . . [There is] widening agreement that Washington's present approach to K–12 education policy—an approach that has scarcely changed since LBJ's time—is broken and needs fixing."[1] There also was growing political support for a "grand bargain"—increased federal education funding and greater flexibility in its use in exchange for expanded accountability for school performance. By the time President Bush took office in January 2001, the ideas and interests surrounding federal education had undergone a dramatic shift from only a few years earlier, and the time was ripe for the policies and institutions of a new policy regime to be put in place.

In retrospect, some observers have been inclined to see the centrist compromises that paved the way for passage of the No Child Left Behind law as inevitable, but the negotiations over the bill encountered a number of substantial challenges and its provisions changed considerably during the legislative process. Agreement on the broad principles of reform by no means implied agreement on the specific measures, timetables, and resources that would be necessary to achieve them. Given the acrimonious national debates over school reform in the 1980s and 1990s, and the considerable remaining differences within and between the Republican and Democratic parties, the ultimate shape that NCLB would take was unclear as it began to wind its way through Congress.

A LEGISLATIVE STRATEGY OF BIPARTISAN CENTRISM

As promised, Bush made education the top domestic priority of his new administration. Bush signaled the importance of education reform in his inaugural address by listing it first among the issues that he would address, remarking,

"Together we will reclaim America's schools, before ignorance and apathy claim more young lives."[2] On his second full day in office, Bush sent an education blueprint based on his campaign proposals to Congress. The "No Child Left Behind Act" (hereafter, NCLB) was the first bill he sent to Congress, and it became the focal point of the new legislature's early deliberations. Two strategic decisions about NCLB proved crucial to how the legislative negotiations unfolded: Bush's decision to submit an *outline* of his education reform ideas rather than detailed legislative language, and his decision to seek a *bipartisan* bill rather than attempt to force a Republican bill through Congress on a narrow party-line vote.

Some Republicans argued that the party should use its narrow majorities in the House and Senate to try to pass a conservative bill that contained vouchers, block grants, and other controversial items that Democrats strongly opposed. Bush declined to follow this strategy, and his pursuit of a bipartisan compromise fundamentally influenced the nature of the final legislation as well as its long-term impact on the politics of federal education policy. Bush opted for the bipartisan approach for a number of reasons, some political, and some having to do with policy. First, though Republicans technically controlled Congress, they did so by a slim margin, and their majority could prove insufficient—particularly in the Senate, which was evenly divided and where the GOP did not have the votes to stop a Democratic filibuster. Second, Bush had pledged to work with Democrats and foster a new spirit of bipartisanship during the campaign, and his controversial victory in 2000 ensured that a partisan approach on his first and highest profile domestic issue would generate a great deal of rancor. By beginning his administration with a bipartisan compromise on school reform, Bush could create an important symbol of his centrist compassionate conservatism. Finally, Bush's views on education reform were actually closer in many respects to those of New Democrats than to conservative Republicans. The administration clearly thought that the way to maximize the political and policy gains from education reform was to create an alliance with moderate Republicans and New Democrats and then to lobby more conservative Republicans to support their new president on his first policy initiative.

When Bush introduced his education blueprint, he publicly distanced himself from the more conservative elements of his party by stating that "change will not come by disdaining or dismantling the federal role in education. Educational excellence for all is a national issue and at this moment is a presidential priority."[3] At a meeting of education leaders held in Austin, Texas, prior to his inauguration, Bush reached out to education leaders from both parties and made it clear that he wanted to pass a bipartisan education bill. Bush invited a number of leading Democrats to attend, including Rep. George Miller (D-CA), a liberal who supported tough new accountability measures, and Sens. Joseph Lieberman (D-CT) and

Evan Bayh (D-IN), centrist Democrats whose "Three R's" plan contained many proposals that Bush had embraced during the campaign. Significantly, however, Sen. Ted Kennedy (D-MA), the leading voice of liberal Democrats on education and a longtime defender of the old equity regime, was not invited. This indicated that Bush's initial strategy was to build a center-right coalition of New Democrats and Republicans. Gradually, however, two things became clear to Bush and his advisers—that the embrace of New Democrats such as Lieberman and Bayh would not lead the majority of Democrats to support NCLB, and that Kennedy was more ready to make a deal on education than previously supposed.[4]

Kennedy—like his fellow liberal stalwart Miller before him—had gradually become convinced that it would take more than money to fix what ailed American public schools. The Bush administration's early talks with Lieberman and Bayh, meanwhile, made Kennedy realize that he would be denied a seat at the table for the drafting of the most important education bill in forty years unless he was willing to compromise on his longstanding opposition to testing and accountability. In a January 2001 meeting at the White House, Bush and Kennedy agreed to work together on the education bill, and Kennedy told reporters that "there are some areas of difference, but the overwhelming areas of agreement and support are very, very powerful."[5] Bush's decision to seek a bipartisan bill and Kennedy's decision to work with the administration ensured that the final version of NCLB would represent a compromise between the Republican and Democratic visions of education reform. As Clinton and Gore adviser Bill Galston observed,

> The entire legislative strategy of the Bush administration in negotiating the bill and pushing it forward was what might be called patient bipartisan centrism. . . . Bush embraced early on the idea of the grand bargain—greatly increased federal spending on education in exchange for major reforms—that I and others had been talking about since the late 1990s. He also embraced the idea that Democrats, even liberal Democrats, were not demons on the issue, and so instead of demonizing the likes of Ted Kennedy and George Miller he co-opted them. And in order to co-opt them he had to make some important concessions. But I don't think the concessions involved any serious points of substance as far as he was concerned—with the exception of vouchers, which were thrown overboard early in the process as a sign of realism and goodwill.[6]

Bush's second important strategic decision on education was to send only a brief, twenty-eight–page blueprint of his reform ideas to Congress (see Table 9.1). He never actually sent "legislation" to Capitol Hill, opting instead to merely sketch out the general contours of ESEA reform that he supported. This approach had several advantages for Bush, although it resulted in somewhat reduced administration influence over the final product. By publicly committing only to general principles rather than specific legislative language, Bush retained the flexibility

Table 9.1. Highlights of Bush's Original No Child Left Behind Proposal

Annual Tests	States would be required to test all students in grades 3–8 in reading and mathematics as a condition of receiving federal Title I aid.
Vouchers	In disadvantaged schools that failed to make adequate yearly progress for three consecutive years, students could use Title I funds to transfer to a higher-performing public or private school, or to pay for supplemental educational services.
School Choice	The secretary of education would award grants for innovative efforts to expand parental choice.
Reading	States that established a reading program "anchored in scientific research" in grades K–2 would be eligible for grants under a new Reading First initiative. An Early Reading First initiative would provide grants for preschool programs, including Head Start.
Flexibility	States and districts would be allowed to enter into a "charter agreement" with the Department of Education to waive the federal regulations placed on categorical grant programs in exchange for presenting a five-year performance agreement.
Rewards and Punishments	High-performing states that narrowed the achievement gap and improved overall student achievement would be rewarded financially. Schools that made the greatest progress in improving the achievement of disadvantaged students would be rewarded with "No Child Left Behind" bonuses. The secretary of education would have the authority to reduce the federal funding available to a state for administrative expenses if the state failed to meet its performance objectives.
Teacher Quality	States and districts would be given flexibility in the use of federal aid to allow them to focus more of their efforts on improving teacher quality.

Source: "Bush Unveils Education Plan," *Education Week,* January 23, 2001, http://www.edweek.org.

to negotiate with all of the different players as Congress debated ESEA reform. In addition, by focusing on broad goals such as accountability and flexibility and indicating his willingness to compromise from the outset, Bush could claim credit for negotiating in a bipartisan manner and for whatever legislation Congress ultimately approved.

Having committed itself to securing bipartisan support for the education bill and desirous of a quick victory, the Bush administration essentially combined the two major Democratic and Republican ESEA proposals from the 106th Congress. The Bush proposal focused on consolidation, accountability, school choice, and flexibility and contained many provisions similar to those found in the New Democrat Three R's plan that had been introduced by Lieberman and Bayh in 1999 and that was reintroduced in 2001. As Sen. Bayh remarked at the time, "80 percent of our proposals are common ground."[7] There were some important differences in the remaining 20 percent, however, as Three R's prohibited the use of federal funds for vouchers and called for greater increases in federal spending and for targeting the new funds at the poorest schools. In addition, the New Democrat plan did not contain a provision comparable to Bush's charter agreements proposal—an idea that was similar to the Straight A's block grant proposal that Republicans had put forward in the late 1990s. These differences, and other disagreements over the specific provisions of the bill, led to a number of heated discussions and at times appeared to threaten the grand bargain itself.

As had been the case during the 1990s, the debate over NCLB revealed four factions in Congress regarding federal education policy: liberal Democrats, New Democrats, conservative Republicans, and moderate "Main Street" Republicans. The liberal Democratic faction wanted to preserve federal education programs and regulations and to obtain large increases in federal spending. It was adamantly opposed to vouchers and generally reluctant to support tough testing or accountability measures. Many in the conservative wing of the Republican Party, meanwhile, continued to oppose any federal influence over elementary and secondary education at all and viewed NCLB as a threat to local control of schools. The key difference in 2001, however, was that growing numbers of moderate Republicans and New Democrats had become increasingly concerned about the status quo in education and were more willing to embrace tough new federal reforms.[8] Patty Sullivan, an education analyst for the Council of Chief State School Officers, has remarked,

> Within the Democratic Party (and with Republicans too) the role of the moderates was important—they came together and put pressure on Kennedy [and though conservative Republicans wanted vouchers] . . . the moderate right realized that if we want a bill this is the way we're going to have to go. It was an odd combination [of forces that came together on NCLB] . . . the moderate Democrats putting pressure on Kennedy, the civil rights community putting tremendous pressure on the Congress to help all kids, and . . . the Republicans calling for this federal intrusion.[9]

In addition to centrist pressure from moderates within both parties, a number of other political and policy factors had converged by 2000 to soften the long-standing opposition of many liberal Democrats and conservative Republicans to rigorous federal school reforms. Bush's activism on education in the presidential campaign and his success in closing the yawning gap between the parties on the issue fundamentally altered the political environment surrounding school reform. Though many conservatives continued to have reservations about expanding federal influence over schools, Republicans saw that Bush reaped great political gain on the issue of school reform, and this furthered an evolution in their thinking about education that had been under way since 1996. As Republican pollster David Winston has observed,

> The Republican view used to be that the federal government's role in education was an obstacle to improvement, but now they are more pragmatic—they talk less

about what government should or shouldn't do and focus more on results and making the system better. . . . Bush sold federal education reforms to Republicans by emphasizing that they would improve schools through the use of the basic conservative concepts of standards and accountability . . . but that they would have to fund changes. A long-term philosophical position of the party had been "don't just throw money at the problem, make the system better by focusing on results," so conservatives generally felt very positive about this shift.[10]

The extent to which Republicans had shifted their positions on the issue by 2001 is illustrated by John Boehner (R-OH), the conservative chair of the House Education and Workforce Committee. Boehner had been a leading opponent of federal influence in education in the 1990s, voting to eliminate the Department of Education and remarking in 1995 that "it is clear that the current experiment of having the federal government heavily involved in education has failed."[11] After Bush's election, however, Boehner acknowledged that "I think we realized in 1996 that our message was sending the wrong signal to the American people about the direction we wanted to go in education."[12] As a result, he became one of the most vocal supporters of NCLB and one of Bush's key allies in mobilizing Republican support for the bill during the legislative process. Boehner observed at the time that "the 2000 campaign paved the way for reform, and conservatives must capitalize by implementing the president's plan. . . . Conservatives have yearned for an opportunity to break the status quo in federal education policy. This could be our moment. On behalf of parents and students, let's seize it."[13]

Democrats, meanwhile, faced their own political and policy challenges on education that ultimately led Kennedy and other liberal Democrats who had long resisted rigorous testing and accountability measures to work with the Bush administration on NCLB. This was largely due to the fact that Republicans had a majority in the House and Senate, and there was concern that they might be able to overcome any Democratic resistance to advance a conservative education bill. As NEA lobbyist Joel Packer has noted, "the political environment was such that even if Democrats opposed Bush he was going to get the bill, so leading Democrats made the decision that it was best to be involved instead of opposing the whole thing (much of which New Democrats supported anyway.)"[14] In addition, Bush's activism on education and the repositioning of the Republican Party on the issue forced the Democratic Party to rethink its own position on school reform. Democrats were concerned that they would be unable to recapture the party's historical electoral dominance on the issue unless liberals abandoned their opposition to standards, testing, and choice.

In addition, discontent with the performance of public schools had grown among blacks and Latinos, two key parts of the Democratic base.[15] Though the NAACP and some other groups remained wary of testing and accountability, a number of minority advocacy groups—such as the Education Trust and the Citizens' Commission on Civil Rights—joined New Democrats in pressuring liberal Democrats to support what they saw as necessary reforms to improve the public schools. As Amy Wilkins from the Education Trust observed,

> The Democrats didn't really evolve much on education until [the Bush administration]. . . . As [they] saw minority—especially African American and Latino—support for vouchers increasing it began to pit two important voting blocks within the Democratic Party against one another. The teachers unions were saying "everything is fine, just give us more money," but increasing numbers of African Americans and Latinos were saying "we want out of these schools." This was forcing the Democrats into a place where they had to deal—they had to do something on education.[16]

It was also becoming clear to many Democrats that the 1994 federal reforms and greatly expanded funding had failed to generate the anticipated improvement in student performance or a reduction in the achievement gap between white and minority students. Democrats saw the country's public education system as a crucial pathway to economic opportunity and an important symbol of the efficacy of government activism and spending. But moderate Democrats and even some of their more liberal colleagues were increasingly convinced that the federal government had to push schools harder to improve, and that a new focus on educational achievement was necessary. Bill Galston has noted that

> it turned out that once Democrats were no longer fighting the voucher wars, even some liberal Democrats were beginning to get quite frustrated with what was widely seen as stagnation in the education system despite a decade of talk about reform. The 1990s, we can now see in retrospect, were not a period of great progress in educational achievement as measured by the standard indices. Nor were the 1990s a period in which the achievement gap between minorities and others continued to close. So it was very hard for liberal Democrats to say that what we were doing was working just fine and we just needed to do more of it. . . . There was more appetite for structural change among liberal Democrats than there had been during the Clinton years . . . and that helped.[17]

Growing public skepticism about the performance of public schools and growing support for vouchers also forced many liberals to believe that the educational status quo was politically unsustainable. As Patty Sullivan has noted,

> There was a growing impatience on the part of some liberal Democrats that poor kids were not getting a good education and that if the public school system was left untended, if pressure wasn't put on the schools to change, the public system would produce too much evidence that we needed a voucher system, and that would ultimately destroy the public school system. There was a lot of data coming out on Title I that showed no improvement in schools . . . and it was getting harder to

argue that we should keep spending money on something that we knew didn't work. There was also a lot of data coming out of the civil rights groups that made the case that we needed accountability to force change at the school building level.[18]

Increasingly, then, many liberal Democrats and even some teachers union leaders (particularly in the American Federation of Teachers) came to realize that they would ultimately have to accept tough school reforms in order to save the institution of public education.

In keeping with his pursuit of a bipartisan bill, Bush's education plan contained elements that each party could support. Democrats were pleased with Bush's call for increased federal spending and activism on education, and Republicans supported the increased flexibility given to states and the emphasis on accountability. But the initial Bush plan also contained elements that each party opposed. Democrats quickly labeled Bush's proposals for private school vouchers a dealbreaker and voiced their opposition to his charter agreements proposals, which they criticized as a block grant that would remove important federal safeguards for disadvantaged and minority students. Bush's call for federally mandated testing, meanwhile, made many on both the left and the right wary. Democrats were concerned about how such tests would be structured and used and their potential disparate impact on poor and minority children. Republicans—who had recently fought to kill Clinton's proposal for a national test—remained nervous about such an expansion of federal influence over schools and their curricula.

Despite these concerns, however, the new political situation created a real opening for a far-reaching reconsideration of the federal role in education. The result was that if Bush was under pressure to pass a bipartisan bill, members of Congress from both parties also felt pressure to support it. As Jay Diskey, the former Republican House Education Committee spokesman noted,

> On the Republican side there were a lot of people who had a lot of unease about many of its provisions but held their tongue out of respect for the first Republican president in eight years. . . . Republicans also thought it was a huge trade-off—that while the federal role grew, accountability grew as well. So there was a sense that okay, we'll give you increased resources but finally we're going to have real federal accountability to see if Title I is working or not. . . . On the Democratic side, you had someone like Kennedy who was being slowly backed into a corner by people like Lieberman with his Three R's proposal and was beginning to feel that pressure. Kennedy felt political pressure, Bush felt pressure, and each of their coalitions felt pressure.[19]

In the final analysis, though Bush's leadership was crucial, the creation of a new federal education policy regime would not have occurred without the willingness of congressional leaders from both parties to reconsider their longstanding opposition to many of the reforms contained in the bill.

THE LEGISLATIVE PROCESS: CONTENTION
AND COMPROMISE

Despite the Bush administration's deep involvement with the bill and the support of leaders from both parties, deliberations in Congress were often contentious, and a number of key elements of NCLB were either defeated or only narrowly survived the legislative process. One of the major sticking points of the Bush proposal was its provision to permit private schools to participate in the school choice programs mandated for failing schools. Vouchers had been the third rail of Democratic education politics for over twenty years, with teachers unions, education groups, and most national civil rights organizations adamantly opposed to using public money for private schools. If opposition to vouchers was a core part of Democratic education strategy in the 1980s and 1990s, however, securing government support for private schools had been a centerpiece of the Republican agenda during the same period. Many conservative groups and members of Congress saw the Republican control of Congress and the White House as a historic opportunity to pass voucher legislation. A number of conservative groups, including the Family Research Council, Focus on the Family, the Eagle Forum, and the Traditional Values Coalition, announced that they would not support the final bill unless it contained vouchers. Moderate Republicans—such as the members of the Republican Main Street Coalition—however, argued that vouchers remained unpopular and were of uncertain effectiveness, and that the party's support for them had been detrimental politically. The overwhelming defeat of voucher ballot initiatives in California and Michigan in 2000 certainly reinforced this point.

Bush's desire for a bipartisan bill and the strong opposition of Democrats and moderate Republicans resulted in the removal of the voucher proposal from the legislation early in the process. Conservative Republicans nonetheless attempted several times, unsuccessfully, to add a voucher program into the House bill. Majority Leader Dick Armey (R-TX) offered a voucher amendment on the House floor, where it was defeated 155–273 (with 68 Republicans voting against it). He offered a second amendment to establish five voucher demonstration programs, but this was also defeated, this time by a vote of 186–241. Although Democrats succeeded in defeating Bush's voucher proposal, they were forced to accept a supplemental services provision that many view as a sort of voucher demonstration project. The provision allows students in failing schools to use federal Title I money for private tutoring, which could set an important precedent for future legislative (and judicial) consideration of federal voucher programs.[20]

Democrats and Republicans also compromised on Bush's block grant proposal by agreeing to fund only a demonstration program. Boehner convinced House Republicans to drop plans to offer a Straight A's amendment in committee that he and the White House feared would cost Democratic support. Kennedy and Miller, meanwhile, were willing to negotiate with the White House and to lobby for Democrats to support the bill, but they made it clear that the price of their cooperation would be a large increase in spending on education. The Bush plan called for an increase in federal spending on ESEA of approximately $1.6 billion, but House Democrats called for a $10 billion increase, and Senate Democrats wanted a $15 billion boost. The latter were ultimately able to win the support of a few Republicans to add additional funding to the bill.

Bush's testing proposal—like Clinton's during the 1990s—encountered stiff resistance from both the left and the right. Whereas liberal Democrats and educators argued that tests were being overused and were unfair to disadvantaged and minority students, conservatives worried that federally mandated tests were the first step toward a national curriculum. During the committee markup in the House, for example, many members spoke in favor of an amendment by Rep. Betty McCollum (D-MN) to strip the testing provisions from the bill entirely. Miller convinced McCollum not to ask for a roll call vote, however, and Boehner declared the amendment defeated on a voice vote. When the bill reached the House floor, the testing provisions came under fire again, this time by an alliance led by Rep. Peter Hoekstra (R-MI), one of the most conservative members of the House, and Rep. Barney Frank (D-MA), one of its most liberal. The amendment drew significant support from conservative Republicans and liberal Democrats but was defeated 173–255. Fifty-two Republicans (and two independents) voted against testing and were joined by 119 Democrats, including the House's two leading Democrats, Minority Leader Richard Gephardt (D-MO) and Minority Whip David Bonior (D-MI). The testing provision was saved by heavy White House lobbying and by the efforts of Boehner and Miller in the House and Kennedy and Judd Gregg (R-NH) in the Senate, who kept the centrist coalition from collapsing under pressure from the left and right. Majority Whip Tom Delay (R-TX), a staunch conservative, also noted at the time "that the majority of our members want to support the president, and the centerpiece of his proposal is testing."[21]

Vocal public support and energetic lobbying by business groups such as the National Alliance of Business, Achieve Inc., and the Business Coalition for Excellence in Education (BCEE) were also crucial in defeating attempts by liberals and conservatives to water down or remove many of the legislation's standards, testing, and accountability provisions.[22] In response to the Hoekstra-Frank amendment, for example, the Business Roundtable urged its members to call on Congress to defeat any attempt to strike out NCLB's testing provisions. In testimony on Capitol Hill, in private meetings with lawmakers, and in interviews with the press, the leaders of business organizations stressed the importance of improving schools and student performance to the vitality of the country's workforce and economy.

In a March hearing of the House Education and Workforce Committee, for example, Keith Bailey of the BCEE called for "a new federal role in K–12 education." He continued,

> Federal funding should support state investments to pursue a common agenda of priorities with clear accountability for achieving results. Real rewards and consequences are essential with the support and flexibility states need to achieve the results. What we are suggesting is a different relationship between the federal government and the states compared to both the categorical program models of the past and the more flexible but less well-defined block grant proposals that impose little direction or priorities for national investments. . . . I want to emphasize that the reforms we are seeking cannot be delayed—the world is changing rapidly and we need to ensure that our educational systems can equip our children with the knowledge and skills to meet the challenges they will face.[23]

The Bush administration's effort to rally disgruntled Republicans and Democrats behind NCLB also received a major boost from public opinion polls that consistently showed high levels of support for the plan, with respondents approving of it by a more than three-to-one margin in the months after it was introduced.[24] Public support for the key reform proposals contained in the plan also was high, with 77 percent supporting giving the states greater authority in deciding how federal funds should be used, 75 percent favoring holding public schools accountable for how much students learn, and 55 percent favoring the increased use of standardized tests for measuring student achievement.[25]

As the Bush administration negotiated compromises on testing, accountability, and funding to placate Democrats, however, many Republicans became more disillusioned with the bill and threatened to vote against it. Conservatives, in particular, felt that Bush gave up too much to Democrats and were concerned that the final bill contained few of the decentralizing and privatizing elements that they had originally sought. Rep. Bob Schaffer (R-CO) bemoaned that "in the end, for the [House] committee and the White House, appeasing Democrats was more important than sending the president's plan to the floor intact."[26] Though there was a great deal of criticism behind the scenes, most Republicans held their fire in public and ultimately threw their support behind the bill for fear of weakening their party's first president in eight years. As Rep. Mark Souder (R-IN) remarked, "The president wanted a bipartisan bill on both sides. While I respect that, I'm not sure it was the wisest negotiating strategy . . . [but] he had a very narrow [election] win, and we don't want anything to jeopardize his number one initiative. But that doesn't mean we like it."[27]

The bill ultimately passed both chambers of Congress by wide margins: the House passed its version of NCLB on May 23, 2001, by a vote of 384–45, and the

Senate passed its version on June 14 with a vote of 91–8. The conference committee was left with two primary tasks—to settle on the level of funding for the bill and to finalize the details of the bill's new accountability system. The key players in negotiating the compromise legislation were Senators Kennedy and Gregg, Representatives Boehner and Miller, and Bush advisers Margaret Spellings and Sandy Kress. The House and Senate versions of the bill called for very different funding levels—the final Senate version called for a $14.4 billion increase in federal education spending, whereas the House version called for only a $4.6 billion increase. It had also become clear that the "adequate yearly progress" (AYP) language contained in the bill approved by the House set unobtainable expectations for improving student test scores. Research by committee staffers had indicated that no state in the country would be able to meet the standard as it was written at that point. The accountability language in the Senate bill, meanwhile, was regarded as too complex to be workable. Many of the early negotiations over the bill between Democrats and Republicans had been cordial and cooperative, but by the time the conference committee convened a number of disagreements had become public, and pressure from the left and right led some observers to question whether a compromise could attract sufficient support to pass both chambers. Educational interest groups that felt threatened by many of the bill's new testing and accountability requirements intensified their efforts to derail the legislation.

At this crucial moment came the terrorist attacks of September 11, 2001. Bush, in fact, was sitting in a school promoting No Child Left Behind when he learned of the news of the airplanes hitting the World Trade Center. The attacks apparently created a sense in the leadership of both parties that completing work on a bipartisan education bill could reassure a jittery public by providing a symbol of a unified and functioning government. As Donald Payne (D-NJ), a member of the House Education Committee, noted, "passage of the education bill had already been a top priority of the Bush administration, and the terrorist attacks of September 11th strengthened the resolve of both Congress and the administration to proceed with the business of the people."[28] Bush and Boehner reiterated their willingness to make the necessary compromises to gain bipartisan passage of the bill. They agreed to preserve support for several education programs—such as those for class size reduction and school construction—that had been targeted for elimination. And though the initial administration proposal had called for only a 3 percent increase in spending on ESEA, the conference committee report settled on a 20 percent increase. A compromise on accountability allowed states to design their own tests and to set their own definitions for student "proficiency" but required them to make adequate yearly progress toward obtaining proficiency for all of their students in twelve years.

THE FINAL BILL

The vote to approve the conference report of NCLB was overwhelming and bipartisan in both the House (381–41) and Senate (87–10). The final version of the legislation was a compromise bill in every sense of the word—there was plenty for politicians of every persuasion to like and dislike about it, and its reforms went too far for some and not far enough for others (see Table 9.2). Given the broad and passionate policy disagreements between Democrats and Republicans during the 1980s and 1990s, however, NCLB's passage with bipartisan support was a remarkable development.

As former House Education Committee coordinator and Department of Education congressional liaison Vic Klatt has remarked,

> The only way that a bill like NCLB could have passed was if a Republican president supported it. There was a lot of stuff in that bill that congressional Republicans would not have put up with under Bill Clinton. Pretty much everybody voted for the NCLB in the end—most people who voted against it were Republican conservatives. This was a unique period of time where you had a new president with a fairly strong mandate on education and there were a few people on the Democratic side (Miller especially, but also Lieberman and, to some degree, Kennedy) who were willing to lead on this and take some flak for it. They thought it was in their best interest to get a bill, and they were willing to take on the unions and some of the education groups in town.[29]

Both sides made major concessions—Republicans dropped vouchers, most of their Straight A's block grant proposals, and their major consolidation effort. And Democrats accepted extensive new federal mandates regarding teacher quality, testing, and accountability. As Wilkins noted,

> It ended up being an unusually bi-partisan bill. . . . NCLB was a defeat for liberals on the left and conservatives on the right—it was a bill that was always designed to run right down the middle so neither extreme won the day. NCLB passes because it is right down the middle. . . . It was about New Democrats and Compassionate conservatives working together. Public opinion polling in the 1990s showed education moving higher and higher on people's agendas and staying there—there was huge dissatisfaction with what was going on in public schools, and this emboldened Congress to act and to pass NCLB.[30]

At the heart of the bill was a fundamental trade-off—it put in place a number of prescriptive new mandates on states and school districts but in exchange for meeting the new demands gave them greater flexibility in how they use increased federal funds.[31] The most important requirements in the new law are that states must adopt academic standards to guide their curricula and adopt a testing and accountability system that is aligned with those standards.[32] States must test all students in grades 3–8 every year (as well as once in high school) in math and reading beginning in the 2005–2006 school year (see Table 9.2). States are required to annually test the English proficiency of students for whom English is not their first language, and by the 2007–2008 school year, states must also test all students in science at certain grade levels. States are free to develop and use their own standards and tests, but every school, school district, and state will have to make student test results publicly available and disaggregated for certain groups of students, including major racial and ethnic groups, major income groups, students with a disability, students with limited English proficiency, and migrant students. States also have to administer the math and reading portions of a national test, the National Assessment of Educational Progress (NAEP), every other year to a sample of their students in grades four and eight to check the effectiveness of state standards and to provide a means of comparability of student performance across states.

NCLB also requires that by 2005–2006, states have a "highly qualified teacher" in every classroom where core academic subjects are taught. States must establish a timetable of intermediate steps to reach this goal. In addition, the act required that all new teachers hired with Title I funds had to be highly qualified. "Highly qualified" is specified as meaning that a teacher must be fully certified or licensed, hold a bachelor's degree, and show competence in subject knowledge and teaching skills. NCLB mandates that every state and school district issue report cards that detail student test scores and identify those schools that have failed to meet proficiency targets and are in need of "program improvement." The law also gives parents, for the first time, the right to request information from schools about teacher qualifications. This wealth of information has never before been made widely available on a consistent basis, and it is certain to provide parents and education reformers alike with a large amount of new data from which to make judgments about the progress of school improvement efforts. NCLB explicitly requires that states use this information to track their efforts to close the achievement gaps on reading and math between different racial, ethnic, and income groups. States are required to establish a timeline (with regular benchmarks) for making "adequate yearly progress" toward eliminating these gaps and moving all students to state proficiency levels within twelve years.

The law's accountability provisions require states to take a number of escalating actions with schools that do not reach their performance objectives. A school that fails to meet state performance targets for two consecutive years must be given technical assistance from the district to help it improve, and students in that school must be given the option to transfer to another public school in the district.

The local school board must pay for some of the cost of transporting students who elect to use the choice option to their new schools. If a school does not improve in the third year, students will be given the option of using their share of Title I funds to pay for tutoring or other supplemental educational services (which can be provided by private companies). Schools that fail for four consecutive years must implement corrective actions such as replacing staff or adopting a new curriculum, and in the fifth year the failing school must be reconstituted with a new governance structure (such as by reopening as a charter school).

In exchange for meeting these new federal demands, NCLB provides a significant increase in federal spending on education and new flexibility in how states can spend it. It provides a 20 percent increase in spending on Title I and also establishes new rules requiring that the additional funds go to the poorest classrooms. School districts can shift up to 50 percent of the federal funds they receive for teaching improvement, innovation, technology, and safe and drug-free schools among the different programs or into Title I. The law also permits some Title I schools to use federal funds for schoolwide projects rather than for just low-achieving students, and it authorizes a number of demonstration projects that relax even more federal regulations in some states and school districts. Up to 150 districts, for example, may take part in flexibility demonstration projects under which they can block grant all of their federal funding in exchange for meeting certain performance goals. The law consolidates a number of federal programs, though not as many as originally proposed by Bush, and also creates a number of new ones, such as Reading First ($900 million per year) and Mathematics and Science Partnerships ($450 million per year). NCLB encourages states to use "scientific, research-based" approaches with documented evidence of effectiveness in these and other programs. Finally, the law includes expanded federal support for public charter schools ($300 million per year).

The new federal focus on accountability and the extension of federal policy to cover every student and every school in the country mark a major shift in the governance of elementary and secondary education in the United States. Richard Elmore calls NCLB "the single largest expansion of federal power over the nation's education system in history," and Andy Rotherham, a former Clinton education adviser, says that it "represents the high water mark of federal intrusion in education."[33]

NCLB builds on reforms at the state and federal levels during the 1980s and 1990s that challenged the original ESEA federal equity paradigm in education and its emphasis on resources, access, and process.[34] Goals 2000 and the 1994 ESEA reforms provided an important ideational foundation for NCLB by shifting the focus of federal education programs from inputs to outputs and by encouraging states to adopt academic standards and assessment systems. But the 1994 reforms

Table 9.2: Highlights of the No Child Left Behind Act as Signed into Law

Annual Testing	By the 2005–06 school year, states must begin administering annual, state-wide assessments in reading and mathematics for grades 3–8. States may select and design their own assessments, but the tests must be aligned with state academic standards. By 2007–08, states must implement science assessments to be administered once during each of the three levels of K–12 education: elementary, middle, and high school. A sample of fourth and eighth graders in each state must participate in the National Assessment of Educational Progress in reading and math every other year to provide a point of comparison for the state's results on its own tests. Test results must include individual student scores and be reported by race, income, and other categories to measure not just overall trends, but also gaps between, and progress of, various subgroups.
Academic Improvement	States must attain academic proficiency—as defined by each state—for all students within twelve years. States must set a minimum performance threshold based on the lowest-achieving demographic subgroup, or the lowest-achieving schools in the state, whichever is higher. Each state must raise the level of proficiency gradually (with "adequate yearly progress") leading to 100 percent proficiency by 2014.
Corrective Action	If a school fails to make adequate progress for two consecutive years, the school will receive technical assistance from the district and must provide public school choice. After a third year of failure to make adequate progress, a school will also be required to offer supplemental educational services chosen by students' parents, including private tutoring. If a school fails to make adequate progress for four consecutive years, the district must implement corrective actions, such as replacing certain staff members or adopting a new curriculum. After five years of inadequate progress, a school would be identified for reconstitution and be required to set up an alternative governance structure, such as reopening as a charter school or turning operation of the school over to the state. States are also responsible for overseeing districts as a whole, identifying those needing improvement, and taking corrective actions when necessary.
Report Cards	Beginning with the 2002–03 school year, states must provide annual report cards with a range of information, including statewide student-achievement data broken down by subgroup and information on the performance of school districts in making adequate yearly progress. Districts must also provide similar report cards, including district-wide and school-by-school data.
Teacher Quality	All teachers hired under Title I, beginning in 2002–2003, must be "highly qualified." In general, under the law, "highly qualified" means that a teacher has been certified (including alternative routes to certification) or licensed by a state and has demonstrated a high level of competence in the subjects that he or she teaches. By the end of the 2005–06 school year, every public school teacher must be "highly qualified."
Reading First	This new program, authorized at $900 million in 2002, provides help to states and districts in setting up "scientific, research-based" reading programs for children in grades K–3.

Table 9.2: (continued)

Transferability	Districts may transfer up to 50 percent of the money from several major ESEA programs; funds may be transferred into, but not out of, Title I. States may transfer up to 50 percent of state-activity funds between several major ESEA programs.
Flexibility Demonstration Projects	Up to 150 districts may enter into performance agreements with the federal Department of Education under which they could consolidate all aid under several major ESEA programs, excluding Title I. Up to seven states may consolidate all state-administration and state-activity funding under several major ESEA programs.
Public Charter Schools	Authorized at $300 million in 2002, the program provides aid to help states and localities support charter schools, including money to help with the planning and design of charter schools, the evaluation of their effectiveness, and facilities costs.

Source: "An ESEA Primer," *Education Week,* January 9, 2002, http://www.edweek.org.

largely stopped at encouragement—due to stiff opposition from the right and the left, the Department of Education was given no tools with which to force states to make the recommended changes. Rotherham noted that "in this system, what passed for accountability was the ability to provide detailed reports of planned and actual spending of federal funds—in other words, a system of accounting, not accountability."[35] The political alignment in education in 1994 still revolved around conservative opposition to federal activism in education and liberal opposition to a more rigorous system of federal testing and accountability.

As a result of these political constraints, the 1994 reforms gave states great flexibility and discretion in designing and implementing their school reform plans. By 2000, however, it was clear that this approach had failed to bring about major policy change at the state level or to improve student achievement. Compliance with the laws' requirements was poor—as of spring 2002, only sixteen states had fully met the requirements of the 1994 law. One observer noted in 2002, for example, that "many of the pieces of the 1994 reform still have not been put in place. . . . In the absence of federal enforcement, states ignored the law's requirements. . . . States have missed the deadlines because the federal government lets them get away with it."[36] NCLB was in many ways a response to the failure of the 1994 reforms and increasing pressure on national leaders to bring about better school results. As Michael Cohen has noted,

NCLB reflects significant impatience in Washington with the pace of state-led improvement and, in particular, with the slow pace at which states have instituted tough accountability systems. The legislation contains new and highly prescriptive testing and accountability requirements for states . . . and spells out in more detail than previously the consequences for schools that fail to make adequate progress toward this goal. These provisions substantially shift the historic balance of federal vs. state control over education.[37]

In essence, Goals 2000 *encouraged* states to create standards, testing, and accountability systems but NCLB *requires* it, and these requirements will have an enormous impact on how public schools are governed and what goes on in classrooms across America. Since the passage of the law, the Department of Education has been reorganized to facilitate the agency's new focus on student achievement and state compliance.[38]

Some observers have downplayed the significance of NCLB because they say it merely builds on earlier state and federal reforms and because the federal share of total education spending remains small (less than 10 percent). But this view underestimates the dramatic impact that the requirements of NCLB are having on state education policies and schools across the nation. Although forty-eight states had standards and tests in place in 2000, for example, only thirteen states were testing students every year in reading and math between the third and eighth grades, as NCLB now requires, and even fewer had strong accountability systems of the sort mandated by the new law. Thus, prior to NCLB, even in the states that had adopted standards and testing reforms, there were few consequences for schools that failed to perform well. NCLB's significance is in mandating that *all* states adopt a standards and testing regime, and that they conform to a federal timetable for achieving student proficiency.

NCLB contains a large number of prescriptive mandates that reach into every major area of education policy and will require states and districts to fundamentally change the way they run their public schools. Although some of the language of the 1994 ESEA is similar to the 2002 legislation, the differences (including those on AYP timetables and mandatory corrective actions) are crucially important, and the substantive impact of the two laws on states and schools has been markedly different. Patty Sullivan of the Council for Chief State School Officers has commented, for example, that

> NCLB is a huge, huge shift for states to have the federal government being as absolutely prescriptive as they are. . . . The federal role in education was much less significant before NCLB—it was money that flowed through state agencies that created capacity through staff at the state agency, and [it] did some good in high-poverty schools. But what the federal government did through Title I was equal to the 6 percent of funding that it provided. NCLB goes well beyond that—it applies accountability to all schools—we're not just talking Title I schools anymore. Under the old law we would say you have to have these things in place. Under the new law it's "you have to have these things in place, you've got to do it on this timeframe, you have to produce and report the information this way, and, by the way, you have to use these reading programs." It is very, very prescriptive. People don't appreciate

that . . . [nor do they] understand the magnitude of the shift in federal education policy.[39]

Future policies regarding funding, teacher certification, academic standards, testing, accountability, school choice, and the release of information to parents will all be heavily influenced by the federal requirements in NCLB. The impact of the new legislation on educational leaders and public schools has been and will continue to be substantial, regardless of whether it succeeds in improving school performance.

2003–2005: THE INITIAL IMPLEMENTATION OF NCLB

How NCLB's new mandates and accountability measures are enforced, however, will prove crucial to the ultimate educational impact of the law.[40] The night after Bush signed No Child Left Behind into law in early 2002, his education secretary, Roderick Paige, met with thirty state education chiefs and warned them that they would be held to the letter of the new law and that he would not grant waivers or tolerate noncompliance as his predecessors had done. In stark contrast to the implementation of previous federal education legislation, the Bush Department of Education has developed tough, detailed regulations in support of NCLB and has threatened to withhold federal funds from states that do not comply with its mandates.[41] Despite the department's tough stance—or perhaps because of it—the initial implementation of the law has not proceeded smoothly. House Education and Workforce Committee staffer Alex Nock has observed that "the department has really struggled in implementing the law—it's a difficult job, but they didn't do it right. They took too long to get out key regulations and guidance, issued contradictory guidance, and did a poor job with providing technical assistance. There was a real rush to implement NCLB's statutory provisions even though the Department of Education really wasn't up to speed."[42]

The beginning of the NCLB era has been eventful as states have struggled to implement the law while strong opposition to it and the expanded federal role in schools has been voiced from many different quarters. Many educators and administrators have gone so far as to call for the law's repeal, but this is not surprising given NCLB's focus on accountability and its challenge to the established operating practices of schools, districts, and states. As Phyllis McClure, a longtime member of the Title I Independent Review Panel, has noted, "NCLB has grabbed the education community's attention like no previous ESEA reauthorization. It has really upset the status quo in state and local offices and has shaken the complacency of educators and parents about their schools' performance. For the first time, district and school officials are actually being required to take serious and urgent action in return for federal dollars."[43]

By 2005, there was growing concern over the capacity of states to comply with the law's programmatic mandates and meet its timetables for moving students to academic proficiency. A July 2004 report by the Education Commission of the States, for example, found that though states had made considerable progress over the preceding year, they continued to struggle with several NCLB requirements. None of the fifty states, for example, was on track to meet the law's requirement of a highly qualified teacher in every classroom or for providing high-quality professional development for teachers. Only nineteen states were on schedule to release annual state report cards on school performance, as required, and fewer than half were meeting goals of making scientifically based technical assistance available to low-performing schools.[44]

In addition, a large number of schools across the country have been identified as "in need of improvement" for failing to meet AYP targets. A report on state implementation of NCLB released by the Center on Education Policy in March 2005 concluded that though student test scores are rising and achievement gaps narrowing in a majority of states and districts, large numbers of schools remain in "in need of improvement" status, and state and district officials have a number of concerns about the law going forward.[45]

Their analysis of state education data found that the number of non–Title I schools identified as in need of improvement (for which states are not required to undertake corrective actions) was 2,370 in 2004–2005.[46] The total number of Title I schools identified as in need of improvement declined slightly in 2004 but has remained basically stable for the past three years at about 6,000 (or 13 percent of all Title I schools).[47] As a result, however, even as states struggled to continue developing the standards and testing frameworks mandated by NCLB, they are also being forced to apply corrective measures to failing Title I schools (such as providing technical assistance and allowing students to choose a better school). In some states this was particularly difficult due to the large number of Title I schools that had failed to meet AYP repeatedly and therefore required more intensive corrective actions, such as reconstitution.[48]

During 2004 a number of state legislatures around the country debated resolutions declaring that NCLB was a violation of states' rights, was inadequately funded, and/or was being administered in an inflexible and unworkable manner. In January of that year, the Republican-controlled Virginia House of Delegates passed an almost unanimous resolution calling on Congress to exempt states such as Virginia—which have "successfully increased student achievement through their own standards and accountability reforms"—from NCLB's accountability provisions.[49] The resolution declared that NCLB "represents the most sweeping intrusions into state and local control of education in the history of the United

States" and will cost "literally millions of dollars that Virginia does not have."[50] Fourteen other states petitioned the department that March for permission to use alternative methods for calculating student academic progress.[51]

State legislatures in Utah, Vermont, New Hampshire, Hawaii, and Maine passed bans prohibiting their states from spending any of their own funds to implement the NCLB. All together, legislators in thirty-one states introduced bills in 2004 seeking greater flexibility or more funding under the law or to limit state participation in it.[52] The Ohio Department of Education released a study estimating that the state would spend about $1.5 billion a year to meet the administrative costs and achievement goals of NCLB, an amount that was more than twice what the state received in ESEA funds. Wisconsin's attorney general suggested in May 2004 that the state had no legal obligation to follow NCLB because the costs of the program exceeded the money provided for it by the federal government.[53] The National Conference of State Legislatures released a report on NCLB in February 2005 that called on the federal government to give states more flexibility across the board regarding NCLB, as well as to "reevaluate" the goal of 100 percent academic proficiency and to "reexamine" the policy of withdrawing federal funds from states that do not comply with NCLB.[54] Adding to what appeared to be an already combustible political mix, several media reports in 2004 declared that public opinion was turning against NCLB.[55]

NCLB clearly has some very loud and visible critics—particularly in the education community—but it appears that predictions of its imminent demise have been overstated. Despite all of the activity in state legislatures, for example, as of 2005 governors in only three states (Maine, Utah, and Vermont) had signed bills critical of NCLB, and only Utah had declared (in April 2005) that it would not follow NCLB provisions that conflict with state education goals. The U.S. Department of Education responded to the growing opposition to NCLB from state legislatures and education officials in 2004 by sending representatives scurrying around the country to deliver a two-pronged message: (1) NCLB is here to stay, so stop complaining and start complying; and (2) if you do not comply with the law you will forfeit your state's share of federal education funds. Commentators are quick to point out that the federal government's share of total education spending is "only" 7–10 percent and to suggest that states may decide to simply end their participation in ESEA if federal mandates are not relaxed.[56] Though this may ultimately prove true, states are hard-pressed to turn down the millions (and often hundreds of millions) of dollars in federal funds that they each receive annually. In addition, because most state and local funds are consumed with fixed costs such as textbooks, building maintenance, and teacher salaries and benefits, federal monies are used by states to fund important supplemental programs and reform efforts. As Patty Sullivan, of the Council of Chief State School Officers, has noted, "Maintaining a good relationship with the federal government that oversees your programs and suing them at the same time is a very difficult proposition."[57]

Much of the opposition to NCLB in 2004–2005 was centered on the perceived unfairness of certain rules governing the calculation of school AYP measures and claims that the U.S. Department of Education had been inflexible in its enforcement of the law and unresponsive to state concerns. In March 2004, the chief school officers of thirty-five states had a two-hour meeting with President Bush and his advisers in which they expressed the difficulties that they were having in complying with NCLB.[58] They secured a promise that the administration would use greater flexibility in the implementation of the law, and a few days later the department relaxed the rules for calculating student participation rates in NCLB's testing program. This change—along with several earlier ones issued by the Department of Education in 2003–2004—made it easier for states to comply with the law's mandates and for more schools to meet annual AYP goals.[59] Through a combination of state improvement efforts and federal rules changes, the percentage of schools that met all of their AYP targets generally held steady or increased from 2003 to 2004. Among the twenty-four states for which preliminary reports were available in September 2004, for example, thirteen increased the number of schools making adequate yearly progress by at least 10 percent, and four had increases of more than twenty percentage points.[60] This trend was observed by Kathy Christie of the Education Commission of the States, who has remarked:

> States have come a long way between 2002 and 2005 in implementing NCLB. States were at very different places on education reform when NCLB [was] passed, so some states had much further to go in complying than others. States are definitely complying with NCLB to a greater and faster extent than they did with the 1994 reforms because NCLB has very specific timelines, and so far those timelines are certainly being enforced. The first year there was a sense of disbelief, especially at the local level, and the hope that NCLB would blow over or just go away. But now people realize that it will not—that NCLB is here to stay.[61]

Growing state opposition to NCLB, the Bush administration's central domestic policy initiative, however, clearly had an effect by 2005. At the start of his second term, Bush replaced Secretary of Education Paige—who was widely criticized for his poor implementation of NCLB and for calling the National Education Association a "terrorist organization"—with Margaret Spellings, a former Bush domestic policy adviser. Secretary Spellings indicated immediately that though she will hold states to the law's core requirements and timetables, she is willing to work with states to a greater extent than did her predecessor.[62] In April 2005, Spellings announced a major policy shift, what she called "a new common sense approach" to NCLB implementation. In "Raising Achievement: A New Path for NCLB," Spell ings identified four "bright lines" in the law that must be met—conducting annual testing, reporting disaggregated subgroup scores, improving teacher quality, and disseminating school information and options to parents.[63] States that meet these principles and demonstrate that student achievement is improving, she wrote, "will get credit for the work they have done to reform their education system as a whole" when seeking additional flexibility. "In other words," she explained, "it is the results that truly matter, not the bureaucratic way that you get there." More specifically, Spellings announced that the department would introduce greater flexibility in the testing of students with learning disabilities as well as look into alternative methods of calculating AYP (such as through growth models). As if to indicate that the new flexibility should not be misconstrued, however, the U.S. Department of Education subsequently fined Texas $450,000 (the largest fine from the department during the Bush administration) for failing to inform parents quickly enough that their children were eligible under NCLB to transfer out of struggling schools.

The announcement of a more flexible approach by the department was not sufficient to prevent the NEA and the state of Connecticut from filing lawsuits against the federal government over NCLB.[64] The legal challenges were based on the general claim that NCLB is an unfunded mandate as well as an NCLB provision—first inserted into ESEA by Republicans in the 1990s—that forbids federal officials to require states to spend their own money to carry out the federal policies outlined in the law.[65] The NEA suit was dismissed by a federal judge in November 2005, and the Connecticut case was still pending as this book went to press.

The intergovernmental negotiations over NCLB will undoubtedly continue—and become even more contentious as the 2014 date for 100 percent student academic proficiency approaches. As Kathy Christie of the Education Commission of the States has remarked, "States are feeling like they really have to speak out about the level of federal intrusion in NCLB. On the other hand, you have a lot of good education leaders at the state and local level who really want to do a better job of serving all kids—they really see it as a civil rights issue—and states are very focused on using education reform to train workers and attract businesses and keep their economies vital. That tension is not going to go away."[66] It remains to be seen, however, whether the changes recently announced by the U.S. Department of Education signify a dramatic change in federal implementation and what impact they will have on state compliance and views of the law. As Frederick Hess noted in his study of state-level reforms, the politics of educational accountability is such that we should expect continued pressure to relax NCLB's rules and timetables for achieving AYP and moving all students to academic proficiency.[67] (In late 2005, for example, Secretary Spellings granted states an extra year to meet NCLB's highly qualified teacher provision.) The ultimate impact of NCLB on students, schools, and state educational policies will therefore be determined by the extent to which federal policymakers are able to resist these pressures and remain committed to enforcing the law's central mandates and timetables.

POLITICS AND THE FUTURE OF THE FEDERAL ROLE
IN EDUCATION

The political future of NCLB and the more assertive federal role in education will likely be determined by the extent and pace of school improvement, whether the public continues to support federal activism in schools, and the degree to which the bipartisan congressional consensus behind the law can be sustained. As long as schools continue to be perceived as underperforming and education reform remains high on the public agenda, the opportunity for elected national officeholders to score political points on the issue through federal activism is likely to prove irresistible. Global economic competition and the shift to a skills-based economy has also made educational quality and attainment more important to individual and national economic success. As James Cibulka has noted, "Education is seen by national elites as a way of meeting the nation's critical need for human capital. It is this nationalization dynamic . . . that will not go away and will continue to drive the politics of education for the foreseeable future."[68]

Crucially, the original bipartisan congressional coalition that passed NCLB remains largely intact. Bush administration officials and congressional Republican education leaders—including committee chairs Senator Gregg and Rep. John Boehner—have remained steadfastly supportive of the law and opposed to making any legislative changes before it comes up for reauthorization in 2007. Boehner, for example, remarked in January 2004,

> Overall, the law is working very much as envisioned. There has been predictable grumbling by the education establishment as it has gradually realized that the Bush administration has no intention of watering down the law through regulatory waivers, as the Clinton administration did with its own education plan. But virtually no one has suggested we should return to the days in which achievement gaps were subsidized and hidden from view. And most important of all, disadvantaged children are finally getting the attention they're due. This is a bipartisan achievement we should build on as a nation in 2004 and beyond.[69]

Though Democrats have criticized Bush for what they believe to be his inadequate funding of the law and called for more flexible enforcement, the Democratic Leadership Council and key liberals such as Rep. George Miller and Sen. Ted

Kennedy have reiterated their support for the law's central principles and reforms. Miller, the ranking Democrat on the House Education Committee, remarked in 2004, "I think the act is actually doing pretty well. I don't want to pretend for a moment that it's easy to implement . . . but it's making a positive change for a lot of children and families who weren't part of the education equation [before]."[70] NCLB's accountability provisions have engendered strong opposition from states' rights advocates and the education community, but congressional leaders from the left and the right continue to see these as essential. Democratic House Education Committee staffer Alex Nock has noted that

> Democrats on the committee believe that having subgroup accountability is criti-
> cally important—that it is the heart of what NCLB is all about and a key reform
> that we have to keep in place. . . . There is definitely still bipartisan support for
> NCLB—especially for its goals—here on Capitol Hill. Lawmakers constantly hear
> from their locals about all of the trouble they're having implementing the law, and
> a lot of that stems from early mistakes made by the Department of Education. But
> there is going to be a long-term interest in educational results by the federal gov-
> ernment. Whether or not AYP remains unchanged is a very different question. Ac-
> countability is here to stay; the only question is what form it will take.[71]

Legislation to make minor changes to NCLB was introduced by Kennedy in September 2004, but he stated at the time, "It's important to acknowledge what this bill does not do. It does not make fundamental changes to the requirements under No Child Left Behind. Those reforms are essential to improving our public schools."[72] Perhaps the clearest sign of the continued strength of the bipartisan consensus behind NCLB was the joint statement by Boehner and Miller in response to Secretary Spellings's 2005 speech announcing new flexibility for states. They wrote that "the integrity of the law must be maintained . . . [while] every effort must be made to ensure smooth and effective implementation. . . . We firmly believe that the effort must be based on the law as it is written, not on a smorgasbord of different waivers for different states and districts."[73] Far from being prepared to abandon the NCLB accountability system, there appears to be strong support in Congress for applying it to Head Start and the Higher Education Act."[74]

Presidential politics and public opinion will also continue to play a major role in determining the direction of federal education policy, as they have for the past twenty years. Some observers of education politics have remarked that the major story of the 2004 presidential election was that education was not a major story. In fact, the major story was that in the first presidential election following the passage of the most intrusive and transformative national education law in forty years, there were remarkably few differences between the parties and candidates on NCLB and the federal role in schools. President Bush repeatedly pointed to NCLB during the 2004 campaign as his major domestic accomplishment and as evidence of his compassion for the plight of the poor and minorities. Far from backing away from the NCLB accountability framework, Bush announced that he would seek to extend it to high schools during his second term. The Republican Party platform declared that "with this success [of NCLB], Republicans have transformed the debate on education. We are the party parents can trust to improve schools and provide opportunity for all children. . . . We are the party willing to embrace new ideas and put them to the test. Americans agree that the status quo in education is no longer acceptable. We have challenged low expectations and poor achievement, and we are seeing results."

Bush's support for NCLB is widely credited—by Democrats and Republicans alike—with improving voters' views of the GOP's position on the education issue and with playing a major role in his election victories in 2000 and, to a lesser extent, 2004. Public opinion surveys indicate that voters continue to support presidential leadership on education. A 2004 PEN/*Education Week* poll found that nearly 60 percent of voters say they are more likely to vote for a presidential candidate with education as an administration centerpiece; crucial swing voters such as independents, voters under age thirty, and homemakers were found to be most likely to support pro-education candidates.[75] Another survey from 2004 revealed that the education gap between the parties continues to close: though 42 percent of respondents in 2004 believed that the Democratic Party was more interested than Republicans in improving education, the GOP has gained ground in each of the past two elections. When respondents were asked which of the presidential candidates they would support if they were voting solely on education issues, Kerry and Bush each drew the same level of support (41 percent).[76] These results are likely to confirm the sense in the GOP that embracing NCLB was a wise move politically as well as educationally and to strengthen the party's commitment to its effective implementation.

Both members of the Democratic ticket in 2004, Sens. John Kerry (D-MA) and John Edwards (D-NC), voted for NCLB and reiterated their support for the law's central principles during the general election.[77] Despite the strong opposition to NCLB from one of the party's most important constituencies, the NEA, Kerry did not call for repealing or substantially changing the law and did not even mention it by name in his acceptance speech at the Democratic convention.[78] On education, the Democratic Party platform only stated that "we will use testing to advance real learning, not undermine it, by developing high-quality assessments that measure the complex skills students need to develop. We will make sure that federal law operates with high standards and common sense, not just bureaucratic rigidity." Kerry called for "fully funding" NCLB and for greater spending on federal education policy through the creation of a $200 billion education trust fund. Kerry's decision to refrain from attacking NCLB—even during its rocky early implementation—is clear evidence that the particular educational and political dynamics that brought about the bipartisan passage of NCLB in 2002 remained in place in 2004.

Public opinion—which has played such an important role in driving the expansion of the federal role in education—appears to be somewhat conflicted about NCLB but continues to support a strong national presence in school reform. An oft-cited 2004 poll conducted by *Education Week* reported that as public awareness of NCLB was increasing, support for the law was decreasing.[79] Although the percentage of voters who said they favor the law remained fairly steady (dropping slightly from 40 percent to 36 percent from 2003 to 2004), the percentage of voters who said they oppose the law increased from 8 percent of voters in 2003 to 28 percent in 2004. However, despite claims that opposition to NCLB has been growing and is widespread, a closer analysis of public opinion data leads to a more complex—and ultimately more supportive—view of public opinion of NCLB and federal activism in education. A 2004 *Phi Delta Kappan* poll, for example, found that overall NCLB continues to be viewed more favorably than unfavorably (24 to 20 percent), and that the favorability ratio has remained roughly constant from 2003, when 18 percent viewed it favorably and 13 percent unfavorably. Those claiming a "great deal" or a "fair amount" of knowledge about the law also viewed it more favorably than unfavorably. A majority (51 percent) of respondents believe that NCLB will help to improve student achievement in public schools in their community "a great deal or a fair amount," while only 32 percent believe it will do so "not very much or not at all." Perhaps the most interesting and important finding from the polls was that 53 percent of respondents said that knowing that a candidate for national office supports NCLB would make them more likely to vote for that candidate, whereas only 25 percent said it would make them less likely to do so.[80]

Other 2004 polls have also reported that more respondents tend to favor NCLB than not. The Educational Testing Service found that respondents were evenly split, with 39 percent approving of it and 38 percent disapproving. A large majority, 74 percent, said that the quality of public schools was a concern, and only 14 percent of respondents felt that the public schools were performing well or pretty well.[81] A poll conducted by the National Education Association—one of NCLB's biggest opponents—found that 37 percent of respondents believe NCLB has had a positive impact on schools, whereas 21 percent believe it has had a negative impact.[82] A Center on Education Policy survey of education officials from forty-seven states, meanwhile, asked them to respond to what degree NCLB will improve student learning. Officials from nineteen states replied that the law will improve student learning "to a great extent," fourteen states said "somewhat," six states said "a little," two state officials said "not at all," and six did not know.[83] A series of focus groups conducted in Kansas City, Missouri, in 2003 concluded that "people are, indeed, concerned about education issues and generally support the kinds of standards, testing, and accountability provisions embodied in NCLB."[84]

What, then, do we make of public opinion on NCLB? When the results of these polls and focus groups are considered together, it appears that the public—and particularly the all-important swing voter—remains very concerned about the performance of American public schools and supports federal leadership in education reform, along with the focus on standards, testing, and accountability at the heart of NCLB. At the same time, however, the public's support for these broad ends and means belies reservations about the specific requirements and timetables mandated by the new federal law and continued support for local control of schools. As a result, the evolution of public opinion about NCLB will likely be determined by perceptions of how effectively and fairly the law is being implemented, and how successful states are in improving school performance.

As Chester Finn and Frederick Hess have noted, the political future of NCLB will also be heavily influenced by how future Democratic administrations and congressional leaders view the law's imperatives. "Only Democratic leaders," they write, "can convince educators and local officials that results-based accountability is a good thing and will not go away. Only liberal voices can ensure that NCLB is not understood as a conservative ploy to undermine public schooling but as a renewed national commitment to equality of opportunity."[85] As noted earlier, Democratic leaders such as Miller and Kennedy have been unwavering in their support of NCLB's core provisions. Support for educational improvement and accountability also remains a key goal of the centrist Democratic Leadership Council as well as many civil rights organizations.[86] In January 2004, the DLC declared that NCLB "is a good law that should be strengthened, not abandoned. . . . Democrats . . . have a special responsibility to force change in Washington, and at the state and local levels, to lift the measurable performance of schools. NCLB remains the best opportunity of this generation to do just that."[87] It is also significant to note that the *New York Times*—a bulwark of liberal elite opinion—recently declared that "with No Child Left Behind, the federal government has set exactly the right goals. It cannot backtrack because the early progress has been rocky. If Washington wavers and begins to cut deals with recalcitrant states like Utah, the effort to remake the country's public schools will fail."[88]

It is also important to note that while there has been pressure to weaken NCLB's mandates to states, a number of education experts and advocacy groups have called for strengthening and extending them. Several studies have identified large gaps between student scores on state and national assessments and argued that many states have set their proficiency levels too low. This has led conservatives such as Diane Ravitch and Chester Finn as well as liberal groups such as the Center for American Progress to call for the creation of national standards and tests that would be applied uniformly across the country.[89] Although there does not appear to be sufficient political support in Congress for such action at this point, these proposals demonstrate the extent to which the debate over the national role in schools has changed fundamentally.

Ultimately, as Timothy Conlan predicted in his classic work on federalism, principled arguments about states' rights have taken and will continue to take a backseat to the strategic political calculations and substantive policy goals of party leaders in determining the direction of federal education policy.[90] And as Paul Peterson has argued, Republicans no longer appear interested in defending federalism going forward: in education and elsewhere, he observed, "the party of local control has become the party of the federal mandate."[91] As a result, despite myriad implementation challenges and robust disagreements over the funding of the law, it seems unlikely that the federal role in education will ever recede to its pre-NCLB level. As former Department of Education official and Republican House Education Committee coordinator Vic Klatt observed,

> The development of a significant federal role in education is a function of the fact that the system is broken and many schools are failing, and this is clear to everyone. You can make the case that the public school system is so resistant to change that only outside pressure like that provided by federal government can force change and improvement. . . . NCLB is the precursor of even more federal involvement to come in education. Federal policymakers have finally decided that this is an area where they have to become involved, and I think you are going to see more and more federal involvement over time, not less. That will change the landscape of education policy.[92]

Democrats and Republicans alike are now publicly committed to active federal leadership in school reform and to holding states accountable for improved academic performance. What John Kincaid has called "coercive federalism" has finally come to education, and it appears to be here to stay.[93]

CONCLUSION

The passage of No Child Left Behind in 2002 fundamentally changed the ends and means of federal education policy from those put forward in the original ESEA legislation and, in so doing, created a new policy regime. The old federal education policy regime, created in 1965, was based on a policy paradigm that saw the central purpose of school reform as promoting equity and access for disadvantaged students, a policymaking arrangement that focused on procedural mandates, and a political alignment in which Republicans opposed federal activism and liberals sought to maintain the federal focus on resources and poor and minority students. The old regime was governed by a largely congressional and interest group–dominated policymaking process made possible by the issue's relatively low salience with the public. Interest groups—the unions and education providers on the left and social, religious, and states' rights conservatives on the right—largely determined the positions of the Democratic and Republican parties on education.

The policy paradigm at the heart of the NCLB regime is centered on the much broader goal of improving education for all students and seeks to do so by significantly reducing federal influence over process and inputs while replacing it with increased accountability for school performance.[94] The adoption of tough new federal timetables and accountability measures in NCLB was seen as essential to force states to comply with the standards and testing reforms introduced in 1994. The new federal focus on accountability, meanwhile, was only possible because of important shifts in the political alignment and policymaking arrangement.

The development of a more competitive national electoral environment and the rise of education to the top of the public agenda in the 1990s eventually led both parties to embrace a more proactive and reform-oriented federal role in improving schools. The convergence of the parties' positions on education was evident in the remarkable degree of bipartisan agreement and broad moderate leadership that characterized the legislative discussions over NCLB, when Democrats and Republicans agreed on substantially increased federal spending, enhanced flexibility and public choice, and the framework of a national accountability system that would have been unthinkable just a few years before. The shift away from the interest group–dominated policy monopoly in education was evidenced by the passage of NCLB with bipartisan support despite the opposition of important conservative groups such as Empower America, the Family Research Council, and Eagle Forum, as well as important liberal groups such as the NEA. Sen. Tom Carper (D-DE) remarked at the time that "even a couple of years ago, no president would have proposed, and no Congress would have passed, the accountability provisions that are part of this bill. What was considered progressive thinking a few years ago . . . has now become accepted."[95]

Public opinion and partisan electoral competition are crucial to understanding the passage of NCLB as well as its likely political future. It is important to acknowledge, however, that the kinds of political pressures that helped to bring about a more aggressive reform-oriented federal role in education could also ultimately undo it: public opinion can turn, and the broader political context can change. Nonetheless, education remains one of the most salient domestic policy issues on the local, state, and national political agendas, and the bipartisan political consensus on federal education policy has much deeper roots than is often assumed and appears to remain strong.

The implementation of NCLB has been difficult and contentious, but much of the media and scholarly coverage has overestimated the extent of the opposition to the new law and underestimated the source, strength, and stability of the political coalition that pushed for passage of NCLB and continues to support it. For much of U.S. history, deference to local control exerted a powerful restraining influence on the size and character of the federal role in education—but that time appears to have passed. Regardless of whether NCLB ultimately improves schools or student achievement, the law has created a new educational federalism in the United States. The U.S. Department of Education now functions as a national schoolmarm, hovering over state school reform efforts and whacking those states that fail to record satisfactory and timely progress toward federal education goals with financial penalties and mandatory corrective actions. Future debates about school reform—whether at the local, state, or national level—will have to adapt to a new politics of federal education policy that is fundamentally different from earlier eras and that has produced an unprecedented level of federal involvement in the country's schools.

10. Conclusion—Education, Swing Issues, and Contemporary American Politics

The passage of the No Child Left Behind (NCLB) Act in 2002 signaled the beginning of a new era of federal education policy and a significantly transformed and expanded national role in our country's schools. The unprecedented attention that has been devoted to the implementation of NCLB by parents, school administrators, the media, and politicians at all levels testifies to the transformative nature of the new law—both in terms of the ambitious scope of its goals and the aggressive federal role in prodding states and school districts to meet them. NCLB is fundamentally a response to the perceived failure of lower levels of government—despite considerable expenditures and reform activity—to improve student performance, particularly in the nation's urban schools and for its most disadvantaged students, since the release of *A Nation at Risk* in 1983. But NCLB and the new accountability regime enshrined in it would not have been possible without major changes in the politics of education that encouraged liberals and conservatives to abandon their longstanding opposition to an active reform-oriented federal role in education. The new federal focus on student achievement is seen by many reformers as an essential precondition to school improvement efforts nationwide and to the campaign for greater equity in educational opportunity.

Though the debate over the new federal role has centered on the efficacy of the specific policies contained in NCLB, the law's long-term success depends in equal measure on developments in the political realm, in particular on the sustainability of the new bipartisan consensus on standards and accountability. This is why it is crucial to understand how and why the politics of federal education policy and the federal role in schools have evolved over time. For decades in the United States, the prevailing thought was that schools should be protected from political influence and would be best served by placing decisions in the hands of educational experts. This may explain why the politics of education has received relatively little attention from scholars. Recently, however, studies by Timothy Hacsi, Mary Smith, and others have emphasized that politics—not empirical evidence on the effectiveness of particular programs—forms the basis for most education policy decisions.[1] The Civic Capacity and Urban Education project has concluded that school reform efforts in U.S. cities have largely failed not because of a lack of knowledge or material resources but because of insufficient attention to the importance of forming and sustaining pro-reform political coalitions over time.[2]

THE DEVELOPMENT OF A REFORM-ORIENTED
EDUCATION POLICY REGIME

As was detailed in Chapter 3, the modern federal role in education policy began with the passage of the Elementary and Secondary Education Act (ESEA) in 1965 as part of President Lyndon Johnson's Great Society. Because of the widespread sentiment at the time among citizens and policymakers that most schools were doing fine and that education was primarily a state and local responsibility, ESEA programs were framed as temporary measures designed to address an extraordinary crisis for a specific group of disadvantaged students. Both the ends and means of ESEA were clearly circumscribed; the national government would limit its efforts to improving educational equity by providing small categorical programs and supplemental funding for poor schools and children. Strong institutional and ideological obstacles to an expansion of the federal role in education persisted long after the passage of ESEA in 1965, and a bipartisan consensus of sorts developed around these limits on the federal role. Liberals fought to keep the federal role redistributive in nature and focused on disadvantaged students. In addition, because of their alliance with teachers unions and the belief that inadequate school resources were the primary problem facing schools, Democrats sought to keep the federal role centered on school inputs rather than on school outputs or governance issues. Conservatives, meanwhile, saw any increase in federal involvement as a threat to local control of schools and sought to minimize the intrusiveness of federal directives and enforcement efforts. Although they supported standards, testing, and accountability reforms, they believed that these should be established at the state rather than federal level. Public opposition to the school integration and busing that was mandated by federal courts in the 1950s and 1960s further fueled opposition to an expanded national role in schools.

A powerful network of interest groups rose up during the 1960s and 1970s to defend the original ESEA policy paradigm and advocate for the expansion of existing programs. These groups allied with powerful congressional committees and subcommittees to lock in the equity orientation of federal education policy and to defeat periodic reform efforts. Federal education policymaking during this early period was a largely closed process dominated by an iron triangle of congressional staffers, educational interest groups, and executive bureaucrats. School reform was not a salient issue in national elections during the 1960s and 1970s because the majority of voters saw public schools as doing a good job, and the major debates around schools centered on equity, integration, and social issues rather than concerns about academic performance.[3] This permitted the scope of conflict around education reform to be narrow and the issue to be dominated by a small group of political actors. Democrats used their control of Congress during most of the 1960s, 1970s, and 1980s to gradually expand existing federal education programs for the poor and to create small new targeted initiatives. Crucially, federal mandates and administrative capacity in education also increased as liberal Democrats sought to force recalcitrant state and local school officials to embrace congressional goals and methods. The story of the 1960s and 1970s for federal education policy, then, was one of expansion—but expansion within the context of a limited focus on ensuring procedural compliance with equity programs and integration mandates for a small group of disadvantaged students.

By 1980, however, the increasingly active and prescriptive federal presence in education—symbolized by the creation of a U.S. Department of Education by Democratic president Jimmy Carter in 1979—led to a backlash from conservatives. Republican president Ronald Reagan made tax cuts, devolution, and privatization the centerpieces of his administration. Social welfare programs generally, and federal education programs specifically, were attacked as being expensive, overly bureaucratic, and ineffective and were targeted for reduction or elimination. The release of the report *A Nation at Risk* in 1983 was a crucial focusing event as it fueled increasing public concern about the decline of public education and, in particular, its impact on the nation's economic competitiveness. Both Democrats and Republicans seized on the report to argue for major changes in federal education policies, but they advocated very different approaches. Democrats argued that the country's educational problems demanded greatly expanded federal funding and control over schools. Republicans argued that *A Nation at Risk* was an indictment of past federal programs and mandates and the public education system generally and called for eliminating federal influence and converting federal education funding into block grants or vouchers. An alternative reform vision, which called for national leadership and reforms centered on academic standards and assessments, also began to develop among many governors and business leaders. These developments altered the political dynamics of education and started the country on a road to major reform, albeit one that would have many significant twists and turns.

The continuing opposition of both liberals and conservatives—and key groups within Democratic and Republican Party coalitions—to a reform-oriented federal role in education persisted throughout the 1980s and into the 1990s. The Democratic position on education continued to be heavily influenced by teachers unions, which were strongly opposed to federal reforms such as rigorous standards, testing, choice, and accountability measures. The Republican Party in the 1980s and 1990s, meanwhile, was heavily influenced by religious conservatives and states' rights groups that opposed any federal influence over schools whatsoever. As a result, the federal role in education remained limited in important ways between 1965 and 1994, and even contracted in the 1980s as part of a broader assault on federal activism and the welfare state. During the 1980s, conservative proposals to abolish the Department of Education and to create private school choice programs were successfully resisted by a coalition of Democrats and moderate Republicans with support from the education establishment. Democratic proposals for a significantly enlarged federal role were also blocked by the Reagan administration's philosophical opposition and a squeeze on discretionary spending due to tax cuts and the defense buildup. Thus, the decade resulted in a stalemate as efforts to eliminate or significantly expand the federal role in education failed.

By the end of the 1980s, however, education was increasingly seen as essential to individual and national economic progress, the central tenants of the old equity policy paradigm had been discredited, and public pressure to improve schools had grown (see Figure 10.1). Moderate Republican George H. W. Bush made a pledge to be an "education president" a major theme of his 1988 election campaign and of his administration. Bush's efforts helped to nationalize the debate over education reform and to shift its focus from school inputs (funding) to outputs (achievement). His America 2000 education standards plan received the support of moderates but was ultimately defeated by an alliance of liberal Democrats who were still wedded to the old policy regime and conservative Republicans who opposed a more assertive federal role. The next president, Democrat Bill Clinton, played a decisive role in moving the standards and choice movements forward and in laying the ideational foundation for a new federal education policy regime. As a centrist New Democrat and former "education governor," Clinton rejected both conservative efforts to eliminate the federal role in education and the liberal emphasis on inputs over outputs. He embraced a greatly expanded federal role and increased investment for schools but also a shift toward promoting school reform and improved student academic performance through the imposition of standards and accountability measures. The first steps in this direction—despite strong resistance from conservatives and from liberals in Clinton's own party—were taken in 1994 with the passage of Goals 2000 and a number of important changes to ESEA. Alongside the existing federal commitment to equalizing educational opportunity for disadvantaged students, a much broader federal commitment to improving the quality of public education for all students began to unfold.

The expanded federal involvement in education precipitated another backlash, however, and Republicans used their newfound control of Congress in 1995 and 1996 to again push a conservative agenda of decentralization and privatization. A coalition of Democrats and moderate Republicans prevented these proposals—including one to abolish the Department of Education—from being enacted. It

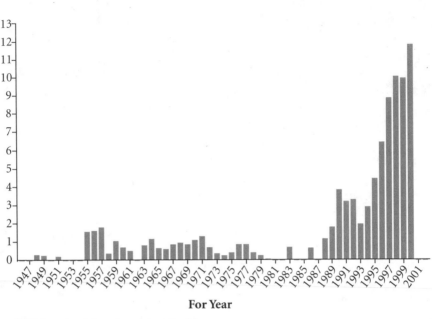

For Year

■ Education Most Important Problem

Figure 10.1. Gallup Surveys of Most Important Problem, 1947–2001

Source: Data Accessed for the Policy Agendas Project at www.policyagendas.org. The data were originally collected by Frank R. Baumgartner and Bryan D. Jones, with the support of National Science Foundation grant SBR 9320922 and were distributed through the Center for American Politics and Public Policy at the University of Washington and the Department of Political Science at Penn State University. Neither the NSF nor the original collectors of the data bear any responsibility for the analysis reported here.

ultimately became clear to many Republicans that these proposals were unpopular with voters and were contributing to a negative image of the party. This was reinforced by Bob Dole's defeat and Clinton's reelection in the 1996 presidential election. Education had by then risen to the top of the public agenda, and the issue was seen by strategists from both parties as central to Clinton's victory. As a result of these political and policy defeats, Republicans called off their assault on the federal role in education and used the remainder of the decade to reshape their message on school reform and social welfare policy. The debate between Democrats and Republicans at the turn of the century was no longer about whether there should be a federal role in education but what the nature of that role should be. The parties' competition to win the education issue resulted in dramatically increased federal spending on schools, a wide array of new federal programs, and a growing embrace of centrist accountability reforms.

Though Republicans and Democrats in Congress had softened their opposition to a new reform-oriented federal role in education by the late 1990s, it would take the election of a former Republican governor, George W. Bush, as president to consolidate a new policy regime. Whereas most earlier Republican presidential candidates had either ignored the issue of education or run in opposition to a federal role, Bush made education the number-one issue of his 2000 campaign and a crucial part of his "compassionate conservative" message. In an effort to close the gap on education and appeal to swing voters—for whom education was a key issue—Bush adopted a pragmatic and centrist education agenda that called for an active but reformed federal role in promoting school improvement. Bush was able to reposition the Republican Party on education and erase the historic Democratic advantage on the issue by citing his experience with education in Texas, by emphasizing specific solutions over ideology, and by painting presidential candidate Al Gore and the Democrats as captives of the teachers unions and unwilling to support meaningful reform. Once in office, Bush leveraged his success on the education issue to push recalcitrant conservatives and liberals to support the grand bargain contained in the No Child Left Behind Act—increased federal spending and activism on education in exchange for expanded flexibility, accountability, and choice.

The political and policy differences between the equity regime of 1965 and the accountability regime of 2002 are striking. The politics of education has been substantially nationalized as voters declared school reform to be one of their highest priorities and as national politicians responded by devoting significant attention and rhetoric to the issue on the campaign trail and while in office. The character of federal education policy has also changed, from a longstanding focus on increasing resources for disadvantaged students to a new much broader goal of improving the academic performance of all schools and students through the imposition of standards and accountability measures. NCLB federalizes education policymaking in the United States to a remarkable extent; though the federal share of total education funding remains relatively small, the broad direction of education reform is now set in Washington.

Some scholars have argued that NCLB merely represents an incremental extension of changes in federal education policy that were made in 1994 and that it is therefore more evolutionary than revolutionary. As noted earlier, Clinton's 1994 Improving America's Schools Act (IASA) did indeed represent an important ideational turning point for federal education policy, and much of the language in NCLB can be found in the earlier statute. But it would be a mistake to underestimate the revolutionary aspects of No Child Left Behind, for two reasons. First, although the existence of new ideas is a necessary condition for major policy change, ideas alone are not sufficient to create a new policy regime. Ideas must

be paired with political will and institutional capacity to be effectively implemented. It is certainly possible (and even likely) that the federal government will
ultimately relax the tough mandates and timetables contained in NCLB, but the
new law has already achieved considerably more compliance—and forced more
changes in schools and state educational policies—in three years than the 1994
reforms achieved in eight. Second, dramatic changes transpired in the positions
of the Democratic and Republican parties on education. In 1994 many Democrats
remained wedded to the idea that increased funding alone could bring about significant improvement in schools and close the achievement gap for disadvantaged
students. Most Republicans, meanwhile, remained adamantly opposed in 1994 to
federal activism in education. As a result, the IASA reforms introduced the idea
of accountability to federal education policy but did little to actually hold states
accountable; thus, their impact as change agents at the state and local levels was
relatively small. Between 1994 and 2002, however, most Democrats became convinced that achievement gaps would only be closed when federal policy held states
accountable for educational results and that continued opposition to meaningful
reform could lead to the loss of their longstanding political advantage on the education issue. Republicans, meanwhile, came to realize that opposition to federal
activism was exacting too high a political cost and that they should shift their efforts to using federal influence to make schools more effective and to give parents
more choice. The result of this evolution of the politics of education was the revolutionary transformation of federal education policy in NCLB. Though it is likely
that the law's specific provisions and timetables will be modified in the coming
years, the active federal role in schools and its focus on standards, testing, and accountability appear firmly entrenched in the American educational landscape.

POLICY REGIMES, POLICY CHANGE, AND CONTEMPORARY AMERICAN POLITICS

The creation of a new federal education policy regime and an expanded national
role in schools reflects and helps to explicate broader changes in American politics
at the end of the twentieth century and the beginning of the twenty-first. Two in-
terrelated developments have been crucial: the demise of the New Deal coalition
and the rise of a new era of partisan parity and electoral competition. The New
Deal coalition structured American political debate for more than thirty years but
began to unravel in the 1970s, throwing the American party system into a period
of reconstruction that continues to this day. During the 1980s, Republicans controlled the presidency and for a time the Senate on the basis of their foreign policy
leadership in the Cold War and their domestic platform of tax cuts and limited

government. The demise of the Soviet Union and an economic recession, however, shifted voters' attention in the early 1990s to economic and domestic policy issues, which were traditionally more advantageous for Democrats. Democrat Bill Clinton's victory in the 1992 election exposed the reality of an American electorate evenly divided in terms of partisan identification.

The dominant feature of the American political environment since the 1980s has been the attempt by both the Democratic and Republican parties to craft new public philosophies and new governing coalitions that could secure sufficient electoral support to provide a stable governing majority.[4] Margaret Weir has observed that "the sharp ideological polarization of political elites in the 1990s meant that politics was no longer simply a contest to enact or reform individual policies but a more fundamental struggle over public philosophies."[5] The 1980s and 1990s witnessed an extended public debate between the Republican and Democratic parties over the proper role of the national government in promoting opportunity and providing social welfare.

The Reagan era left an important legacy by discrediting many of the policies of the New Deal and welfare state liberalism generally. Clinton won the 1992 election by campaigning as a New Democrat and proposing a "third way" between liberalism and conservatism. But conservatives rode opposition to some of the Democrats' big government proposals (such as nationalizing health care) to congressional majorities in the 1994 midterm election. This success led Dole and many other Republicans to run on conservative policy positions in the 1996 elections. Clinton's easy reelection in 1996 was widely viewed as the victory of centrist rhetoric and pragmatic policy proposals over ideological extremism. Republicans responded by moderating some of their positions on salient issues in the late 1990s, and George W. Bush made his claim to be a compassionate conservative the centerpiece of his successful 2000 presidential campaign. This book has described how education not only was influenced in important ways by this broader ideological debate but also came to play a pivotal role in it. Democrats largely won the debate over federal activism in education, but Republicans emerged victorious on the character that the activism would take. The dominant paradigm of educational policymaking in the contemporary era is not completely liberal or conservative, progovernment or promarket, but instead a unique amalgamation that embraces federal government activism founded on market principles of standards, accountability, choice, and competition.

The case of education thus demonstrates that the combination of partisan parity and ideological reconstruction has transformed American politics and policymaking in important ways. It has produced what Marc Landy and Martin Levin have called "a new politics of public policy" that is centered on issues and more open to public pressures.[6] In particular, the political environment since the

1980s has encouraged national politicians to emphasize ideas and symbols in their rhetoric and to make more frequent public appeals for political support; this is especially true for presidents and presidential candidates.[7] As Martha Derthick and Paul Quirk have noted, "The decisive features of the political system [are], above all, leadership that is responsive to broad audiences; widespread competition for leadership, both within Congress and between Congress and other institutions; and extreme receptivity by leaders and other officials, including rank-and-file members of Congress, to the materials of policy advocacy; that is, argument, symbols, and ideas."[8] In contemporary times, the process of campaigning for public support is no longer confined to occasional election contests but is now a never-ending process, a "permanent campaign."[9]

The competitive national electoral context has also forced both Republicans and Democrats to appeal to centrist swing voters. Parity in partisan identification—combined with the large number of independents and weak identifiers who tend to be moderate in their political views—means that national elections in the contemporary era are typically won in the middle with moderate voters. This is why Landy and Levin argue that both parties and their candidates have been focused on "seeking the center" of the ideological spectrum in their campaigns and policymaking.[10] Presidents Bill Clinton and George W. Bush, for example, operated under the same macropolitical reality—an era of partisan parity and divided government in which no political philosophy or governing coalition has been dominant. In such an environment, presidents have strong incentives to establish a moderate image by forging bipartisan solutions to high-profile policy issues. As Jeffrey Cohen has concluded, "in this media-saturated age, there are powerful pressures for presidents to follow public opinion."[11]

Presidential candidates from both parties struggle to craft winning coalitions by attracting moderate voters without alienating established constituencies. One of the primary ways they accomplish this is by strategically repositioning their broad rhetoric about the role of government in society and their specific positions on salient policy issues. This is approached in both an offensive and a defensive manner, as politicians seek to capitalize on the resonance of their popular policy positions with the electorate and to inoculate themselves from the potential electoral damage of their party's unpopular issue positions. But party leaders who attempt to modify policy positions or rhetoric that is unpopular with the general public will often encounter opposition from party constituencies wedded to the status quo.[12] As a result, the story of partisan politics and policymaking is as much a story of intraparty struggles as it is a story of interparty struggles—in fact, the two struggles occur simultaneously.[13]

Given the power of the bully pulpit and presidents' desire to appear innovative and moderate to swing voters, presidents often become the key players in driving policy change and in bringing about the destruction and reconstruction of policy regimes. National politicians have seized on education in recent years because of its importance to citizens, its powerful resonance with deeply held American values, and its relationship to a wide variety of other economic and social issues. In their study of the politics of urban school reform, Clarence Stone, Jeffrey Henig, Bryan Jones, and Carol Pierannunzi describe education as a "high-reverberation" policy system—one "characterized by frequent reshuffling of mobilized stakeholders, multiple and strongly-felt competing value and belief systems, deeply held stakes by both educators and parents, and ambiguous boundaries."[14] Education has long been a dominant issue in state and local politics, and when *Brown v. Board of Education* and later *A Nation at Risk* provided the impetus for expanded federal involvement, the education issue came to reverberate loudly at the national level as well.

Beginning with George H. W. Bush in 1988 and continuing with Clinton and George W. Bush, presidents seized on new concerns about educational quality and staked out popular centrist positions that went against the views of many in their own parties. This was a conscious strategy in two ways: it was designed to reap political gain on a salient issue with voters, and it was presented as a symbol of the candidates' general independence and pragmatism. This "triangulation" (in Dick Morris's famous formulation) was also used to demonstrate the presidential candidates' centrism by contrasting their positions on education with the more ideological views of the congressional wing of their parties. Education reform thus helped Clinton's effort to be seen as a New Democrat and the younger Bush's efforts to craft a compassionate conservative image and enabled both men to attract the moderate swing voters that have become crucial to winning presidential elections.[15] In the end, the elder Bush was unable to persuade his party to follow his lead on education, but Clinton and George W. Bush were able to do so and succeeded in passing important school reform legislation that dramatically increased federal involvement in education.

It is important to note that the contemporary political climate encourages policy change and responsiveness only on certain kinds of issues. The majority of policy issues under consideration in the political system at any particular point in time are low-visibility and low-salience issues on which there is little public interest or pressure for reform. A few issues, however, achieve high visibility and high salience with the public and take on wider political significance. These "swing issues" are policy issues that are given top priority by swing voters and have the power to swing elections in an era of partisan parity and narrow electoral margins. They have become central to the electoral and governing strategies of politicians and parties, with several important consequences for policymaking. In an effort to appeal to swing voters on these issues, politicians and parties will often adopt popular moderate positions even if they conflict with longstanding ideological convictions or the preferences of allied interest groups. This political maneuvering forces both parties to the center and can generate compromises on salient issues over which there may have long been great conflict. Through this "strategic centrism" politicians may thus be able to come across as responsive or centrist generally when in fact they are only being responsive (or centrist) on a few selected issues. This may result in responsiveness on only a limited number of issues, but these will tend to be the issues of greatest importance to the public. As a result, though iron triangles or subgovernments may dominate policymaking for most issues, at times policymaking becomes more public and contested, and periods of extensive nonincremental change are possible, often in ways that bring important policies more in line with public opinion.[16]

Public policy scholars have long emphasized that policy subsystems are highly durable and that major policy change is, as a result, extremely difficult and rare. Earlier policy case studies from the 1970s and 1980s—such as those by Martha Derthick, Gary Mucciaroni, and Richard Harris and Sidney Milkis, for example—emphasized the closed nature of the political and policymaking environment and the ability of powerful interest groups to block reform and preserve the status quo. The policy struggles described in their works were dominated by "inside" actors—bureaucrats, interest groups, and members of Congress and their staff. These were not public debates—in part because of the closed nature of the policymaking process at the time and in part because the issues in question were not particularly salient with citizens.[17] The case of federal education policy is entirely different because the debate over how to reform schools became a central issue in partisan debates and political campaigns during the 1990s. The closed policymaking process that existed before the 1990s thus has given way to a new, more open policymaking regime. Developments in American politics and institutions—particularly the existence of partisan parity and intense political competition for swing voters—have elevated the importance of public opinion and electoral pressures to the rise and fall of policy regimes.

To argue that policymakers respond to public priorities and demands at first brush does not seem like a particularly controversial statement. Yet as noted in Chapter 2, the political science literature on policymaking is, in fact, quite divided on the question of the degree to which politicians are responsive to public opinion.[18] There is a sizable body of research that argues that policymakers tend to be influenced more by narrow constituent groups than by the demands of the mass public.[19] The evolution of federal education policy provides a case study of how politicians and parties struggle to negotiate the tension between public and private demands. It sheds light on the conditions under which policymaking can be transformed from a closed interest-group model to a more open mass politics model—when the focus of party leaders shifts from satisfying narrow interest-group demands to appealing for broad electoral support.

The development of an expansive, active, and reform-oriented federal role in education can only be understood in light of the shattering of the old interest-group–dominated policymaking regime. Studies of federal policymaking in education have emphasized the importance—even the dominance—of particular interest groups within each party. On the Democratic side, the teachers unions—which are the largest single source of campaign contributions to the party—wield enormous influence. The NEA (the largest union) has adamantly opposed school choice and national testing and accountability measures. On the Republican side, religious and states' rights conservatives are a crucial part of the party's primary and donor base. They have vociferously opposed increased federal spending or control in education and have fought for the elimination of the federal Department of Education.

The equity regime created in 1965 was marked by its closed and consensual nature—federal education policymaking was dominated by a few groups, with little public input, and bipartisan support for the limited ends and means of federal policy. As a result, efforts to substantially expand or reform the federal role during the 1960s, 1970s, and 1980s were defeated. In the late 1980s and 1990s, however, mounting evidence of problems in the public school system and the strategic use of the issue by both parties for electoral gain combined to expand the scope of conflict around education. Public pressure began to grow for increased federal involvement and for a shift to more rigorous reforms, many of which were opposed by important interest groups committed to the previous policy regime. As citizens and politicians alike pushed for federal fixes for what was perceived as a broken school system, the antifederal reform views of powerful interest groups on the left and right were gradually pushed aside. Education became a top public priority, and politicians became more interested in how the issue would help (or harm) them with voters than they were in satisfying the demands of their allied interest groups.

The case of education demonstrates that the ability of an interest group to influence policy outcomes is not determined by its power alone—indeed, the NEA and the religious right were at the peak of their power and influence within the Democratic and Republican parties, respectively, when they "lost" on education reform. Rather, the application of interest-group power is crucially contextual. The ability of a group to affect policy outcomes is dependent on four factors: the salience and visibility of the particular issue with the public (and thus its wider political significance), the extent to which the interest group's views on the issue are considered mainstream or extreme, its ability to prevent the entrance of new groups and perspectives, and the centrality of the issue in the campaign and governing agendas of the parties. In the case of education, interest groups (such as the NEA and conservative religious groups) were able to exert a strong influence on policy for many years when the issue had low public visibility and salience and when it played only a minor role in national politics and elections. In the 1990s, however, Democrats and later Republicans began to shift their positions on education in response to increasing public pressure for reform-oriented national leadership despite its unpopularity with major interest groups within each party.[20]

It is important to note that public opinion did not determine the specific content of federal education policy; as various scholars have shown, citizens have relatively low levels of information about school reform issues and often hold conflicting positions.[21] But public preferences were clear and strong on a number of important points and set the broad parameters within which deliberations about school reform at the national level took place. Polls taken in the 1990s demonstrated that clear majorities of citizens supported public school choice but opposed private school vouchers; supported increased federal spending on schools but believed that more money alone would not solve schools' problems; wanted expanded federal leadership in education reform but supported local control of schools; and believed that more rigorous standards, testing, and accountability measures were necessary to improve student and school performance.[22] Politicians were forced to respond to these public preferences even as they sought to reshape them. As a result, Democrats in the 1990s, led by Clinton, and Republicans in 2000, led by George W. Bush, ultimately embraced positions on education that went against the preferences of strong constituent groups within their parties. Democrats came to support national standards and accountability and some choice, and Republicans pushed through legislation expanding the federal role in education to an unprecedented degree. In each case, party leaders opted to go against powerful but narrow constituent groups in the pursuit of political gain among the broader electorate. A key consequence of these maneuvers was the nationalization of education policy.

Throughout this book I have demonstrated how a historically based policy regimes model can illuminate the evolution of specific policy areas and account for periods of dynamic change amidst long periods of policy stasis. In studying policy change, it is necessary to place political and policymaking developments in their broader historical context, to create, in Paul Pierson's phrase, a "moving picture."[23] Doing so emphasizes both how earlier decisions and events influence and constrain later policy development and how such constraints can sometimes be overcome when features of the political and policymaking environment change. Political scientists have tended to look at federal education policy only in narrow terms, by focusing on individual events, actors, or policies. Historical analyses have enlarged the scope of inquiry but have failed to offer explanations for how and why broader political forces interacted to produce policy development. Early historical interpretations of federal education policy thus tended to emphasize the fundamental limits on the national government's role, and later accounts have tended to portray the expanded federal role as inevitable. Previous accounts of federal education policy by historians and political scientists have also failed to account for conflicts and pressures that could have pushed the federal role in different directions and that contributed to the particular shape federal policy ultimately took.

The case study of federal education policy presented here offers an alternative interpretation of major policy change. Rather than fitting the punctuated equilibrium model (see Chapter 1) of a longstanding policy monopoly that is rapidly punctured and replaced in a single decisive stroke, federal education policy demonstrates how the *gradual* shifting of ideas, interests, and institutions in a policy area and their interaction with changes in the broader political context over time ultimately brings about major reform. The No Child Left Behind Act of 2002 is best understood as a response to shifts in the policy regime and the broader political milieu that played out over a three-decade period. The history of federal education policymaking is thus best characterized not as one of intermittent punctuated equilibria amidst long periods of policy stasis, but rather of gradual regime construction, maintenance, enervation, and reconstruction that unfolded in fits and starts over time.

The theory of path dependence in political science, along with the older disciplinary emphasis on the power of interest groups and the apathy and ignorance of citizens, emphasizes the static nature of politics and policymaking. These approaches—and their implication of policy stasis and unresponsiveness—may indeed be accurate for the majority of policy issues, but the case of education presented here paints a very different picture. The ends and means of national school policy have changed dramatically since 1965 in ways that were opposed by many key interest groups and that violate the general predictions of much of the policymaking literature. In marked contrast to the earlier pluralist mode of decision-making in which crucial policy debates occurred behind closed doors between unelected administrative officials and interest-group representatives, debates over the federal role in education involved sustained and highly visible public appeals.

The evolution of federal education policy thus offers some encouragement for those who long for greater public deliberation and influence over the policymaking process. The political science literature is replete with studies that cast doubt on the accuracy of public opinion polls as true measures of citizens' views. Scholars of political behavior have emphasized that the conditions for issue voting do not exist—voters have been found to possess relatively little detailed information about policy issues, to pay little attention to electoral campaigns, and to vote largely on partisan labels and candidate characteristics rather than specific issue positions. Taken together, these lines of research have cast considerable doubt over whether public preferences receive serious consideration in the policymaking process and whether it is even rational for politicians to weigh them heavily. The interviews conducted for this book, however, revealed that politicians and political strategists place tremendous importance on public opinion and monitor polls closely, and that prospective and retrospective issue evaluations by voters weigh heavily in the formulation of party and candidate issue positions and policy agendas. In the case of education, this enabled the public to exert extensive influence over the broad direction of national school reform efforts.

It is too early to know whether the new accountability regime at the heart of federal education policy will ensure that no child is left behind in the United States. Regardless of whether NCLB ultimately improves schools or student achievement, the law will have—and is already having—a massive impact on the direction of education policy at every level in this country. The debate over reforming federal education policy has also had a major, if underappreciated, impact on American politics more generally. Swing issues such as education are thus an important political phenomenon—their unique characteristics facilitate major policy change even as they influence the outcome of wider ideological debates and electoral conflicts.

Appendix: Interviews Conducted for This Study

Lesley Arsht, president, Standards Work; former counselor to U.S. Secretary of Education Lamar Alexander and director of communications at the Department of Education; former deputy press secretary to President Reagan. January 16, 2003, Washington, DC.

Julian Bond, president, National Association for the Advancement of Colored People. March 29, 2001, Charlottesville, VA.

Alice Johnson Cain, senior professional staff member, Committee on Education and the Workforce, U.S. House of Representatives. Telephone interview, May 13, 2005.

Kathy Christie, vice president for Knowledge Management and Clearinghouse, Education Commission of the States; previously worked on education issues for the National Conference of State Legislatures. Telephone interview, March 18, 2005.

Michael Cohen, director, Achieve; former assistant secretary of education in the Clinton administration. August 27–28, 2004, Charlottesville, VA.

Jay Diskey, president, Diskey and Associates, an education public relations consulting firm; former director of communications for the Committee on Education and the Workforce, U.S. House of Representatives, 1996–1999; former special assistant to the U.S. secretary of education for communications in George H. W. Bush's administration. May 5, 2003, Washington, DC.

Chester Finn, president, Thomas B. Fordham Foundation; former assistant secretary for research and improvement and counselor to the secretary of the U.S. Department of Education in the Reagan and George H. W. Bush administrations. January 7, 2003, Washington, DC.

Jason Foster, policy director, Republican Main Street Partnership. March 11, 2003, Washington, DC.

Bill Galston, professor of political science, University of Maryland; former deputy assistant for domestic policy in the Clinton administration and former campaign adviser to Al Gore. Telephone interview, March 18, 2003.

Siobhan Gorman, education reporter, *National Journal*. January 29, 2003, Washington, DC.

Jack Jennings, director, Center on Education Policy; former subcommittee staff director and general counsel to the Committee on Education and Labor, U.S. House of Representatives. January 15, 2003, Washington, DC.

Krista Kafer, senior policy analyst for education, Heritage Foundation; former legislative director for U.S. Rep. David McIntosh (R-IN) and legislative assistant for Rep. Bob Schaffer (R-CO). January 29, 2003, Washington, DC.

Edward Kealy, executive director, Committee for Education Funding; former director of federal programs, National School Boards Association. Telephone interview, March 26, 2003.

Nancy Keenan, education policy director, People for the American Way; former state school superintendent for Montana. January 26, 2003, Washington, DC.

Victor Klatt, vice president, Van Scoyoc Associates; former education and human capital policy coordinator, the Committee on Education and the Workforce, U.S. House of Representatives; former deputy assistant secretary for Congressional Affairs at the U.S. Department of Education during the George H. W. Bush administration. March 10, 2003, Washington, DC.

Charles Kolb, president, Committee for Economic Development; former deputy assistant to President George H. W. Bush for domestic policy; also held positions in the U.S. Department of Education and the Office of Management and Budget during the Reagan administration. January 15, 2003, Washington, DC.

Sandy Kress, senior education policy adviser to President George W. Bush and chief administration negotiator for No Child Left Behind; member, Education Commission of the States. Telephone interview, May 23, 2003.

Bruno Manno, senior program associate, Annie E. Casey Foundation; former assistant secretary of education and director of the Office of Educational Research and Innovation and America 2000 task force during the George H. W. Bush administration. January 16, 2003, Washington, DC.

Jennifer Marshall, education policy analyst and government relations liaison, Empower America; former education policy analyst and director of family studies at the Family Research Council. Telephone interview, March 26, 2003.

Will Marshall, president, Progressive Policy Institute; former policy director, Democratic Leadership Council. Telephone interview, March 26, 2003.

Carmel Martin, education adviser to Sen. Edward Kennedy (D-MA) and Democratic professional staff member, Education Committee, U.S. Senate; former associate director for domestic policy, Center for American Progress; former education policy adviser to Senator Jeff Bingaman (D-NM). Telephone interview, May 5, 2005.

Alex Nock, Democratic professional staff member, the Committee on Education and the Workforce, U.S. House of Representatives. Telephone interview, May 6, 2005.

Paul O'Neill, former treasury secretary under George W. Bush; chair of George H. W. Bush's Presidential Advisory Commission on Education (PEPAC); former CEO of ALCOA. Telephone interview, March 20, 2003.

Joel Packer, lobbyist, National Education Association. March 3, 2003, Washington, DC.

Nina Shokraii Rees, deputy undersecretary for innovation and improvement, U.S. Department of Education, George W. Bush administration; former education adviser to Vice President Dick Cheney; former education adviser to George W. Bush campaign; former chief education analyst for the Heritage Foundation. Telephone interview, May 22, 2003.

Diane Stark Renter, deputy director, Center on Education Policy; former legislative associate for the Committee on Education and Labor, U.S. House of Representatives, 1988–1994. January 16, 2003, Washington, DC.

Richard Riley, former secretary of education during the Clinton administration; former governor of South Carolina. August 27–28, 2004, Charlottesville, VA.

Andrew Rotherham, director, Twenty-first Century Schools Project, Progressive Policy Institute; former special assistant to President Clinton for education and domestic policy. August 22, 2002, Washington, DC.

Marshall Smith, education program director, Hewlett Foundation; former acting deputy secretary of the U.S. Department of Education during the Clinton administration; former professor of education and dean of the Graduate School of Education at Stanford University; former chief of staff to the first secretary of education in the Carter administration and adviser to the National Education Goals panel and the National Council of Education Standards and Testing. Telephone interview, March 23, 2003.

Patricia Sullivan, director of federal-state relations, Council of Chief State School Officers; former lobbyist and director of Education Policy for the National Governors' Association; former staff member for Achieve Inc. and the Committee on Education and Labor, U.S. House of Representatives. Telephone interview, March 27, 2003.

Bob Sweet, senior Republican staff member, the Committee on Education and the Workforce, U.S. House of Representatives. Telephone interview, April 30, 2003.

William Taylor, executive director, Citizens' Commission on Civil Rights; former staff director, U.S. Commission on Civil Rights. Telephone interview, May 22, 2003.

Susan Traiman, director, Education Initiative, Business Roundtable; former staffer at the National Governors' Association and the National Commission on Excellence in Education. January 19, 2003, Washington, DC.

Kristina Twitty, education policy analyst, Eagle Forum. Telephone interview, March 7, 2003.

Paul Weinstein, senior fellow, Progressive Policy Institute; former senior adviser for policy planning and coordination for Vice President Al Gore; chief of staff of the Clinton Domestic Policy Council; special assistant for domestic policy during the Clinton administration. March 10, 2003, Washington, DC.

Amy Wilkins, executive director, the Trust for Early Education; former director of the Education Trust's Policy, Governmental Affairs, Research, and Communications Office; former staffer at the Children's Defense Fund; former staffer at the Democratic National Committee and the White House Office of Media Affairs. Telephone interview, March 13, 2003.

David Winston, president, the Winston Group, a polling and consulting firm that advises the Republican Party; former director of planning for Speaker of the House Newt Gingrich; analyst for Voter News Service; polling editor for PollTrack on PoliticsNow; chief information officer for Republican National Committee; former staffer at Heritage Foundation. Telephone interview, May 9, 2003.

Joan Wodiska, director, Education, Early Childhood, and Workforce Committee, National Governors Association. Telephone interview, May 19, 2005.

Christine Wolfe, chief of staff, Office of the Under Secretary, U.S. Department of Education, George W. Bush administration; former education staffer at Heritage Foundation and on the Committee on Education and Labor, U.S. House of Representatives. Telephone interview, May 5, 2003.

NOTES

CHAPTER ONE: INTRODUCTION

1. Mary McGuire, "Are Political Scientists Ignoring Education Policy at Their Own Risk?" Paper presented at the Midwest Political Science Association Meeting, April 2004, 1.

2. Jennifer Hochschild, "Three Puzzles in Search of an Answer from Political Scientists," *Political Science and Politics* 37 (2004): 225–229.

3. David Clark and Terry Astuto, "The Disjunction of Federal Educational Policy and National Educational Needs in the 1990s," in Douglas Mitchell and Margaret Goertz, eds., *Education Politics for the New Century* (London: Falmer Press, 1990), 11.

4. John Jennings, *Why National Standards and Tests? Politics and the Quest for Better Schools* (Thousand Oaks, CA: Sage, 1998), viii.

5. Frederick Wirt and Michael Kirst, *The Political Dynamics of American Education* (Berkeley, CA: McCutchan Publishing, 1997), 260.

6. From a survey of research on the politics of education, for example, Stroufe concluded that it has been concerned predominantly with policy analysis rather than political analysis and that there has been inadequate focus on the influence of political structures and processes on policymaking. He concluded that "while it is clearly a moral responsibility to pay attention to policy concerns at any point in time, it is equally imperative for scholars to explain why such policies exist and under what circumstances they might be changed. Such analysis cannot be accomplished apart from considerations of the political system." Gerald Stroufe, "Politics of Education at the Federal Level," in Jay Scribner and Donald Layton, eds., *The Study of Educational Politics* (London: Falmer Press, 1995), 79.

7. See, for example, David Broder, "Long Road to Reform: Negotiators Forge Education Legislation," *Washington Post*, December 7, 2001, A1.

8. Lorraine McDonnell, "No Child Left Behind and the Federal Role in Education: Evolution or Revolution?" *Peabody Journal of Education* 80, 2 (2005): 21. See also K. A. McDermott and E. H. DeBray, "Accidental Revolution: State Policy Influences on the No Child Left Behind Act," in L. D. Fusarelli, B. C. Fusarelli, and B. S. Cooper, eds., *The Rising State: How State Power Is Transforming Our Nation's Schools* (Albany: State University of New York Press, forthcoming).

9. See Paul Manna, "Federalism, Agenda Setting, and the Dynamics of Federal Education Policy" (Ph.D. dissertation, University of Wisconsin, 2003).

10. Education Commission of the States, *ECS Report to the Nation: State Implementation of the No Child Left Behind Act* (Denver: ECS, July 2004), iv.

11. Michael Mintrom and Sandra Vergari, "Education Reform and Accountability Issues in an Intergovernmental Context," *Publius: The Journal of Federalism* 27 (Spring 1997): 14.

12. Timothy Conlan, *From New Federalism to Devolution: Twenty-Five Years of Intergovernmental Reform* (Washington, DC: Brookings Institution Press, 1998), 313.

13. Ibid., 303.

14. Wirt and Kirst, *The Political Dynamics of American Education*, 342.

CHAPTER TWO: THE POLITICS OF POLICY REGIMES

1. Louis Hartz, *The Liberal Tradition in America* (New York: Harcourt, 1985); Seymour Martin Lipset, *American Exceptionalism* (New York: W. W. Norton, 1997).

2. Suzanne Mettler, *Dividing Citizens* (Ithaca, NY: Cornell University Press, 1998); Jill Quadagno, *The Color of Welfare* (Oxford: Oxford University Press, 1994).

3. Anthony Downs, *Inside Bureaucracy* (Boston: Little, Brown, 1967); James Q. Wilson, *Bureaucracy* (New York: Basic Books, 1989); Terry Moe, "The Politics of Bureaucratic Structure," in *Can the Government Govern?* (Washington, DC: Brookings Institution Press, 1989).

4.. The power of interest groups in policy formation has been emphasized in Ralph Miliband, *State in Capitalist Society: An Analysis of the Western System of Power* (New York: Basic Books, 1969); David Truman, *The Governmental Process: Political Interests and Public Opinion* (New York: Greenwood, 1971); Morris Fiorina, *Congress: Keystone of the Washington Establishment* (New Haven, CT: Yale University Press, 1989); Jeffrey Berry, *The Interest Group Society* (New York: Longman, 1989); Paul Sabatier and Hank Jenkins-Smith, eds., *Policy Change and Learning: An Advocacy Coalition Approach* (Boulder, CO: Westview Press, 1993); and Thomas Dye, *Top Down Policymaking* (New York: Chatham House, 2001).

5. C. Wright Mills, *The Power Elite* (Oxford: Oxford University Press, 1956); E. E. Schattschneider, *The Semi-Sovereign People* (New York: Wadsworth, 1975); Theodore Lowi, *The End of Liberalism* (New York: W. W. Norton, 1979).

6. Lawrence Jacobs and Robert Shapiro, *Politicians Don't Pander: Political Manipulation and the Loss of Democratic Responsiveness* (Chicago: University of Chicago Press, 2000).

7. Frank Baumgartner and Bryan Jones, *Agendas and Instability in American Politics* (Chicago: University of Chicago Press, 1993).

8. Deborah Stone, *Policy Paradox and Political Reason* (New York: HarperCollins, 1988).

9. John Kingdon, *America the Unusual* (New York: St. Martin's Press, 1999); *Agendas, Alternatives, and Public Policies,* 2d ed. (New York: HarperCollins, 1995).

10. Schattschneider, *The Semi-Sovereign People,* 34–35.

11. Paul Pierson, "When Effect Becomes Cause: Policy Feedback and Political Change," *World Politics* 45, 4 (July 1993): 595–628; Douglas North, *Institutions, Institutional Change, and Economic Performance* (Cambridge: Cambridge University Press, 1994); Jacob Hacker, *The Divided Welfare State* (Cambridge: Cambridge University Press, 2002).

12. Paul Pierson, *Politics in Time: History, Institutions, and Social Analysis* (Princeton, NJ: Princeton University Press, 2004), 54–55.

13. Charles Lindblom, "The Science of Muddling Through," *Public Administration Review* 19 (1960): 79–88; Aaron Wildavsky, *The Politics of the Budgetary Process* (Boston: Little, Brown, 1984); Michael Hayes, *The Limits of Policy Change* (Washington, DC: Georgetown University Press, 2001).

14. Martha Derthick, *Policymaking for Social Security* (Washington, DC: Brookings Institution Press, 1979), 413.

15. Pierson, *Politics in Time,* 66–67.

16. David Mayhew, *Congress: The Electoral Connection* (New Haven, CT: Yale University Press, 1974). See also Anthony King, "Running Scared," *Atlantic Monthly,* January 1997, www.theatlantic.com. King writes that "the American electoral system places politicians in a highly vulnerable position. Individually and collectively, they are more vulnerable, more of the time, to the vicissitudes of electoral politics than are the politicians of any other democratic country. Because they

are more vulnerable, they devote more of their time to electioneering, and their conduct in office is more governed by electoral considerations."

17. James Stimson, Michael MacKuen, and Robert Erikson, "Dynamic Representation," *American Political Science Review* 89 (September 1995): 545, 559.

18. Schattschneider, *The Semi-Sovereign People*, 18. He also wrote that "the role of the people in the political system is determined largely by the conflict system, for it is conflict that involves the people in politics and the nature of conflict determines the nature of public involvement" (126).

19. Anthony Downs, "Up and Down with Ecology—The Issue Attention Cycle," *Public Interest* 28 (1972): 28–50.

20. Anthony Downs, *An Economic Theory of Democracy* (New York: Harper and Brothers, 1957); William Riker, *The Art of Political Manipulation* (New Haven, CT: Yale University Press, 1986).

21. Michael Mintrom, *Policy Entrepreneurs and School Choice* (Washington, DC: Georgetown University Press, 2000).

22. Derthick has shown, for example, that as problems within the social security program grew larger and more visible, political and economic developments encouraged elites inside and outside of government to reconsider the core assumptions and structure of the program. The result was that "a greater variety of participants [became] involved, long established doctrines have been challenged, and longstanding procedures revised. The policymaking system and the program are both changing and, as always, interacting with each other as well as the society to determine the nature of social security politics. During much of the history of social security they interacted in a way that dampened contention. In the later 1970s, they are interacting in a way that will admit more of it." *Policymaking for Social Security*, 428.

23. Kingdon, *Agendas, Alternatives, and Public Policies*.

24. W. Russell Neuman, "The Threshold of Public Attention," *Public Opinion Quarterly* 54, 2 (Summer 1990): 174.

25. Marc Landy and Martin Levin, eds., *The New Politics of Public Policy* (Baltimore: Johns Hopkins University Press, 1995).

26. See Heclo, in Lawrence C. Dodd and Calvin Jillson, eds., *The Dynamics of American Politics: Approaches and Interpretations* (Boulder, CO: Westview Press, 1994), 383. For Heclo, "the 'action' is at the intersection, where the influence among the three elements is reciprocal." Ultimately, "interests tell institutions what to do; institutions tell ideas how to survive; ideas tell interests what to mean."

27. Frank Baumgartner and Bryan Jones, *Agendas and Instability in American Politics* (Chicago: University of Chicago Press, 1993); Frank Baumgartner and Bryan Jones, eds., *Policy Dynamics* (Chicago: University of Chicago Press, 2002).

28. Baumgartner and Jones, *Policy Dynamics*, 297.

29. See especially two articles in the *Journal of Policy History* by Julian Zelizer ("Clio's Lost Tribe: Public Policy History since 1978" in 2000 and "History and Political Science: Together Again?" in 2004) and articles by Skowronek, John Gerring, and Richard Bensel in the spring 2003 issue (vol. 17) of *American Political Development*.

30. Pierson, *Politics in Time*, 1–2.

31. This discussion is indebted to Carter Wilson's recent article "Policy Regimes and Policy Change," *Journal of Public Policy* 20, 3 (2000): 247–274.

32. Richard Harris and Sidney Milkis, *The Politics of Regulatory Change* (New York: Oxford University Press, 1988).

33. Ibid., 48.

34. Ibid., 279.

35. Daniel Tichenor, *Dividing Lines: The Politics of Immigration Control in America* (Princeton, NJ: Princeton University Press, 2002).

36. Ibid., 18.

37. Ibid., 10.

38. Robert Reich observed that he was "struck by how much the initial definition of problems and choices influences the subsequent design and execution of public policies. The act of raising the salient public question . . . is often the key step, because it subsumes the value judgements that declare something to be a problem, focuses public attention on the issue, and frames the ensuing public debate." See Robert Reich, ed., *The Power of Public Ideas* (Cambridge, MA: Ballinger Publishing, 1988), 5. For more on the importance of ideas in policymaking see Martha Derthick and Paul Quirk, *The Politics of Deregulation* (Washington, DC: Brookings Institution Press, 1986); Harvey Feigenbaum, Jeffrey Henig, and Chris Hamnett, *Shrinking the State: The Political Underpinnings of Privatization* (Cambridge: Cambridge University Press, 1998); and Steven Teles, *Whose Welfare? AFDA and Elite Politics* (Lawrence: University Press of Kansas, 1998).

39. As Deborah Stone has noted, "in the polis, change occurs through the interaction of mutually defining ideas and alliances. . . . The representation of issues is strategically designed to attract support to one's side, to forge some alliances and break others. . . . Ideas are the very stuff of politics. People fight about ideas, fight for them, and fight against them." *Policy Paradox and Political Reason*, 25.

40. Karen Orren and Stephen Skowronek, "Beyond the Iconography of Order: Notes for a New Institutionalism," in Dodd and Jillson, *The Dynamics of American Politics*, 320–321.

41. Karen Orren and Stephen Skowronek, *The Search for American Political Development* (Cambridge: Cambridge University Press, 2004), 184.

42. For more on the use of public opinion surveys in analyzing education politics, see Jennifer Hochschild and Bridget Scott, "Trends: Governance and Reform of Public Education in the U.S.," *Public Opinion Quarterly* 62, 1 (Spring 1998): 79–120.

43. George Markus, "The Impact of Personal and National Economic Conditions on the Presidential Vote," *American Journal of Political Science* 32 (1988): 137–154.

44. See in particular the different perspectives presented in Jeff Manza, Fay Lomax Cook, and Benjamin Page, eds., *Navigating Public Opinion* (Oxford: Oxford University Press, 2002).

45. Lawrence Jacobs and Robert Shapiro, "Public Opinion and the New Social History: Some Lessons for the Study of Public Opinion and Democratic Policymaking," *Social Science History* 13, 1 (Spring 1989): 1–24.

46. Carl Kaestle, "The Public Schools and the Public Mood," *American Heritage* 41 (February 1990): 68.

47. *A Nation at Risk* was only one of many studies released during the 1970s and 1980s that questioned the effectiveness of U.S. public schools and of previous federal reform efforts. I have chosen to focus on *A Nation at Risk*, however, because it received by far the most media coverage and because it became a powerful symbol of the new reform movement.

48. For more detailed analyses of the evolution of politics and policy, see the following: on poverty, Michael Harrington, *The Other America: Poverty in the United States* (New York: Macmillan, 1962); on the environment, Rachel Carson, *Silent Spring* (Boston: Houghton Mifflin, 2002 [1962]); and on deregulation, Martha Derthick and Paul Quirk, *The Politics of Deregulation* (Washington, DC: Brookings Institution Press, 1985).

49. In this respect, the influence of the education issue in U.S. politics has been similar to

(though less extensive than) the role of race as described by Edward Carmines and James Stimson in *Issue Evolution: Race and the Transformation of American Politics* (Princeton, NJ: Princeton University Press, 1989).

CHAPTER THREE: THE EARLY FEDERAL ROLE IN EDUCATION

1. As Hugh Davis Graham has noted, "Prior to the 1960s, one of the most distinctive attributes of America's political culture had been the tenacity with which the United States, unlike other nations, had resisted a national education policy." Hugh Davis Graham, *The Uncertain Triumph: Federal Education Policy in the Kennedy and Johnson Years* (Chapel Hill: University of North Carolina Press, 1984), xvii.

·   2. For a thorough discussion of the educational views of the Founders and of the early role of education in the United States, see Lorraine Pangle and Thomas Pangle, *The Learning of Liberty: The Educational Ideas of the American Founders* (Lawrence: University Press of Kansas, 1993).

3. The latter ordinance asserted that "religion, morality, and knowledge, being necessary to good government and the happiness of mankind, schools and the means of education shall forever be encouraged." David Tyack and Thomas James, "Education for a Republic: Federal Influence on Public Schooling in the Nation's First Century." American Political Science Association (available from http://www.apsanet.org/CENnet/thisconstitution/tyack.html).

4. Led by Horace Mann, Massachusetts began to establish a statewide system of common schools in the late 1830s and passed the nation's first compulsory school attendance law in 1852, but it was not until 1918 that such laws were in force in the other forty-nine states.

5. For more on the establishment and activities of the U.S. Office of Education, see Harry Kursh, *The United States Office of Education: A Century of Service* (New York: Chilton Books, 1965).

6. U.S. Department of Commerce, *Education of the American Population* (Washington, DC: U.S. Census of Population, 1999), table 8.

7. See, for instance, Paul Peterson, *The Politics of School Reform: 1870–1940* (Chicago: University of Chicago Press, 1985), 5–22; Michael Katz, *Reconstructing American Education* (Cambridge, MA: Harvard University Press, 1987), 16–20; or Diane Ravitch, *Left Back: A Century of Failed School Reforms* (New York: Simon and Schuster, 2000), 241–247.

8. Whereas in 1940 just 38.1 percent of 25–29-year-olds had graduated from high school and just 5.9 percent had completed four years of college, by 1970, 75.4 percent had finished high school and 16.4 percent had completed four years of college. U.S. Department of Commerce, *Education of the American Population*, table 8.

9. For more on this development see Diane Ravitch, *The Troubled Crusade: American Education, 1945–1980* (New York: Basic Books, 1983), 10–16.

10. For more on the Supreme Court's *Brown* and *Brown II* decisions and southern desegregation efforts see J. Harvie Wilkinson III, "The Supreme Court and Southern School Desegregation, 1955–1970," *Virginia Law Review* 64, 4 (May 1978): 485 559.

11. For an extensive account of the context and consequences of the *Brown* decision, see James Patterson, *Brown vs. Board of Education* (Oxford: Oxford University Press, 2001).

12. James Guthrie, "The Future of Federal Education Policy," *Teachers College Record* 84, 3 (Spring 1983): 674.

13. Even the opponents of federal involvement in education recognized its significance, with Barry Goldwater writing during consideration of the bill that it reminded him "of an old Arabian proverb: 'If the camel once gets his nose in the tent, his body will soon follow.' If adopted, the

legislation will mark the inception of aid, supervision, and ultimately control of education in this country by federal authorities." Quoted in James Sundquist, *Politics and Policy: The Eisenhower, Kennedy, and Johnson Years* (Washington, DC: Brookings Institution Press, 1968), 178.

14. Graham, *The Uncertain Triumph*, xv.

15. Kennedy's efforts to enact a federal aid to education bill were also complicated by his Catholicism (which heightened fears about federal aid to private and parochial schools) and his narrow victory in the 1960 presidential election (which left him without a strong popular mandate).

16. Johnson won the 1964 presidential election by what was then the largest margin in American history—16 million votes. Johnson's popularity was also widely credited with helping the Democratic Party significantly increase its control of Congress by expanding its majority to 36 in the Senate and 155 in the House. Johnson used his strong popular mandate and the gratitude of many Democratic senators and representatives for the strength of his coattails, to effectively lobby for support of his education agenda.

17. As cited in Julie Roy Jeffrey, *Education for Children of the Poor: A Study of the Origins and Implementation of the Elementary and Secondary Education Act of 1965* (Columbus: Ohio State University Press, 1978), 3.

18. Tinsley Spraggins, "New Educational Goals and Direction: A Perspective of Title I, ESEA," *Journal of Negro Education* 37, 1 (Winter 1968): 46.

19. As cited in Phillip Meranto, *The Politics of Federal Aid to Education in 1965* (Syracuse, NY: Syracuse University Press, 1967), 104.

20. As cited in Harold Howe, "LBJ as the Education President," in Kenneth Thompson, ed., *The Presidency and Education* (Lanham, MD: University Press of America, 1990), 102.

21. Meranto, *The Politics of Federal Aid to Education in 1965*, 132.

22. Joel Spring, *Conflict of Interests: The Politics of American Education* (Boston: McGraw-Hill, 1999), 96–97.

23. Howe, "LBJ as the Education President," 101–102.

24. For a thorough discussion of the political context surrounding the passage of ESEA, see Meranto, *The Politics of Federal Aid to Education in 1965*; Eugene Eidenberg and Roy Morey, *An Act of Congress: The Legislative Process and the Making of Education Policy* (New York: W. W. Norton, 1969); and Graham, *The Uncertain Triumph*.

25. "Remarks in Johnson City, Texas, Upon Signing the Elementary and Secondary Education Bill, April 11, 1965," *Public Papers of the Presidents of the United States: Lyndon B. Johnson, 1965*, vol. I, entry 181 (Washington, DC: Government Printing Office, 1966), 412–414.

26. The legislation contained four additional titles. Title II of the ESEA created a five-year program (funded at $100 million for the first year) to fund the purchase of library resources, instructional material, and textbooks by state educational agencies (which were then to loan them out to local public and private school students.) Title III created a five-year program of matching grants to local educational agencies to finance supplemental education centers and services. (It was also allocated $100 million for the first year.) Title IV gave the U.S. Commissioner of Education the authority to enter into contracts with universities and state educational agencies to conduct educational research, surveys, and demonstrations. This title received $100 million in funding for the five-year period. Finally, Title V provided $25 million over five years to strengthen state departments of education.

27. As cited in Joel Spring, *The Sorting Machine: National Educational Policy Since 1945* (New York: David McKay, 1976), 225.

28. Eidenberg and Morey, *An Act of Congress*, 247.

29. For a detailed explanation of the typology of public policies and what is meant by distribution and redistribution, see Theodore Lowi, "American Business, Public Policy Case Studies, and Political Theory," *World Politics* 16 (July 1964): 677–715.

30. As Diane Ravitch has noted, "From the middle 1950's to the end of the 1960's, a vast literature was produced which sought to account for the low achievement of poor and minority children in urban schools. Books, articles, symposia, seminars, and conferences proliferated around the theme of how to educate the 'culturally deprived,' the 'culturally disadvantaged,' the 'underprivileged,' and the 'lower-class child.'" *The Troubled Crusade*, 150.

31. Ibid., 158.

32. Paul Peterson and Barry Rabe, "The Role of Interest Groups in the Formation of Educational Policy," *Teachers College Record* 84, 3 (Spring 1983): 717.

33. Eidenberg and Morey, *An Act of Congress*, 93.

34. As quoted in Sundquist, *Politics and Policy*, 16.

35. Ibid., 215.

36. As Terry Moe has noted, institutions are sticky—"they constitute an institutional base that is protected by all the impediments to new legislation inherent in separation of powers, as well as by the political clout of the agency's supporters. Most of the pushing and hauling in subsequent years is likely to produce only incremental change." Terry Moe, "The Politics of Bureaucratic Structure," in John Chubb and Paul Peterson, eds., *Can the Government Govern?* (Washington, DC: Brookings Institution Press, 1989), 285.

37. Graham, *The Uncertain Triumph*, 193.

38. Jack Jennings, "Title I: Its Legislative History and Its Promise," *Phi Delta Kappan* (March 2000): 4.

39. See Paul Peterson, Barry Rabe, and Kenneth Wong, *When Federalism Works* (Washington, DC: Brookings Institution Press, 1986), 136–140, for a more detailed discussion of the local tendency to shift federal funds from redistributive programs to other purposes.

40. Graham, *The Uncertain Triumph*, 204.

41. Joel Berke, *Answers to Inequity: An Analysis of the New School Finance* (Berkeley, CA: McCutchan Publishing, 1974), 143.

42. The USOE was ill-suited to a compliance role—it had long been a small, passive organization that focused on collecting and disseminating statistical data on education and did little else. The result, as John and Anne Hughes noted, was that "if USOE had limitations on its policy-making authority and capability—and these have been legion—its ability to enforce its policies has been even more limited. The state agencies and the local districts, by and large, were used to going their own ways, which often meant disregarding federal requirements." John Hughes and Anne Hughes, *Equal Education: A New National Strategy* (Bloomington: Indiana University Press, 1972), 50.

43. Ibid., 57.

44. Ravitch, *The Troubled Crusade*, 271.

45. For more on the judicial and political context of this period, see Gary Orfield and Susan Eaton, eds., *Dismantling Desegregation: The Quiet Reversal of Brown vs. Board of Education* (New York: Free Press, 1996); David Armor, *Forced Justice: School Desegregation and the Law* (New York: Oxford University Press, 1995); and Marian Wright Edelman, "Southern School Desegregation, 1954–1973: A Judicial-Political Overview," *Annals of the American Academy of Political and Social Science* 407 (May 1973): 32–42.

46. See, for example, Edward Carmines and James Stimson, *Issue Evolution: Race and the Transformation of American Politics* (Princeton, NJ: Princeton University Press, 1989).

47. John E. Chubb, "Excessive Regulation: The Case of Federal Aid to Education," *Political Science Quarterly* 100, 2 (Summer 1985): 287.

48. Ravitch, *The Troubled Crusade*, 312.

49. National Center for Education Statistics, *The Condition of Education 2000* (Washington, DC: NCES, 2000), 395.

50. Deil Wright, *Understanding Intergovernmental Relations* (Pacific Grove, CA: Brooks/Cole, 1988), 195.

51. Paul Hill, "The Federal Role in Education," in Diane Ravitch, ed., *Brookings Papers on Education Policy* (Washington, DC: Brookings Institution Press, 2000), 25–26. By 1993, state education agencies nationwide relied on federal funds for on average 41 percent of their operating budgets, with the federal share as high as 77 percent in some states.

52. Michael Newman, *America's Teachers* (New York: Longman, 1994), 166.

53. Ravitch, *The Troubled Crusade*, 267.

54. Michelle Fine, "Who's 'At Risk'?" *Journal of Urban and Cultural Studies* (November 1, 1990): 55, 64.

55. Shep Melnick, "Separation of Powers and the Strategy of Rights: The Expansion of Special Education," in Marc Landy and Martin Levin, eds., *The New Politics of Public Policy* (Baltimore: Johns Hopkins University Press, 1995), 24.

56. The move was widely regarded as a political payback for the endorsement and support of the National Education Association and the American Federation of Teachers during the 1976 election. Legislation to create a new federal department for education had been introduced 130 times between 1908 and 1975, but the idea had always generated a great deal of political opposition from a variety of interests. D. T. Stallings, "A Brief History of the U.S. Department of Education, 1979 2002," *Phi Delta Kappan* 83, 9 (May 2002): 677.

57. For more on the politics surrounding the creation of the department, see David Stephens, "President Carter, the Congress, and NEA: Creating the Department of Education," *Political Science Quarterly* 98, 4 (Winter 1983–1984): 641–663.

58. For an extended discussion of the expansion of federal compensatory education programs and the accompanying increase in federal education regulations, see Paul Peterson, "Background Paper," in *Making the Grade: Report of the Twentieth-Century Fund Task Force on Federal Elementary and Secondary Education Policy* (New York: Twentieth Century Fund, 1983), 73–76.

59. See, for example, those by Stephen Bailey and Edith Mosher, *ESEA: The Office of Education Administers a Law* (Syracuse, NY: Syracuse University Press, 1968); Joel Berke and Michael Kirst, *Federal Aid to Education* (Lexington, MA: Heath, 1972); Joel Berke, *Answers to Inequity: An Analysis of the New School Finance* (Berkeley, CA: McCutchan Publishing, 1974); Milbrey McLaughlin, *Evaluation and Reform: The Elementary and Secondary Education Act of 1965, Title I* (New York: Harper Information, 1975); Norman C. Thomas, *Education in National Politics* (New York: David McKay, 1975); and Jeffrey, *Education for Children of the Poor*.

60. Berke and Kirst, *Federal Aid to Education*, 45.

61. As cited in Jeffrey, *Education for Children of the Poor*, 143.

62. Gareth Davies, *From Opportunity to Entitlement: The Transformation and Decline of Great Society Liberalism* (Lawrence: University Press of Kansas, 1996), 78.

63. Ibid., 1–9.

64. Marshall Kaplan and Peggy Cuciti, eds., *The Great Society and Its Legacy* (Durham, NC: Duke University Press, 1986), 217.

65. Charles Murray, *Losing Ground: American Social Policy 1950–1980* (New York: Basic Books, 1984).

66. For an in-depth examination of Reagan's political philosophy, see James Ceaser, "The Theory of Governance of the Reagan Administration," in Lester Salmon and Michael Lind, eds., *The Reagan Presidency and the Governing of America* (Washington, DC: Urban Institute Press, 1984).

67. *Historic Documents of 1980* (Washington, DC: Congressional Quarterly, 1981), 583–584.

68. As cited in Sar Levitan and Clifford Johnson, "Did the Great Society and Subsequent Initiatives Work?" in Kaplan and Cuciti, *The Great Society and Its Legacy,* 73.

69. Parris N. Glendening and Mavis Mann Reeves, *Pragmatic Federalism* (Los Angeles: Palisades Publishers, 1984), 243.

70. As D. T. Stallings has noted, "The new administration planned to move the Department of Education away from awarding categorical grants and toward the awarding of block grants, with the goal of eventually eliminating federal grants entirely, which would cause the federal role to revert to what it had been in 1838—nothing more than collecting statistics." "A Brief History of the U.S. Department of Education," 678.

71. Graham, *The Uncertain Triumph,* 22.

72. Ravitch, *The Troubled Crusade,* 320.

73. Edward Fiske, "George Bush as the Education President," in Kenneth Thompson, ed., *The Presidency and Education* (Lanham, MD: University Press of America, 1990), 125.

74. Gerald Holton, "An Insider's View of 'A Nation at Risk' and Why It Still Matters," *Chronicle of Higher Education,* April 25, 2003, B13.

75. National Commission on Excellence in Education, *A Nation At Risk: The Imperative for Educational Reform* (Washington, DC: Government Printing Office, 1983).

76. Fiske, "George Bush as the Education President," 126.

77. As cited in Gerald Holton, "An Insider's View of 'A Nation at Risk' and Why It Still Matters," *Chronicle of Higher Education,* April 25, 2003, B15.

78. "Time Is Running Out for Nation's Schools" *U.S. News and World Report,* July 18, 1983, 52.

79. However, even at the height of Reagan's popularity, he could not alleviate the public perception that Democrats were more concerned with ensuring opportunity for all than were Republicans. For instance, when a 1984 poll asked voters, "Which [candidate] would do a better job of insuring that government programs and policies are fair to all people," respondents preferred Mondale over Reagan by a 53 percent to 40 percent margin. Roper Center, Public Opinion Online, accession number 0005299, question number 51, September 1984.

80. Gallup poll conducted April 30–May 9, 1984. Retrieved from Roper Center at University of Connecticut, Public Opinion Online, accession number 32687, question number 8.

81. ABC news poll conducted September 25–26, 1981. Retrieved from Roper Center at University of Connecticut, Public Opinion Online, accession number 1045, question number 11.

82. Gallup poll conducted August 5–8, 1983. Retrieved from Roper Center at University of Connecticut, Public Opinion Online, and accession number 30609, question number 4.

83. Deborah A. Verstegen and David L. Clark, "The Diminution in Federal Expenditures for Education During the Reagan Administration," *Phi Delta Kappan* 70, 2 (October 1988): 137.

84. Thomas Toch, *In the Name of Excellence* (Oxford: Oxford University Press, 1991), 36.

85. Paul Manna, "Federalism, Agenda Setting, and the Dynamics of Federal Education Policy," paper presented at the annual meeting of the American Political Science Association, August 29–September 1, 2002.

86. A new weekly newspaper devoted exclusively to covering elementary and secondary education—*Education Week*—had begun publication in 1981, and it provided more expansive and regular coverage of school issues than had ever been seen in the United States.

87. Gallup poll conducted April 25–May 10, 1987. Retrieved from Roper Center at University of Connecticut, Public Opinion Online, accession number 24833, question number 237.

88. *Washington Post* poll conducted June 15–19, 1988. Retrieved from Roper Center at University of Connecticut, Public Opinion Online, accession number 130212, question number 19.

89. Gallup poll conducted April 8–10, 1987. Retrieved from Roper Center at University of Connecticut, Public Opinion Online, accession number 45133, question number 11.

90. Gordon Black polls conducted January 27, 1987. Retrieved from Roper Center at University of Connecticut, Public Opinion Online, accession number 148953, question number 8, and accession number 183758, question number 8.

91. Roper poll conducted February 14–28, 1987. Retrieved from Roper Center at University of Connecticut, Public Opinion Online, accession number 128241, question number 13.

92. Gallup poll conducted April 10–13, 1987. Retrieved from Roper Center at University of Connecticut, Public Opinion Online, accession number 44505, question number 25.

93. Ibid., accession number 44511, question number 31.

94. As cited in Toch, *In the Name of Excellence,* 9.

95. Sixty percent of respondents reported having a highly or moderately favorable opinion of the department whereas only 35 percent had a not too favorable or unfavorable opinion of it. Roper poll conducted April 25–May 2, 1987. Retrieved from Roper Center at University of Connecticut, Public Opinion Online, accession number 128460, question number 13.

96. Harris poll conducted September 1–6, 1988. accession number 0060945, question number 3. Retrieved from Roper Center at University of Connecticut Public Opinion Online, http://web.lexis-nexis.com/universe/form/academic/s_roper.html.

97. Tom Loveless, "The Structure of Public Confidence in Education," *American Journal of Education* 105, 2 (February 1997): 7.

CHAPTER FOUR: FROM DEVOLUTION TO NATIONAL GOALS IN EDUCATION

1. For in-depth analyses of the 1988 election, see Gerald Pomper, ed., *The Election of 1988: Reports and Interpretations* (Chatham, NJ: Chatham House Publishers, 1989); and Paul Abramson, John Aldrich, and David Rohde, *Change and Continuity in the 1988 Elections* (Washington, DC: Congressional Quarterly Press, 1991).

2. ABC News/*Washington Post* poll conducted October 28–November 1, 1988, accession number 0178335, question number 47. Retrieved from Roper Center at University of Connecticut Public Opinion Online, http://web.lexis-nexis.com/universe/form/academic/s_roper.html.

3. "The Education President," *New Republic* 198, 5 (May 9, 1988): 3.

4. Muriel Cohen, "The Presidential Campaign," *Boston Globe,* October 9, 1988, A2.

5. For an analysis of this and other trends in public opinion, see Jennifer Hochschild and Bridget Scott, "Trends: Governance and Reform of Public Education in the U.S.," *Public Opinion Quarterly* 62, 1 (Spring 1998): 79–120.

6. Poll conducted April 1987, accession number 0044505, question number 25. Retrieved from Roper Center at University of Connecticut Public Opinion Online, http://web.lexis-nexis.com/universe/form/academic/s_roper.html.

7. Abramson, Aldrich, and Rohde, *Change and Continuity in the 1988 Elections,* 291–292.

8. Interview with author, January 15, 2003.

9. "The Basic Speech: George Bush," *New York Times*, February 4, 1988, B10.

10. David Hoffman, "Bush Details Proposals on Education Spending," *Washington Post*, June 15, 1988, A8.

11. As quoted in Regan Walker, "Bush: Capturing the 'Education' Moment?" *Education Week*, October 19, 1988, http://www.edweek.org.

12. Lamar Alexander, a former governor and member of Bush's education advisory panel, noted that "Mr. Dukakis is the endorsed candidate of the NEA, so he basically stands for the status quo. The Republicans are offering 'the candidate of change' and a 'new agenda' in education." As quoted in ibid.

13. Ibid.

14. Chester Finn, "Two Cheers for Education's G-Men," *National Review* 38 (August 15, 1986): 35.

15. "Republican Party Platform 1988," *Historical Documents of the United States for 1988* (Washington, DC: Congressional Quarterly Press, 1989), 46A–75A.

16. E. J. Dionne, "Democrats in Race for '88 Are Forcing Accord on Issues," *Washington Post*, June 22, 1987, A4.

17. Kirsten Goldberg, "Drafting Planks: Parties Begin 'Battle of Ideas,'" *Education Week*, June 8, 1988, http://edweek.org.

18. Barbara Vobejda, "New ABCs for Campaigning on Education," *Washington Post*, September 18, 1988, A11.

19. E. J. Dionne Jr., "Dukakis Scorns Bush Vow of Education Leadership," *New York Times*, September 2, 1988, A16.

20. Gwen Ifill, "Dukakis Turns Focus to Bush," *Washington Post*, April 23, 1988, A4.

21. Senate Majority Leader Robert Byrd (D-WV) remarked that "we understand that the number of well-educated children, not the number of tanks and missiles, is the sure measure of our strength." Sen. Edward Kennedy (D-MA) added that "we cannot be satisfied to see American students rank 15th among industrial nations in science and math. We must strengthen education, not attack it. . . . We must invest in Star Schools here on earth, not Star Wars in the sky. . . . We must make America once again the best educated society in the world." Rep. Bill Richardson's (D-NM) speech also tied the party's commitment to education to its commitment to equal opportunity, stating that "we must make real the promise of American education for all of our citizens, or the American dream will be real for none of us." As reported in "The Democrats on Education," *Education Week*, August 3, 1988, http://edweek.org.

22. Peter Schmidt, "Teachers' Unions Jockey to Sway Races in Pivotal Election Year," *Education Week*, October 10, 1990, http://edweek.org.

23. "National Education Group Backs Dukakis for President," *New York Times*, September 9, 1988, A14.

24. Harris poll conducted October 14–17, 1988, accession number 0062369, question number 4. Retrieved from Roper Center at University of Connecticut Public Opinion Online, http://web.lexis-nexis.com/universe/form/academic/s_roper.html.

25. Norpoth and Buchanan found that "in promising to bring about '30 million new jobs' and to be the 'education president,' George Bush raised issues commonly associated with the Democratic Party. If that was an effort to aim for voters beyond his partisan parameters, it failed." They believe that the attempt failed not because voters were skeptical of Bush's promises on jobs and education but because they mistakenly associated those promises with his Democratic opponent. Helmut Norpoth and Bruce Buchanan, "Wanted: The Education President: Issue Trespassing by Political Candidates," *Public Opinion Quarterly* 56, 1 (Spring 1992): 98.

26. Analysis conducted by author of the Public Papers of the Presidents of the United States, accessed online at http://www.gpo.gov/nara/pubpaps/srchpaps.html.

27. Charles Kolb, *White House Daze: The Unmaking of Domestic Policy in the Bush Years* (New York: Free Press, 1994), 126.

28. Julie Miller, "After Victory, Speculations about 'Education President,'" *Education Week*, November 16, 1988, http://edweek.org.

29. As cited in Kolb, *White House Daze,* 132.

30. Julie Johnson, "So Far, Educators Give Bush No Passing Grade," *New York Times*, April 26, 1989, B8.

31. CBS News/*New York Times* poll conducted November 10–16, 1988, accession number 0019675, question number 28. Retrieved from Roper Center at University of Connecticut Public Opinion Online, http://web.lexis-nexis.com/universe/form/academic/s_roper.html.

32. Sen. Claiborne Pell (D-RI), chairman of the Senate subcommittee on education, for example, commented that though Bush's plan offered "a constructive approach to advance excellence in education," it was "disappointing" because "any serious education package must begin with significant increases in the [current] need-based programs." Julie Miller, "Bush's Long-Awaited Education Plan Greeted with Skepticism in Congress," *Education Week*, April 12, 1989, http://edweek.org.

33. Interview with the author, January 7, 2003.

34. For a detailed discussion of state-level standards-based school reforms (and the role of business in them) in the 1980s, see Thomas Toch, *In the Name of Excellence: The Struggle to Reform the Nation's Schools, Why It's Failing, and What Should be Done* (Oxford: Oxford University Press, 1991).

35. Interview with the author, January 7, 2003.

36. For a detailed description of the meeting, see Maris Vinovskis, "The Road to Charlottesville: The 1989 Education Summit" (Washington, DC: National Education Goals Panel, 1999).

37. Bernard Weinraub, "Bush and Governors Set Education Goals," *New York Times*, September 29, 1989, A10.

38. Ibid.

39. Susan Martin, "The 1989 Education Summit as a Defining Moment in the Politics of Education," in Kathryn Borman and Nancy Greenman, eds., *Changing American Education* (Albany: SUNY Press, 1992), 141.

40. "Assessing the Education Summit: 'Pap' or Progress," *Education Week*, October 25, 1989, http://edweek.org.

41. Diane Ravitch, *National Standards in American Education* (Washington, DC: Brookings Institution Press, 1995), 58.

42. Interview with the author, January 7, 2003.

43. Bill Goodling, "Quality Education: How to Get There?" *Roll Call*, May 21, 1990, http://www.rollcall.com.

44. Michael Heise, "Goals 2000: Educate America Act: The Federalization and Legalization of Educational Policy," *Fordham Law Review* 63 (November 1994): 11.

45. Interview with the author, January 16, 2003.

46. As one article noted about Bush, "As the midpoint of his presidency approaches, he's showing himself to be virtually all promise and no performance in addressing the problems of the nation's schools. So far, the Bush administration's record on education has been largely one of superficial rhetoric, halfhearted initiatives and a devastating deficiency of leadership at the U.S. Department of Education." Thomas Toch, "The President's Worst Subject," *U.S. News and World Report*, August 6, 1990, 46.

47. February 1990 poll, accession number 0000988. Retrieved from Roper Center at University of Connecticut Public Opinion Online, http://web.lexis-nexis.com/universe/form/academic/s_roper.html.

48. *Times Mirror* poll conducted April 5–8, 1990, accession number 0107150, question number 42. Retrieved from Roper Center at University of Connecticut Public Opinion Online, http://web.lexis-nexis.com/universe/form/academic/s_roper.html.

49. *Los Angeles Times* poll conducted January 8–12, 1991, accession number 0152902, question number 14. Retrieved from Roper Center at University of Connecticut Public Opinion Online, http://web.lexis-nexis.com/universe/form/academic/s_roper.html. See also Lynn Olsen and Julie Miller, "The 'Education President' at Midterm: Mismatch Between Rhetoric, Results?" *Education Week*, January 9, 1991, http://edweek.org.

50. CBS News poll conducted May 30–June 2, 1990, accession number 0013595, question number 6. Retrieved from Roper Center at University of Connecticut Public Opinion Online, http://web.lexis-nexis.com/universe/form/academic/s_roper.html.

51. NBC News/*Wall Street Journal* poll conducted August 28, 1991, accession number 0159232, question number 5. Retrieved from Roper Center at University of Connecticut Public Opinion Online, http://web.lexis-nexis.com/universe/form/academic/s_roper.html.

52. Toch, "The President's Worst Subject," 46.

53. *Los Angeles Times* poll conducted December 8–12, 1990, accession number 0146856, question number 2. Retrieved from Roper Center at University of Connecticut Public Opinion Online, http://web.lexis-nexis.com/universe/form/academic/s_roper.html.

54. Cavazos had been a holdover from the Reagan administration but was widely criticized by Democrats and Republicans alike for being an ineffective spokesman for education reform. His opposition to private school choice—which the Bush administration was now planning to push—also played a role in his dismissal.

55. Bush's presidential advisory committee on education, chaired by Alcoa CEO Paul O'Neill, formally recommended in January 1991 that there should be national (but not federal) standards and examinations. A second group—headed by former New Jersey governor Tom Kean—also issued a report calling for national standards and tests at about the same time.

56. White House Fact Sheet on the President's Education Strategy, April 18, 1991. Accessed from http://bushlibrary.tamu.edu/papers/1991/91041807.html.

57. John Yang, "Bush Unveils Education Plan," *Washington Post*, April 19, 1991, A1.

58. "President's Message to the Congress Transmitting Proposed Legislation to Promote Excellence in Education," May 22, 1991. Retrieved from http://bushlibrary.tamu.edu/papers/1991/91052204.html.

59. Interview with author, January 16, 2003.

60. Ibid.

61. Michael Frisby, "Bush Education Plan Is Criticized," *Boston Globe*, April 24, 1991, 3.

62. One observer noted that "Mr. Kennedy opposes the idea of new experimental schools, national standards, testing, and almost everything else. The Senator is, of course, in a double bind. He is both a captive of the educational establishment, which is more than happy with the status quo, and chagrined that the president might have seized the initiative on a long-held Democratic monopoly." Many liberals agreed with University of Chicago professor Gary Orfield that "America 2000 is not a plan for American education but a plan for re-electing the president." See "School Haze," *New Republic* 205, 25 (December 16, 1991): 7.

63. See, for example, Karen DeWitt, "Teachers' Union Chief Faults Bush School Plan," *New York Times*, July 12, 1991, A13.

64. Julie Miller, "Reform Measure Dies—Except as Campaign Issue?" *Education Week*, October 7, 1992, http://edweek.org.

65. Interview with the author, March 23, 2003.

66. Interview with the author, January 16, 2003.

67. Rep. Dick Armey (R-TX), for example, argued that "rather than relying on federal bureaucrats and Washington diktats, America 2000 turns to parents, school boards, and state and local government. It puts power in the hands of education consumers and takes it away from the providers—the teachers' unions and bureaucrats that have been dictating education policy to students and parents for far too long. . . . the biggest obstacle to education progress remains the Democrat-controlled Congress. The House Education and Labor Committee took the Bush proposals and mutilated them beyond recognition. The committee has taken the funding in the Bush proposal and started filling items on the NEA wish list." Dick Armey, "The Case for Choice in Schools," *Roll Call*, January 27, 1992, http://www.rollcall.com.

68. "Bush Administration Targets NEA," *NEA Today* 11, 3 (October 1992): 3.

69. In a speech at a Republican Party fundraiser, Bush emphasized that "we're fighting for choice in education. . . . we think that parents and students, not the bureaucrats, should choose which school is best for them . . . [but] our bill has been gathering some dust, a hostage to the education lobby." "President Bush's Remarks at a Republican Party Fundraising Dinner in Salt Lake City, Utah," September 18, 1991. Retrieved from http://bushlibrary.tamu.edu/papers/1991/91091806.html.

70. Various polls, accession numbers 0017984, August 1988; 0086602, November 1989; 0007851, January 1990; 0142075, October 1990; 0156207, June 1991; 0165776, December 1991; 0168504, January 1992; 0191039, December 1992. Retrieved from Roper Center at University of Connecticut Public Opinion Online, http://web.lexis-nexis.com/universe/form/academic/s_roper.html.

71. "Remarks of President Bush at the New Education Choice Initiative Ceremony," June 25, 1992, Federal News Service. Retrieved from http://web.lexis-nexis.com/congcomp/printdoc.

72. The shift on vouchers was also due to the publication of John Chubb and Terry Moe's book *Politics, Markets, and America's Schools* (Washington, DC: Brookings Institution Press, 1990), which received a great deal of notoriety and established a solid intellectual argument for a radical restructuring of public education through choice.

73. Michael Oreskes, "Political Memo: GOP Plagued with Political Problems," *New York Times*, December 15, 1990, A1.

74. Interview with author, May 5, 2003.

75. White House spokesman Marlin Fitzwater went so far as to comment publicly that "we just want to make it clear that we want conservatives to come back. We understand there is a protest vote out there but we need their help in November and we want their support." Karen Hosler, "Americans Face Great Divide: Chameleon Bush Panders to Republican Right Wing," *Toronto Star*, March 5, 1992, A16.

76. Kolb, *White House Daze*, 159.

77. Interview with the author, March 20, 2003.

78. Interview with the author, March 10, 2003.

79. Interview with the author, May 5, 2003.

80. Diane Ravitch, *National Standards in American Education* (Washington, DC: Brookings Institution Press, 1995), 145.

81. CBS News/*New York Times* poll conducted October 20–23, 1992, accession number 0186417, question number 41. Retrieved from Roper Center at University of Connecticut Public Opinion Online, http://web.lexis-nexis.com/universe/form/academic/s_roper.html.

82. As cited in Meg Sommerfeld, "Few Trust Politicians to Improve Schools, Gallup Poll Shows," *Education Week*, September 9, 1992, http://edweek.org.

83. Yankelovich poll conducted December 17–22, 1991, accession number 0193339, question number 31. Retrieved from Roper Center at University of Connecticut Public Opinion Online, http://web.lexis-nexis.com/universe/form/academic/s_roper.html.

84. Sommerfeld, "Few Trust Politicians to Improve Schools."

85. As cited in Deborah Cohen, "National School Goals: Old Idea Surfaces with Newfound Intensity," *Education Week*, September 27, 1989, http://edweek.org.

86. Interview with author, January 16, 2003.

87. Abramson, Aldrich, and Rohde, *Change and Continuity in the 1988 Elections*, 291–292.

88. Harris poll conducted July 17–19, 1992, accession number 0183491, question number 2. Retrieved from Roper Center at University of Connecticut Public Opinion Online, http://web.lexis-nexis.com/universe/form/academic/s_roper.html.

CHAPTER FIVE: LAYING THE FOUNDATION FOR A NEW ACCOUNTABILITY REGIME

1. See, for example, Jon Hale, "The Making of the New Democrats," *Political Science Quarterly* 110, 2 (Summer 1995): 207.

2. Julie Miller, "Teacher Delegates Turn Out in Force to Hail Clinton's Record on Education," *Education Week*, August 5, 1992, http://www.edweek.org.

3. Olson and Miller, "Self-Styled 'Education President.'"

4. "Bush's GOP Challengers Omit Education as a Key Issue in the Campaign," *Education Week*, February 12, 1992, http://www.edweek.org.

5. Gary Bauer, the president of the conservative Family Research Council, for example, noted, "I suspect that including [vouchers] in the budget was an effort to signal conservatives that . . . he is still philosophically committed to the choice idea." Olson and Miller, "Self-Styled 'Education President.'"

6. As one observer noted, "the notion of empowering parents to choose the schools their children attend by allowing them to spend public money at private schools has become the flagship of President Bush's education agenda. It is the education issue he mentions even in speeches that are not specifically about education." Julie Miller, "Bush Stand on School Choice Is Seen Bolder," *Education Week*, September 9, 1992, http://www.edweek.org.

7. As quoted in Julie Miller, "Education Issues Get Scant Attention from Republicans," *Education Week*, September 9, 1992, http://www.edweek.org.

8. *Historic Documents of 1992* (Washington, DC: Congressional Quarterly Press, 1993), 809.

9. A 1991 Gallup poll demonstrated that public opinion on vouchers remained somewhat murky, with 62 percent favoring public school choice and 50 percent favoring choice among public or private schools, but 68 percent opposed to "allowing students and parents to choose a private school to attend at public expense." As cited in Miller, "Bush Stand on School Choice Is Seen Bolder."

10. Jon Hale, "The Making of the New Democrats," *Political Science Quarterly* 110, 2 (Summer 1995): 207.

11. Clinton was uniquely positioned to take advantage of the increased salience of domestic issues in the 1992 campaign. As a governor—and former chairman of the National Governors Association—Clinton could claim substantial experience in working to improve economic de-

velopment, health care, the environment, and education—issues that voters identified as the most important facing the country in 1992. Though Clinton adopted a liberal position on some social issues, such as abortion, these were balanced by his more moderate positions on crime, welfare, education, and the military. And whereas Democrats had long been identified as the party of the poor, Clinton aggressively courted middle-class voters. For a more detailed discussion of Clinton's 1992 campaign strategy, see Joshua Muravchik, "Why the Democrats Finally Won," *Commentary* 95, 1 (January 1993): 17.

12. *Historic Documents of 1992* (Washington, DC: Congressional Quarterly Press, 1993), 697–698.

13. Interview with the author, March 27, 2003.

14. Rupert Cornwell, "Bush Critics Do Their Homework on Schools," *Independent* 31 (October 1991): 16.

15. Chris Black, "Clinton Targets Schools," *Boston Globe,* May 15, 1992, 12.

16. Clinton's approach to balancing the need for genuine reform with the need to maintain the support of the unions in Arkansas is illuminating and offered a preview of how he would cope with a similar challenge as president. Clinton dramatically increased state spending on education—including a large ($4,000) teacher pay raise—and this helped to win back many in the education establishment who had initially opposed his reforms.

17. "Time for a Real Education President," *NEA Today* 11, 2 (September 15, 1992): 3. A poll of AFT members showed that Clinton was strongly favored even in the more reform-minded union, with 68 percent favoring him and only 19 percent backing Bush. See also "Shanker Bashes Bush, Spearheads AFT Endorsement of Clinton," *Education Week,* September 9, 1992, http://www.edweek.org.

18. The NEA had every state affiliate establish a Clinton-Gore campaign coordinator and a team to turn out union voters on behalf of the Democratic ticket, and it produced twice as many campaign materials as it had in past years. "Unions Putting Time, Money, Energy to Task of Campaigning for Clinton," *Education Week,* October 14, 1992, http://www.edweek.org.

19. The NEA had earlier passed a resolution that flatly opposed government-mandated testing programs of any kind and the use of tests to compare schools or school districts. The AFT had long been the more reform-minded of the two major teachers unions, and it had announced its support for national standards and tests.

20. Interview with the author, March 27, 2003.

21. Robert Koenig, "Voters Hear Variety of Plans to Improve Schools," *St. Louis Post-Dispatch,* February 23, 1992, B1.

22. Interview with the author, August 22, 2002.

23. Interview with the author, March 10, 2003.

24. Roper Center for Public Opinion Online: Carnegie Foundation poll conducted July-August 1992, accession number 0189591, question 14.

25. Roper Center for Public Opinion Online: *Los Angeles Times* poll conducted October 2–5, 1992, accession number 0188389, question 13.

26. Olson and Miller, "Self-Styled 'Education President.'"

27. Louis Bolce, Gerald DeMaio, and Douglas Muzzio, "The 1992 Republican 'Tent': No Blacks Walked In," *Political Science Quarterly* 108, 2 (Summer 1993): 260.

28. Roper Center for Public Opinion Online: accession number 0187515, question 3.

29. "Ballot Box: Education President II," *Education Week,* April 22, 1992, http://www.edweek.org.

30. As cited in Koenig, "Voters Hear Variety of Plans to Improve Schools," B1.

31. Olson and Miller, "Self-Styled 'Education President.'"

32. Thomas Toch and Jerry Buckley, "The Blackboard Jumble," *U.S. News and World Report* 112, 20 (May 25, 1992): 23.

33. The liberal magazine *The Nation*, for example, had expressed displeasure at Clinton's centrism during the campaign but noted hopefully after the election that "the new Congress is likely to have a slew of new leftish Democrats" who could be part of a "post-election mobilization" to push the Clinton administration leftward. Muravchik, "Why the Democrats Finally Won," 17.

34. Interview with the author, March 27, 2003.

35. Stanley Elam and Ben Brodinsky, *The Gallup/Phi Delta Kappan Polls of Attitudes Towards the Public Schools, 1968–1988* (Bloomington, IN: Phi Delta Kappan, 1989).

36. Roper Center for Public Opinion Online: Greenberg-Lake poll conducted January 4–5, 1993, accession number 0191610, question 37.

37. Two of the top domestic policy advisers on Clinton's transition team, Al From and Bruce Reed, for example, came from the DLC. Mark Walsh, "Think-Tank Proposals Mirror Clinton Education Agenda," *Education Week*, December 16, 1992, http://www.edweek.org.

38. Interview with the author, March 18, 2003.

39. Elena Neuman, "Clinton on the Education Fence," *Insight on the News* 8, 46 (August 1992): 6.

40. On February 22, 1994, Clinton gave a major speech on education that emphasized the importance of education and urged Congress to pass his school agenda. His advisers noted at the time that "an enormous fraction of the [administration's] legislative agenda" revolved around education and that the speech was intended to put the issue on the "front burner." Mark Pitsch, "President Puts Education on the Front Burner," *Education Week*, March 2, 1994, http://www.edweek.org.

41. Richard Riley, "Reflections on Goals 2000," *Teachers College Record* 96, 3 (Spring 1995): 2–3.

42. Peter Cookson noted that national standards represented a "new federalism" in education and were "a striking departure from traditional liberal reform strategies, which emphasize equality of inputs and tinkering, as it were, with the existing system. It [also] directly challenges the conservative reform paradigm in that, while it nods its head in the direction of volunteerism . . . [it] is not sympathetic to market solutions for educational problems. The conservative issues of choice and freedom are muted in the discussion of standards and accountability." Peter Cookson Jr., "Goals 2000: Framework for the New Educational Federalism," *Teachers College Record* 96, 3 (Spring 1995): 3.

43. Robert Schwartz and Marian Robinson, "Goals 2000 and the Standards Movement," in Diane Ravitch, ed., *Brookings Papers on Education Policy 2000* (Washington, DC: Brookings Institution Press, 2000), 179.

44. The NESIC was a nineteen-member presidentially appointed council made up of educators, administrators, parents, business leaders, and others and was charged with establishing national content standards, national student performance standards, and national opportunity-to-learn standards to serve as models for the states. Although the NESIC was to certify these model national standards, they were actually to be written by private organizations. (Thus the standards for government were drafted by the Center for Civic Education and the science standards were created by the National Academy of Sciences.) The NEGP (which already existed but would be written into law) would report on state and national progress toward achieving the national goals. It was to be made up of eighteen members, including presidential appointees, governors, members of Congress, and state legislators, and was given the power to review—and approve or disapprove—the standards developed by the NESIC. The NEGP and NESIC were also given

the controversial authority to oversee the states in developing their standards and ultimately to evaluate and certify the standards that the states proposed. The NSSB's mission was to define skills for all kinds of work and to devise skill certification programs for use by states. In addition, a National Board for Professional Teaching Standards was created by congressional amendment to develop and implement national teacher assessment and certification standards.

45. Riley, "Reflections on Goals 2000," 2.

46. Interview with the author, March 18, 2003.

47. Judd Gregg, "Goals 2000 Will Gum Up School Plans," *Insight on the News* 10, 10 (March 7, 1994): 32.

48. Interview with the author, March 18, 2003.

49. In a subsequent response to the concerns of the National Governors Association, President Clinton also wrote, "The key to meaningful long-term education reform lies in clearly stated national goals coupled with maximum feasible flexibility for states and localities to devise and implement their own plans for achieving those goals. Schools should be held accountable for results—not for complying with a discouraging maze of micromanaged bureaucratic prescriptions." Diane Ravitch, *National Standards in American Education* (Washington, DC: Brookings Institution Press, 1995), 179.

50. The language (which became Sections 318 and 319 of the act) states: "The Congress agrees and reaffirms that the responsibility for control of education is reserved to the States and local school systems and other instrumentalities of the States and that no action shall be taken under the provisions of this Act by the Federal Government which would, directly or indirectly, impose standards or requirements of any kind through the promulgation of rules, regulations, provision of financial assistance and otherwise, which would reduce, modify, or undercut State and local responsibility for education."

51. Heather Bodell, *Goals 2000: A National Framework for America's Schools* (Fairfax, VA: Education Funding Research Council, 1994), 8.

52. Interview with the author, August 22, 2002.

53. Tom Loveless, "The Politics of National Standards," in Nina Cobb, ed., *The Future of Education* (New York: College Board, 1995), 51.

54. Richard Riley, "The Role of the Federal Government in Education—Supporting a National Desire for Support for State and Local Education," *St. Louis University Public Law Review* 17, 9 (1997).

55. Michael Kirst saw Goals 2000 as a good example of "Clintonian federalism" in which the Department of Education was willing to support a wide variety of existing state reform efforts. "That's much different," he noted, "than Democratic administrations in the past [where] the view was there were some states that couldn't be trusted." With Goals 2000, he continued, "applications are being approved on the basis of, 'you keep doing what you've been doing. . . . Goals 2000 allows for 50 different patterns [and the Education Department is] permitting wide state variation." As cited in Mark Pitsch, "States Seek Goals 200 Aid for Existing Efforts," *Education Week,* September 21, 1994, 1.

56. Riley, "Reflections on Goals 2000," 1

57. Robert Schwartz and Marian Robinson, "Goals 2000 and the Standards Movement," in Diane Ravitch, ed., *Brookings Papers on Education Policy 2000* (Washington, DC: Brookings Institution Press, 2000), 174.

58. Michael Usdan, "Goals 2000: Opportunities and Caveats," *Education Week,* November 23, 1994, http://www.edweek.org.

59. Marshall Smith, Brett Scoll, and Valena Pliskp, "The Improving America's Schools Act: A

New Partnership," in Jack Jennings, ed., *National Issues in Education: Elementary and Secondary Education Act* (Washington, DC: Phi Delta Kappa, 1995), 7.

60. The administration's proposal to refocus federal Title I funding on the nation's poorest schools also encountered strong opposition in Congress because it would have taken funds away from many wealthier congressional districts.

61. Interview with the author, March 23, 2003.

62. Congressional letter from September 24, 1993.

63. As was the case with Goals 2000, the ESEA debate also provided an opportunity for conservatives to offer a series of amendments on school prayer, homosexuality, and sex education related to the wider culture wars.

64. Jack Jennings, *Why National Standards and Tests?* (Newbury Park, CA: Sage Publications, 1998), 127–128.

65. Ibid., 126.

66. Interview with the author, May 5, 2003.

67. For more on the impact of the 1994 federal reforms on state and local school policies, see Susan Furhman, "Clinton's Education Policy and Intergovernmental Relations in the 1990s," *Publius* 24, 3 (Summer 1994): 92.

68. For a detailed description of the politics and provisions of the 1994, ESEA reauthorization, see Jennings, *National Issues in Education.*

69. Remarks on signing the Improving America's Schools Act of 1994, *Weekly Compilation of Presidential Documents* 30, 42 (October 24, 1994): 2084.

70. Interview with the author, March 23, 2003.

71. Interview with the author, March 27, 2003.

72. Gary Bauer, "The Reauthorization of ESEA," in Jennings, *National Issues in Education,* 145.

73. Ibid., 148–149.

74. Interview with the author, March 13, 2003.

75. Usdan, "Goals 2000: Opportunities and Caveats."

76. Jack Jennings, "School Reform: The Making of Two New National Policies," in Jennings, *National Issues in Education,* 193.

77. Interview with the author, August 22, 2002.

78. Interview with the author, March 27, 2003.

79. Interview with the author, March 23, 2003.

80. Gordon Ambach, "Goals 2000: A New Partnership for Student Achievement," in Jennings, *National Issues in Education,* 68–69.

81. "The Candidates on Education," *Roll Call,* January 27, 1992, http://www.rollcall.com.

82. Interview with the author, March 27, 2003.

83. "A GOP Divided: O.B.E Drives Wedge in Party," *Education Week,* June 15, 1994, http://www.edweek.org.

84. Interview with the author, March 23, 2003.

85. Interview with the author, January 15, 2003.

CHAPTER SIX: SHOWDOWN

1. For more on the positions and activities of Christian conservatives, see Catherine Lugg, "Reading, Writing, and Reconstructionism: The Christian Right and the Politics of Public Education," *Educational Policy* 14, 5 (November 2000): 622–637; Catherine Lugg, "The Christian

Right: A Cultivated Collection of Interest Groups," *Educational Policy* 15, 1 (January 2001): 41–57; George Kaplan, "Shotgun Wedding: Notes on Public Education's Encounter with the New Christian Right," *Phi Delta Kappan* 75, 9 (May 1994): K1.

2. Roper Center for Public Opinion Online: Kaiser/Harvard Election Night Survey of voters conducted November 8, 1994, accession number 0225196, question 19.

3. Democrats were preferred over Republicans on education 45 percent to 30 percent in one poll and 34 percent to 21 percent in another. Roper Center for Public Opinion Online: ABC News/*Washington Post* poll conducted October 20–23, 1994, accession number 0229437, question 24; and NBC News/*Wall Street Journal* poll conducted October 14–18, 1994, accession number 0223612, question 31.

4. Roper Center for Public Opinion Online: ABC News/*Washington Post* poll conducted October 20–23, 1994, accession number 0229437, question 24.

5. Roper Center for Public Opinion Online: Kaiser/Harvard Election Night Survey of voters conducted November 8, 1994, accession number 0231522, question 20.

6. Lynn Olson, "Undo School Programs, Heritage Urges," *Education Week*, December 7, 1994, http://www.edweek.org.

7. Lamar Alexander, William Bennett, and Daniel Coats, "Local Options: Congress Should Return Control of Education to States, School Boards, and Parents," *National Review* 46, 42 (December 19, 1994): 3.

8. Rep. Lindsay Graham, "Take Washington Out of Education," *The Hill*, June 14, 1995, http://www.hillnews.com.

9. Rep. John Shadegg (R-AZ) and forty-six cosponsors introduced "The Goals 2000 Elimination Act" in 1996 to convert federal education assistance to block grants that would be given to local school districts without any conditions attached. As Rep. Shadegg noted in a press release, "The bill is about getting the federal government out of education, returning power to the local level and giving parents, teachers, and local school boards the freedom they need to educate students in a way that meets the unique needs of their area." Press release of September 18, 1996.

10. Michael Heise, "Goals 2000: Educate America Act: The Federalization and Legalization of Educational Policy," *Fordham Law Review* 63 (November 1994): 1.

11. Jack Jennings, *Why National Standards and Tests?* (Newbury Park, CA: Sage, 1998), 36.

12. As cited in Lynn Olson, "The Future Looks Cloudy for Standards-Certification Panel," *Education Week*, April 12, 1995, http://www.edweek.org.

13. Interview with the author, March 18, 2003.

14. Roper Center for Public Opinion Online: NBC News/*Wall Street Journal* poll conducted January 14–17, 1995, accession number 0228828, question 28.

15. Roper Center for Public Opinion Online: NBC News/*Wall Street Journal* poll conducted June 2–6, 1995, accession number 0237493, question 24; NBC News/*Wall Street Journal* poll conducted July 29–August 1, 1995, accession number 0240197, question 74; Princeton Survey Associates poll conducted November 6–10, 1996, accession number 0277736, question 21; and Lake, Snell, Perry, and Associates poll conducted June 1998, accession number 0320054, question 52.

16. Roper Center for Public Opinion Online: NBC News/*Wall Street Journal* poll conducted March 4–7, 1995, accession number 0232151, question 16.

17. A Times Mirror poll released in December 1994 found that 64 percent of respondents wanted to increase federal spending on education and that support for federal education programs was second only to anticrime initiatives (on a list of fourteen programs). As cited in *USA Today*, April 6, 1995, 14. A poll taken in October 1996 showed continued strong support for federal spending on education, with 64 percent in favor of increasing it, 25 percent wanting to keep

it about the same, and only 9 percent in favor of decreasing it. Roper Center for Public Opinion Online: CBS News/*New York Times* poll conducted October 10–13, 1996, accession number 0266675, question 65.

18. Interview with the author, March 23, 2003.

19. Interview with the author, March 18, 2003.

20. Fred Siegel and Will Marshall, "Liberalism's Lost Tradition," *New Democrat* (September–October 1995): 12–13.

21. Interview with the author, March 27, 2003.

22. "DLC Drafts Alternative to Republican Contract," *Education Week*, December 14, 1994, http://www.edweek.org.

23. As cited in Mark Pitsch, "Polls Confirm Key Role of Education in Political Arena," *Education Week*, June 19, 1996, http://www.edweek.org.

24. As cited in Morton Kondracke, "Clinton Trying New Strategy: Stress Education," *Roll Call*, April 10, 1995, http://www.rollcall.com.

25. "Remarks to the California Democratic Party in Sacramento," *Weekly Compilation of Presidential Documents* 31, 15 (April 17, 1995): 584.

26. Ibid.

27. "Remarks to the National Education Association," *Public Papers of the Presidents* 2 (July 6, 1995): 1057–1062.

28. Richard Stengel and Eric Pooley, "Masters of the Message: Inside the High-Tech Machine that Set Clinton and Dole Polls Apart," *Time*, November 18, 1996, 76.

29. As cited in Alison Mitchell, "State of the Union—The Overview," *New York Times*, January 24, 1996, A1.

30. Important support for federal education spending also came, not surprisingly, from the education community itself. While seventy seven education-related organizations continued to lobby Congress through the Committee for Education Funding, a new group, the Education First Alliance, was created in May 1995 to build grassroots support for education spending. Michael Edwards, an Alliance member and lobbyist for the NEA, noted that "this idea is to take the debate out of Washington and into local communities to show the direct relationship between [federal budget cutting] and what is happening in local communities. The idea is to make education a fundamental public policy issue from now until whenever—1996 or beyond." As cited in Mark Pitsch, "Education Lobby Aims to Rally Public Support," *Education Week*, May 31, 1995, http://www.edweek.org.

31. Diane Ravitch, "Goals 2000: Four Ways to Fix It," *Washington Post*, January 12, 1995, A27.

32. Chester Finn, "Blindspots on the Right: Conservative Illusions about Education Policy," *National Review* 47, 18 (September 25, 1995): 68.

33. As cited in James Barnes, "Politics—Rightward March?" *National Journal*, August 6, 1994, http://nationaljournal.com.

34. Interview with the author, March 11, 2003.

35. As cited in Mark Pitsch, "GOP Liberal Goes against the Grain," *Education Week*, April 12, 1995, http://www.edweek.org.

36. For more on the business view and role on standards, see Milton Goldberg and Susan Traiman, "Why Business Backs Education Standards," in Diane Ravitch, ed., *Brookings Papers on Education Policy* (Washington, DC: Brookings Institution Press, 2001).

37. Jack Jennings, *Why National Standards and Tests?* (Newbury Park, CA: Sage, 1998), 161.

38. Paul Starobin, "Politics-Right Fight," *National Journal*, November 9, 1995, http://www.nationaljournal.com.

39. As cited in Mark Pitsch, "Dole Campaign Weighs Options on Education," *Education Week,* May 1, 1996, http://www.edweek.org.

40. Interview with the author, May 5, 2003.

41. Roper Center for Public Opinion Online: Tarrance Group and Mellman, Lazarous, and Lake poll conducted April 2–4, 1995, accession number 0234547, question 43; NBC News/*Wall Street Journal* poll conducted July 29–August 1, 1995, accession number 0240173, question 50; Princeton Survey Associates poll conducted September 28–October 1, 1995, accession number 0243699, question 46.

42. Interview with the author, March 26, 2003.

43. As cited in "Republicans Join in Call to Boost ED Budget," *Education Week,* September 25, 1996, http://www.edweek.org.

44. Ibid.

45. Chester Finn, "Can We Educate Republicans?" *National Review* 48, 11 (June 17, 1996): 44.

46. As cited in Mark Pitsch, "Polls Confirm Key Role of Education in Political Arena," *Education Week,* June 19, 1996, http://www.edweek.org.

47. Roper Center for Public Opinion Online: *Los Angeles Times* poll of registered voters conducted October 6–7, 1996, accession number 0275482, question 1; Princeton Survey Research Associates poll conducted September 6–16, 1996, accession number 0286041, question 023; and Louis Harris and Associated poll of registered likely voters conducted October 17–20, 1996, accession number 0266837, question 11.

48. "There is a widespread sense that the schools are not working," said Deborah Wadsworth of the Public Agenda Foundation, which monitored public opinion. "The schools seem to mirror for most people the things that they believe are most problematic in society. . . . [Politicians] are responding to the abundance of research that has indicated that people are unhappy with public education." Richard Wolf, "Dole, Clinton Courting Votes with Education Proposals," *USA Today,* September 25, 1996, 5D.

49. Interview with the author, March 13, 2003.

50. Chester Finn, "Can We Educate Republicans?" *National Review* 48, 11 (June 17, 1996): 44.

51. "Democratic Party Platform," in *Historic Documents of 1996* (Washington, DC: Congressional Quarterly Press, 1997), 629–630.

52. James Barnes, "Politics—Rightward March?" *National Journal,* August 6, 1994, http://www.nationaljournal.com.

53. As cited in "1996 Presidential Candidates: Profiles and Education Policy," *Education Week,* February 7, 1996, http://www.edweek.org.

54. "Republican Party Platform," in *Historic Documents of 1996* (Washington, DC: Congressional Quarterly Press, 1997), 527–528.

55. As cited in Mark Pitsch, "GOP Hopefuls of One Mind on Education," *Education Week,* February 7, 1996, http://www.edweek.org.

56. Interview with the author, May 9, 2003.

57. As cited in Mark Pitsch, "GOP Themes Boost Choice, Hamper Dole," *Education Week,* October 30, 1996, http://www.edweek.org.

58. Interview with the author, March 26, 2003.

59. A September survey conducted by ABS News, for example, found that 46 percent of respondents thought that unions have a positive impact on schools; 31 percent indicated that unions had a negative impact. As cited in Pitsch, "GOP Themes Boost Choice, Hamper Dole."

60. As cited in David Hoff, "Teachers' Unions Flex Political Muscles as Election Nears," *Education Week,* October 16, 1996, http://www.edweek.org.

61. As cited in Stephen Hegarty, "Both Tickets Give Education Issue a Ride," *St. Petersburg Times*, November 2, 1996, 1A.

62. Roper Center for Public Opinion Online: Louis Harris and Associates poll of registered likely voters conducted November 1–3, 1996, accession number 0267644, question 3.

63. Roper Center for Public Opinion Online, Gallup poll of registered voters conducted October 30–31, 1996; accession number 0332381, question number 28. One reporter quipped shortly before the election that "four years ago after they won election to the White House, Bill Clinton and Al Gore took a ceremonial bus trip to Washington for the inauguration. If they win another four years, perhaps they should consider riding a big yellow school bus into town. The Clinton/ Gore team has already gotten quite a ride out of the education issue. . . . It is surprising how large a role education has played in this presidential election. Clinton and Gore have made 'education, Medicare, and the environment' the campaign mantra." Hegarty, "Both Tickets Give Education Issue a Ride," 1A.

64. Richard Riley, "Education Reform through Standards and Partnerships, 1993–2000," *Phi Delta Kappan* 83, 9 (May 2002): 701.

65. Interview with the author, April 30, 2003.

66. Roper Center for Public Opinion Online: NBC News/*Wall Street Journal* poll of nationally registered voters conducted October 19–22, 1996, accession number 0267308, question 60.

67. Interview with the author, March 26, 2003.

68. Media coverage of George W. Bush's emphasis on education in the 2000 election and his administration's school reform proposals (which became the basis for the No Child Left Behind Act) have generally emphasized the extent to which they broke with longstanding Republican positions on the federal role in education. This chapter has demonstrated that the national Republican Party began to shift its position on education not in 2000, but several years earlier—following Dole's defeat in 1996 and the resignation of Newt Gingrich as Speaker of the House.

CHAPTER SEVEN: STALEMATE

1. Dan McLean, "GOP Poised to Launch Offensive on Education," *The Hill*, December 10, 1997, http://www.hillnews.com.

2. Ibid. The GOP's vocal opposition to choice in abortion—something a majority of women supported—was certainly also important in turning women away from the Republican Party, but this was a position that was less alterable than education for many party members.

3. Dan Balz, "Stands on Education Cost GOP among Women, Governors Told," *Washington Post*, November 27, 1996, p. A6.

4. Ibid.

5. "Triumphs and Traps: What's Ahead for Conservatives," *Policy Review* 81 (January–February 1997): 18.

6. Ibid.

7. Michael Castle, "Republicans Really Are a Pro-Education Party," *Roll Call*, June 2, 1997, http://www.rollcall.com.

8. Ibid.

9. Interview with the author, May 9, 2003.

10. Biographer David Maraniss noted after the 1996 election that Clinton's advisers "say he wants to be remembered as the education president, just as he developed a reputation in Arkan-

sas as the education governor." Cited in Mark Pitsch, "Education Seen Key to Forging Clinton Legacy," *Education Week,* November 13, 1996, http://www.edweek.org.

11. William Jefferson Clinton, "Second Inaugural Address," January 20, 1997.

12. "A New Nonpartisan Commitment to Education," *Education Week,* February 12, 1997, http://www.edweek.org.

13. Interview with the author, March 26, 2003.

14. Two of Clinton's biggest priorities, however—national tests and a major school construction program—encountered strong resistance and were not enacted during 1997.

15. Interview with the author, January 29, 2003.

16. Romesh Ratnesar, "A Tempest over Testing," *Time,* September 22, 1997, 168.

17. Ibid.

18. David Hoff, "Clinton's 100,000 Teacher Plan Faces Hurdles," *Education Week,* February 4, 1998, http://www.edweek.org.

19. "An Education Primer," *New Democrat,* March 1, 1998.

20 David Hoff, "GOP Skeptical of Clinton's New School Plans," *Education Week,* February 18, 1998, http://www.edweek.org.

21. Subcommittee on Oversight and Investigations, House Committee on Education and the Workforce, xi–xvii.

22. Roper Center for Public Opinion Online: Lake, Snell, Perry, and Associates poll of nationally registered women voters conducted June 1998, accession number 0320026, question 24.

23. Interview with the author, April 30, 2003.

24. For more on these meetings, see Andrew Rudalevige, "No Child Left Behind: Forging a Congressional Compromise," in Paul Peterson and Martin West, eds., *No Child Left Behind? The Politics and Practice of School Accountability* (Washington, DC: Brookings Institution Press, 2003), 31–32.

25. "Clinton: New Ideas, Expanded Programs," *Education Week,* February 2, 2000, http://www.edweek.org.

26. All quotes from "GOP: More Money, Local Control," *Education Week,* February 2, 2000, http://www.edweek.org.

27. Chester Finn and Michael Petrilli, "Two Views of Education Reform Making the Rounds of Washington," *Dayton Daily News,* July 15, 1999.

28. Interview with the author, March 26, 2003.

29. Anjetta McQueen, "Moderates Reveal Plan to Overhaul Federal Law," Associated Press Newswire, November 16, 1999.

30. David Broder, "Serious on Schools," *Washington Post,* November 21, 1999.

31. Joetta Stack, "Moderate Democrats Aim to Restructure K-12 Programs," *Education Week,* February 12, 2000, http://www.edweek.org.

32. Interview with the author, March 27, 2003.

33. Erik Robelen, "Civil Rights Group Decries Implementation of Title I," *Education Week,* September 22, 1999, http://www.edweek.org.

34. For a lengthy discussion of the issue of vouchers in the African-American community, see Patrick McGuinn, "Race and School Choice: The Disconnect Between African-American Elite and Mass Opinion." Paper presented at the August 2001 meeting of the American Political Science Association, San Francisco, CA.

35. Interview with the author, May 5, 2003.

36. Poll data cited in Thomas Toch and Major Garrett, "Will Teachers Save Public Schools?" *U.S. News and World Report,* July 20, 1998, 16.

37. The unions themselves were beginning to recognize that their opposition to even relatively moderate reforms was increasing support for more radical structural reforms such as vouchers. A public relations study done for the NEA in the mid-1990s, for example, had warned that inertia would be politically costly and that if the union failed to support the school reform movement it risked "further marginalization and possibly even organizational death." And in a major 1996 speech, NEA president Bob Chase remarked that "we cannot go on denying responsibility for school quality. We must revitalize our public schools from within or they will be dismantled from without." Toch and Garrett, "Will Teachers Save Public Schools?" 16.

38. Ibid.

39. A bill to expand the Ed-Flex (Education Flexibility Partnership Demonstration) program that had been created as part of Goals 2000 did, however, ultimately pass with the support of Clinton and a coalition of Republicans and moderate Democrats. It allowed the Department of Education to grant waivers from many federal education regulations to all fifty states in exchange for showing academic improvement.

40. Interview with the author, April 30, 2003.

41. The large increases in the late 1990s contributed to a 69 percent increase in federal on-budget funds for elementary and secondary education in constant dollars between Fiscal Year 1990 and FY 2001. National Center for Education Statistics, *Federal Support for Education: 1980–2001* (Washington, DC: U.S. Department of Education, Office of Educational Research and Improvement, 2002), 3.

42. "Remarks and a Question and Answer Session with the Education Writers Association in Atlanta, Georgia," April 14, 2000, *Public Papers of the Presidents: William J. Clinton—2000*, vol. 1 (Washington, DC: Government Printing Office, 2001), 706–707.

43. As Clinton remarked at the National Education Summit in Palisades, New York, on September 30, 1999, "We have made significant progress, particularly in the ideas governing the way we look at this. More and more we're leaving behind the old divisions between one side saying 'we need more money,' and the other side saying, 'we shouldn't invest any more money in our public schools, it's hopeless.' By and large, there is a new consensus for greater investment and greater accountability, greater investment and higher standards, and higher quality teachers to help students reach the standards; holding schools accountable for the results." *Public Papers of the Presidents: William J. Clinton—1999*, vol. 2 (Washington, DC: Government Printing Office, 2000), 1640–1645.

44. Interview with the author, May 6, 2005.

CHAPTER EIGHT: MANEUVER

1. Donald Kettl, "Schoolhouse Tango," *Governing Magazine*, December 1999, 12.

2. Some scholars believe issues had become more important in elections generally during this period; as Opfer has noted, "the recent emergence of education in the electoral process is not a unique phenomenon but represents a more general rise in issue-oriented voting." V. Darleen Opfer, "Elections and Education—A Question of Influence," *Educational Policy* (January/March 2002): 5.

3. Roper Center for Public Opinion Online: CNN/*USA Today* poll conducted between January 13 and 15, 2000, accession number 0349833, question 16.

4. Roper Center for Public Opinion Online: CNN/*USA Today* poll conducted between August 4 and 5, 2000, accession number 0365874, question 39.

5. Roper Center for Public Opinion Online: CNN/*USA Today* poll conducted between April 7 and 9, 2000, accession number 0365045, question 14.

6. See Joetta Sack, "Gore Stumps in Iowa with Focus on Education Themes," *Education Week*, May 26, 1999, http://www.edweek.org; and Robert Johnston, "Bush Record on Education Defies Labels," *Education Week*, September 22, 1999, http://www.edweek.org.

7. Twenty-eight percent thought it was better, and 15 percent thought it was about the same. Roper Center for Public Opinion Online: CNN/*USA Today* poll conducted between April 7 and 9, 2000, accession number 0365046, question 15.

8. Thirty-six percent were somewhat or completely satisfied. Roper Center for Public Opinion Online: Gallup poll conducted between August 24 and 27, 2000, accession number 0368628, question 1.

9. Many voters who supported the idea that government should do less in general nonetheless supported government doing more in the area of education. Seventy-eight percent of voters who supported leaving more things to business and individuals also supported at least one government solution in education. Kathleen Frankovic and Monika McDermott, "Public Opinion in the 2000 Election: The Ambivalent Electorate," in Gerald Pomper, ed., *The 2000 Election* (New York: Chatham House, 2001), 89.

10. Roper Center for Public Opinion Online: Gallup poll conducted between April 7 and 9, 2000, accession number 0365047, question 16.

11. Dan Baltz and Richard Morin, "Education Voters Pose a Tough Test," *Washington Post*, June 30, 2000, A1.

12. Frankovic and McDermott, "Public Opinion in the 2000 Election," 77.

13. Roper Center for Public Opinion Online: Penn, Schoen, and Berland Associates poll conducted between June 17 and 20, 1999, accession number 0343650, question 40.

14. Frankovic and McDermott, "Public Opinion in the 2000 Election," 89.

15. Denis Doyle, "The Presidential Sweepstakes 2000," *Phi Delta Kappan* (October 2000): 121.

16. Melissa Marschall and Robert McKee, "From Campaign Promises to Presidential Policy: Education Reform in the 2000 Election," *Educational Policy* (January/March 2002): 110.

17. James Ceaser and Andrew Busch, *The Perfect Tie: The True Story of the 2000 Presidential Election* (Lanham, MD: Rowman and Littlefield, 2001), 36.

18. Ibid., 116.

19. "In Their Own Words: Excerpt from a July 22 Speech by Texas Gov. George W. Bush on Faith-based Organizations," *Minneapolis Star Tribune*, July 29, 1999, A16.

20. As one observer has noted, "Bush's compassionate conservatism could be a vehicle for criticizing how government works without declaring government is unnecessary. With ambiguous eloquence Bush has said: 'My guiding principle is government if necessary but not necessarily government.'" E. J. Dionne, "A Fourth Way," *Washington Post*, March 30, 1999, A17. This approach was both reviled and admired—with one writer calling him "George W. Clinton"—for what appeared to many to be an attempt to triangulate between conservative Republicans and liberal Democrats.

21. As one observer noted, "Compassionate conservatism is, in part, a renunciation of 1980s conservatism. By accepting that government can be 'effective and energetic' (Mr. Bush's own phrase), compassionate conservatism made it easier for Republicans to vote for spending proposals that were anyway popular. It therefore helped to move the party beyond its one-dimensional anti-government message." "Preparing America for Compassionate Conservatism," *Economist*, July 29, 2000, http://www.economist.com.

22. Interview with the author, May 23, 2003.

23. Interview with the author, March 18, 2003.

24. David Rosenbaum, "Bush and Gore Stake Claims to Federal Role in Education," *New York Times*, August 30, 2000.

25. For more on Bush's education reforms in Texas, see Robert Maranto, "The Politics behind George W. Bush's No Child Left Behind: Ideas, Elections, and Top-Down Education Reform," in Bryan Hillard, Tom Lansford, and Robert Watson, eds., *George W. Bush: Evaluating the President at Midterm* (Albany: State University of New York Press, 2004).

26. Interview with the author, May 23, 2003.

27. Charles Hokanson, "Where Gore and Bush Stand on Education," *World and I* (September 2000): 34.

28. As cited in Michael Kinsley, "…And His Wise-Fool Philosophy," *Washington Post*, September 5, 2000, A25.

29. Dan Balz, "On Federal Role in Education, Bush Walks a Fine Line," *Washington Post*, November 4, 1999, p. A2.

30. As cited in Eric Pooley, "Who Gets the 'A' in Education?" *Time*, March 27, 2000, 38.

31. He remarked that "we need a president who not only speaks up for parental choice but who will shut down the U.S. Department of Education. George Bush won't. I will." Buchanan attributed responsibility for the "hellish mess of American education" to the "dismal triangle" of federal bureaucrats, judges, and the teachers unions. Erik Robelen, "No Lack of Candidates—or Ideas—for Schools," *Education Week*, June 21, 2000; http://www.edweek.org.

32. As cited in "Image and Reality on Education," *New York Times*, August 1, 2000, A20.

33. The Republican Party's 2000 platform, accessed at http://www.rnc.org/GOPInfo/Platform/2000platform3.

34. As cited in Erik Robelen, "GOP Calls for Limiting Federal Role in Education," *Education Week*, July 31, 2000, http://www.edweek.org.

35. Denis Doyle, "Bush's Approach on Education Is Right on the Mark," *Houston Chronicle*, September 22, 1999, 48.

36. Interview with the author, May 5, 2003.

37. Donald Kettl, "Schoolhouse Tango," *Governing Magazine*, December 1999, 12.

38. Interview with the author, May 9, 2003.

39. Interview with the author, January 15, 2003.

40. Interview with the author, March 13, 2003.

41. David Bositis, *1999 National Opinion Poll: Education* (Washington, DC: Joint Center for Political and Economic Studies, 1999). Another survey, the 2000 *Phi Delta Kappan*/Gallup poll of the public's attitudes toward public schools, found that blacks graded their community public schools much more poorly than did whites and that 58 percent of blacks supported allowing parents to send their school-age children to any public, private, or church-related school they chose at government expense. Gallup Organization, *Phi Delta Kappan's Thirty-Second Annual Survey of the Public's Attitudes Toward the Public Schools*, 169.

42. Interview with the author, March 29, 2001.

43. George W. Bush, "Address to the Republican National Convention," *Vital Speeches*, August 15, 2000, 642.

44. As cited in Peter Schrag, "Education and the Election," *Nation*, March 6, 2000.

45. Jill Zuckerman, "Teachers Back Gore with Money, Muscle," *Boston Globe*, June 3, 2000, A1.

46. Interview with the author, March 26, 2003.

47. Press release for Speech to Conference of Black Mayors, April 28, 2000.

48. Interview with the author, March 18, 2003.

49. Albert Gore Jr., "Vice-President Al Gore's Plans for Education in America," *Phi Delta Kappan* (October 2000): 123.

50. Gerald Pomper, "The Presidential Election," in Pomper, *The 2000 Election*, 145.

51. Marschall and McKee, "From Campaign Promises to Presidential Policy," 101.

52. James Barnes, "The GOP's Shifting Terrain," *National Journal*, November 11, 2000, 3609.

53. Interview with the author, May 9, 2003.

54. See discussion in Barnes, "The GOP's Shifting Terrain," 3609.

55. Interview with the author, May 9, 2003.

56. As cited in Joetta Sack, "Candidates' K–12 Policies Share Themes," *Education Week*, September 6, 2000, http://www.edweek.org.

CHAPTER NINE: CONVERGENCE

1. Checker Finn, Bruno Manno, and Diane Ravitch, "Education 2001: Getting the Job Done— A Memorandum to the President-Elect and the 107th Congress" (Washington, DC: Thomas B. Fordham Foundation, 2000), 1–2.

2. "George Walker Bush Inaugural Address," January 20, 2001. Accessed from http://odur.let. rug.nl/'usa/P/gwb43/speeches/gwbush1.htm on March 19, 2002.

3. "Reform School: Bush Seeks Compromise on Education Proposals," ABCNews.com, January 23, 2001.

4. Sen. Tom Harkin (D-IA), a liberal senior member of the Senate Education Committee, for example, remarked that the New Democrat education plan was "not the Democratic Party's plan. . . . [Lieberman] does not speak for us. He's not even on the Education Committee. What [New Democrats] are trying to do is move an agenda on false promises. You're not going to do anything to help schools in this country unless you're willing to invest considerably more money per student." As cited in Susan Crabtree, "Changing His Tune, Kennedy Starts Work with Bush on Education Bill," *Roll Call*, January 25, 2001, http://www.rollcall.com.

5. Crabtree, "Changing His Tune, Kennedy Starts Work with Bush on Education Bill."

6. Interview with the author, March 18, 2003.

7. As cited in David Nather, "Broad Support Is No Guarantee for Bush's Legislative Leadoff," *CQ Weekly*, January 27, 2001, 221.

8. The appointment of Rep. Michael Castle (R-DE) as chair of the new Subcommittee on Education Reform within the House Education and Workforce Committee was very important in this regard. Castle is a moderate and is chair of the centrist Republican Main Street Coalition's education task force. The chair of the Senate Health, Education, Labor, and Pensions Committee, meanwhile, was another moderate, Sen. James Jeffords (R-VT). In fact, Jeffords's positions on education were viewed as being closer to those of liberal Democrats than Republicans. The education bill that he introduced (and passed) in committee did not contain two of Bush's central proposals—vouchers and block grants. The Bush administration eventually tried to circumvent Jeffords by using Sen. Judd Gregg as the point person in its negotiations with Senate Republicans. In part as a reaction to this snub, Jeffords dropped his affiliation with the Republican Party in May 2001. By voting (as an independent) with the Democratic caucus, Jeffords effectively threw control of the Senate to the Democrats. As a result, Kennedy became chair of the Education Committee.

9. Interview with the author, March 27, 2003.

10. Interview with the author, May 9, 2003.

11. As cited in Siobhan Gorman, "The Education of House Republicans," *National Journal*, March 31, 2001, 955.

12. Ibid.

13. John Boehner, "Making the Grade," *National Review Online*, April 6, 2001, http://www.nationalreview.com.

14. Interview with the author, March 11, 2003.

15. See, for example, "Blacks v. Teachers; Blacks and Vouchers," *Economist*, March 10, 2001, 1.

16. Interview with the author, March 13, 2003.

17. Interview with the author, March 18, 2003.

18. Interview with the author, March 27, 2003.

19. Interview with the author, May 5, 2003.

20. Congress established a federally funded voucher program for the District of Columbia in 2004.

21. David Nather, "As Education Bills Head for Floor Votes, Big Ideological Tests Loom in House," *CQ Weekly*, May 19, 2001, 1157.

22. For more on business support of education reform, see Milton Goldberg and Susan Traiman, "Why Business Backs Education Standards," in Diane Ravitch, ed., *Brookings Papers on Education Policy* (Washington, DC: Brookings Institution Press, 2001).

23. Keith Bailey, "Testimony before the Committee on Education and the Workforce, U.S. House of Representatives," March 29, 2001. Accessed from http://edworkforce.house.gov/hearings/107th/fc/hr132901/bailey.htm.

24. A February 10, 2001, poll found that 73 percent of respondents approved of Bush's reform proposals whereas only 22 percent opposed them, and a poll taken in March 2001 found an 80 percent/15 percent split. *Newsweek* poll conducted between February 8 and 9, 2001, accession number 0378681, question number 5. Harris poll conducted between February 22 and March 3, 2001, accession number 0379989, question number 3. Support for Bush's handling of education had declined somewhat by the summer, but polls continued to show that respondents were supportive by more than a two-to-one margin. Fox News poll conducted between June 6 and 7, 2001, accession number 0383115, question number 9. ABC News poll conducted between September 6 and 9, 2001, accession number 0386555, question number 5. All polls accessed from Roper Center for Public Opinion Online.

25. Roper Center for Public Opinion Online: Gallup poll conducted between May 23 and June 6, 2001, accession number 0385817, question numbers 23–25.

26. David Nather, "Democrats Leaving Their Stamp on Bush's Education Bill," *CQ Weekly*, May 12, 2001, 1079.

27. As cited in David Nather, "Compromises on ESEA Bills May Imperil Republican Strategy," *CQ Weekly*, May 5, 2001, 1009.

28. Donald Payne, "Reflections on Legislation: Reauthorization of ESEA, Challenges throughout the Legislative Process," *Seton Hall Legislative Journal* 315 (2003): 26.

29. Interview with the author, March 10, 2003.

30. Interview with the author, March 13, 2003.

31. For a detailed analysis of the provisions of NCLB, see *No Child Left Behind: A Desktop Reference* (Washington, DC: Department of Education, 2002). Available online at http://www.ed.gov/pubs/edpubs.html. See also Erik Robelen, "An ESEA Primer," *Education Week*, January 9, 2002, http://www.edweek.org; Learning First Alliance, "Major Changes to ESEA in the NCLB Act," http://www.learningfirst.org; and Center on Education Policy, "A New Federal Role in Education," January 2002, http://www.ctredpol.org.

32. For detailed analyses of the NCLB from the viewpoint of state implementers, see Education Commission of the States, "State Requirements under NCLB," January 2003, http://www.ecs.org; and National Governors Association, "NGA Summary of the Timeline Requirements of NCLB," www.nga.org.

33. Richard Elmore, "Unwarranted Intrusion," *Education Next* (Spring 2002): 31–35; Andrew Rotherham interview with the author, August 22, 2002.

34. For more on the influence of state education reforms on federal education policy, see Paul Manna, "Education Policy Change and Bottom-Up Agenda Setting," paper presented at the annual meeting of the Midwest Political Science Association, Chicago, April 2001.

35. Andrew Rotherham, "A New Partnership," *Education Next* (Spring 2002): 38.

36. William Taylor and Dianne Piche, "Will New School Law Really Help?" *USA Today*, January 9, 2002, 13A.

37. Michael Cohen, "Unruly Crew," *Education Next* (Fall 2002).

38. The department has added a new office of communications and outreach to oversee public affairs and intergovernmental and interagency affairs as well as a variety of new entities—an office of innovation and improvement, the Academy of Education Sciences, and an office of planning, evaluation, and policy development—to evaluate the effectiveness of departmental programs and state improvement efforts. See Michelle Davis, "Spellings Puts Her Stamp on Department," *Education Week,* March 15, 2005, http://www.edweek.org.

39. Interview with the author, March 27, 2003.

40. For more on the challenges of implementing NCLB, see Dan Goldhaber, "What Might Go Wrong with the Accountability Measures of the No Child Left Behind Act?" and Michael Cohen, "Implementing Title I Standards, Assessments, and Accountability." Papers presented at the Thomas B. Fordham Foundation conference entitled "Will No Child Truly Be Left Behind?" on February 13, 2002.

41. In March 2003, for example, the Department of Education threatened to withhold $783,000 in federal funds from Georgia for the state's failure to meet the testing requirements of the 1994 law. For more information on this, see Erik Robelen, "Department Levies $783,000 Title I Penalty on GA," *Education Week,* May 28, 2003, http://www.edweek.org.

42. Interview with the author, May 6, 2005.

43. Phyllis McClure, "Grassroots Resistance to NCLB," in *Education Gadfly*, March 18, 2004, accessed at http://www.edexcellence.net/foundation/gadfly/index.cfm#1723.

44. Education Commission of the States, *ECS Report to the Nation: State Implementation of the No Child Left Behind Act* (Denver: ECS, 2004), B2–B6.

45. Center on Education Policy, *From the Capital to the Classroom: Year 3 of the No Child Left Behind Act* (Washington, DC: Center on Education Policy, 2005). Available online at http://www.ctredpol.org/pubs/nclby3/press/cep-nclby3_21Mar2005.pdf.

46. "Title I schools" are high-poverty schools that receive funds from Title I of ESEA. The distinction between Title I and non–Title I schools is very important because the mandatory corrective actions spelled out in the new law for failing schools only apply to Title I schools. The other provisions of the law (such as those regarding standards, testing, and school report cards) apply to Title I and non–Title I schools alike.

47. Center on Education Policy, *From the Capital to the Classroom: Year 3 of the No Child Left Behind Act* (Washington, DC: Center on Education Policy, 2005). Available online at http://www.ctredpol.org/pubs/nclby3/press/cep-nclby3_21Mar2005.pdf.

48. See, for example, Bess Keller, "Michigan May Feel Full Force of Federal Law," *Education Week*, February 11, 2004, http://www.edweek.org.

49. Opposition to NCLB among states has been of a bifurcated nature. Resistance to the new federal mandates has generally been strongest among states that had done either the most or the least standards-based reform on their own.

50. Jo Becker and Rosalind Helderman, "Virginia Seeks to Leave Bush Law Behind," *Washington Post*, January 24, 2004, A1.

51. For more on this, see Diana Jean Schemo, "Fourteen States Ask U.S. to Revise Some Education law Rules," *Education Week*, March 25, 2004, http://www.edweek.org.

52. Lynn Olson, "States Revive Efforts to Coax NCLB Changes," *Education Week*, February 2, 2005, http://www.edweek.org.

53. Attorney General Peg Lautenschlager stated that "the states are entitled to take Congress at its word that it did not intend to require states to implement programs that will cost more than the federal government is providing" and that it was a "stark reality" that NCLB was underfunded. As quoted in Alan Borsuk, "No Child Left Behind May Not Be Enforceable, Lautenschlager Says," *Milwaukee Journal Sentinel Online*, May 13, 2004.

54. The report is available at http://www.ncsl.org/programs/educ/nclb_report.htm.

55. See, for example: Erik Robelen, "Opposition to School Law Growing, Poll Says," *Education Week*, April 7, 2004, http://www.edweek.org.

56. Kathryn McDermott, for example, has argued that "given that federal funds are still less than 10 percent of total education spending, it is unclear how long the federal 'tail' can go on using mandates to wag the state and local 'dog.' If the financial and political costs of compliance with federal mandates get high enough, some states may decide that it is no longer worth their while to receive ESEA funds." "Changing Conceptions of Federalism and Education Policy Implementation: Where Did the No Child Left Behind Act Come From and Where Is It Going?" paper presented at the annual meeting of the American Political Science Association conference, August 2003, 31.

57. As quoted in Alan Borsuk, "Law's Foes Unable to Stir Change," *Milwaukee Journal Sentinel Online*, July 12, 2004.

58. David Hoff, "Chiefs Sense a New Attitude in Meeting with Bush," *Education Week*, March 31, 2004, http://www.edweek.org.

59. In December 2003, testing rules for students with disabilities were relaxed, and in February 2004, the rules governing limited English proficiency students were made more flexible. In March 2004, extra flexibility was provided for teachers in rural communities and for science teachers in meeting the "highly qualified" mandate and streamlined alternative means for current teachers seeking to demonstrate subject-matter mastery in multiple subjects. Also in March 2004, the department allowed states to modify the way they calculate student test-participation rates by averaging participation over a two- or three-year period and by omitting students who miss the tests because of a medical emergency. "Changing the Rules," *Education Week*, April 7, 2004, http://www.edweek.org. For a detailed list of amendments to state accountability plans under NCLB submitted to the U.S. Department of Education, see Center on Education Policy, "Rule Changes Could Help More Schools Meet Test Score Targets for the No Child Left Behind Act," October 22, 2004, http://www.ctredpol.org/nclb/StateAccountabilityPlanAmendmentsReportOct2004.pdf.

60. Lynn Olson, "Data Show Schools Making Progress on Federal Goals," *Education Week*, September 8, 2004, http://www.edweek.org.

61. Interview with the author, March 5, 2005.

62. Signs of this new flexibility were displayed in early 2005 when the Education Department approved North Dakota's and Utah's requests to use their existing measure of veteran teacher

quality to satisfy the NCLB requirement and indicated that transfers from failing schools might not have to be undertaken if they resulted in overcrowding. Sam Dillon, "New U.S. Secretary Showing Flexibility on 'No Child' Act," *New York Times,* February 14, 2005. At the same time, however, the department denied a request from Connecticut to test less frequently than NCLB demands and forced California to classify more struggling school districts as failing.

63. The new plan is available online at http://www.ed.gov/news/pressreleases/2005/04/04072005.html.

64. It is interesting to note that Connecticut issued an open invitation to other states to join the lawsuit against the federal government and NCLB, but none decided to do so.

65. A 2004 General Accounting Office (GAO) report concluded that NCLB was technically not an unfunded mandate since states and districts participated voluntarily as a condition of receiving federal aid. The GAO analysis of NCLB and other federal mandates was released in June 2004 and is available online at http://www.gao.gov/new.items/d04637.pdf.

66. Interview with the author, March 5, 2005.

67. Frederick Hess, "Refining or Retreating? High Stakes Accountability in the States," in Paul Peterson and Martin West, eds., *No Child Left Behind? The Politics and Practice of School Accountability* (Washington, DC: Brookings Institution Press, 2003), 55–79.

68. James Cibulka, "The Changing Role of Interest Groups in Education: Nationalization and the New Politics of Education Productivity," *Educational Policy* 15, 1 (January–March 2001): 36.

69. Press release from January 7, 2004, available online at http://johnboehner.house.gov.

70. As quoted in Erik Robelen, "Bush Marks School Law's Second Anniversary," *Education Week,* January 14, 2004, http://www.edweek.org.

71. Interview with the author, May 6, 2005.

72. As quoted in Erik Robelen, "Kennedy Bill Would Give States, Districts Leeway," *Education Week,* September 22, 2004, http://www.edweek.org.

73. House Committee on Education and the Workforce press release, April 7, 2005.

74. The imposition of federal accountability measures on higher education would be particularly ironic. The historically hands-off approach of the national government in its support for colleges and universities was often cited during the 1980s and early 1990s as the model that should be followed in elementary and secondary education reform. The prescriptive new model of elementary and secondary education now may be applied to higher education, with the federal government demanding improved performance and efficiency in exchange for its financial support.

75. Public Education Network/*Education Week,* "The Public's Responsibility for Public Education," 2004 National Survey of Public Opinion, available online at http://publiceducation.org/portals/Learn_Vote_Act/default.asp.

76. Lowell Rose and Alec Gallup, *The Thirty-sixth Annual Phi Delta Kappa/Gallup Poll of the Public's Attitudes toward the Public Schools, 2004;* available online at http://www.pdkintl.org/kappan/k0309pol.pdf.

77. During the Democratic primary, Kerry (as well as most of the other Democratic candidates) was more critical of NCLB, calling it a "one-size-fits-all" approach. Early Democratic primary frontrunner Howard Dean made his vocal opposition to NCLB and his promise to repeal the law a major part of his campaign, but he ultimately fell behind Kerry and dropped out of the race, in large measure because his rhetoric and policy positions were seen as too liberal to enable him to be competitive against President Bush in the general election. See Erik Robelen, "Kerry Softens Rhetoric on 'No Child Left Behind,'" *Education Week* August 2, 2004, http://www.edweek.org.

78. In a speech to the Democratic convention on July 27, 2004, NEA president Reginald Weaver called NCLB "a one-size-fits-all federal mandate that sets the wrong priorities—too much paperwork, bureaucracy, and testing." Erik Robelen, "NEA President Goes beyond Party Line in 'No Child' Critique," *Education Week*, July 29, 2004, http://www.edweek.org.

79. Public Education Network/*Education Week*, "The Public's Responsibility for Public Education."

80. Rose and Gallup, *The Thirty-sixth Annual Phi Delta Kappa/Gallup Poll of the Public's Attitudes Toward the Public Schools, 2004*. The 2004 poll indicated, however, that the public continues to have only low levels of knowledge about NCLB, with 55 percent of respondents indicating that they "don't know enough" to express an opinion about the law. There is also strong opposition (67 percent) to using students' performance on a single test to judge whether a school is in need of improvement.

81. Educational Testing Service, *Equity and Adequacy: Americans Speak on Public School Funding*, http://ftp.ets.org/pub/corp/2004summary.pdf.

82. "Attitudes on No Child Left Behind Law," *Education Week*, January 21, 2004, 29.

83. As cited in "State Views on No Child Left Behind Act," *Education Week*, February 4, 2004, http://www.edweek.org.

84. Mid-continent Research for Education and Learning, "Digging Deeper: Where Does the Public Stand on Standards-based Education?" July 2003, 7. Available online at http://www.mcrel.org/PDF/Standards/5032IR_IssuesBrief0703_DiggingDeeper.pdf.

85. Chester Finn and Frederick Hess, "On Leaving No Child Behind," *Public Interest* 157 (Fall 2004): 55.

86. In a recent statement, the Achievement Alliance (which includes the National Council of La Raza and the Citizen's Commission on Civil Rights) declared that "the NEA's lawsuit is unfortunate and ill-considered. It will not help teachers—many of whom are union members—who are working hard every day to boost student achievement and close achievement gaps. Many of these teachers have struggled, essentially single-handedly, to help their students overcome the obstacles of racism and poverty. NCLB has strengthened their position and put the weight of the federal government behind their efforts. The NEA is attacking what may be the best hope this nation has of closing achievement gaps and leveraging more funding for and attention to our nation's public schools. Since the passage of NCLB, poor children and children of color—particularly at the elementary school level—have received more focused attention and their schools have received a major infusion of federal dollars." Available online at http://www.cccr.org/news/press.cfm?id=16.

87. "An Educational Mission That Must Not Fail," *New Democrat Daily*, January 7, 2004.

88. "Fixing 'No Child Left Behind,'" *New York Times*, April 5, 2005.

89. See Diane Ravitch, "Every State Left Behind," *New York Times*, November 7, 2005, A23; Chester Finn, "National Standards: Do We Have the Will?" *Education Gadfly* 5, 40 (November 10, 2005); and Cindy Brown and Elena Rocha, "The Case for National Standards, Accountability, and Fiscal Equity" (Washington, DC: Center for American Progress, 2005).

90. Timothy Conlan, *From New Federalism to Devolution: Twenty-five Years of Intergovernmental Reform* (Washington, DC: Brookings Institution Press, 1998), 313.

91. Paul Peterson, "The Changing Politics of Federalism," in *Evolving Federalisms: The Intergovernmental Balance of Power in America and Europe* (Syracuse, NY: Maxwell School of Syracuse University, 2003), 29.

92. Interview with the author, March 10, 2003.

93. John Kincaid, "From Cooperative to Coercive Federalism," *Annals of the American Academy of Political and Social Science* 509 (May 1990): 139–152.

94. Though improving educational "equity" clearly remains a central goal of federal education policy, NCLB defines this goal very differently from the original ESEA. The old "equity regime" had equalization of school resources and access as its central objectives. NCLB, meanwhile, defines equity in terms of closing racial and socioeconomic achievement gaps as measured on standardized tests. It also supplements this goal with a concern for improving the educational performance of all students in the United States.

95. David Nather, "Student-Testing Drive Marks an Attitude Shift for Congress," *CQ Weekly*, June 30, 2001, 1560.

CHAPTER TEN: CONCLUSION

1. Hacsi studied policy debates over Head Start, bilingual education, class size, social promotion, and the impact of money on student achievement and concluded that "being reelected drives most politicians . . . [and] evidence about what works is usually well down the list of factors influencing policy. . . . Politics is often at the heart of education, and of arguments about how to change or 'reform' education." Timothy Hacsi, *Children as Pawns: The Politics of Educational Reform* (Cambridge, MA: Harvard University Press, 2002), 209–213. For more on the importance of politics in educational policymaking, see Mary Smith, *Political Spectacle and the Fate of American Schools* (New York: Routledge Falmer, 2004), and Jay Scribner and Donald Layton, eds., *The Study of Educational Politics* (London: Falmer Press, 1994).

2. The project's findings are presented in Clarence Stone, Jeffrey Henig, Bryan Jones, and Carol Pierannunzi, *Building Civic Capacity: The Politics of Reforming Urban Schools* (Lawrence: University Press of Kansas, 2001).

3. This is not to say that education was absent from public or governmental agendas or from political campaigns during this period. As noted in Chapter 3, federal pressure to integrate public schools and end discriminatory practices in the aftermath of the *Brown* decision and the civil rights and Elementary and Secondary Education Acts received a great deal of publicity and created tremendous resistance and resentment in many parts of the country. However, though busing and integration became major political issues in the 1960s and 1970s, improving student academic performance did not emerge as a major issue until the 1980s.

4. James Ceaser has defined a public philosophy as a set of core ideas that define a particular approach to governance, a program of policy initiatives, and an attempt to shape how people think about the political world. *What Is the Public Philosophy?* (Oxford: Oxford University Press, 1999).

5. Margaret Weir, ed., *The Social Divide: Political Parties and the Future of Activist Government* (Washington, DC: Brookings Institution and Russell Sage Foundation, 1998), 8.

6. Marc Landy and Martin Levin, *The New Politics of Public Policy* (Baltimore: Johns Hopkins University Press, 1995), 277–297.

7. Samuel Kernel, *Going Public: New Strategies of Presidential Leadership* (Washington, DC: Congressional Quarterly Press, 1986).

8. Martha Derthick and Paul Quirk, *The Politics of Deregulation* (Washington, DC: Brookings Institution Press, 1986), 253.

9. Sidney Blumenthal, *The Permanent Campaign* (New York: Simon and Schuster, 1982).

10. See Martin Levin and Marc Landy, "Durability and Change," in Martin Levin, Marc Landy, and Martin Shapiro, eds., *Seeking the Center: Politics and Policymaking at the New Century* (Washington, DC: Georgetown University Press, 2002), 3–32.

11. Jeffrey Cohen, *Presidential Responsiveness and Public Policy-Making* (Ann Arbor: University of Michigan Press, 2000), 248.

12. As Milkis revealed in his study of FDR and the New Deal, reconstitutive party leaders inevitably face opposition from factions that have principles or interests that are threatened by the proposed shifts. Sidney Milkis, *The President and the Parties* (Oxford: Oxford University Press, 1995).

13. The growth of the federal role in education policy is commonly attributed to the successful efforts of the Democratic Party in the face of Republican opposition. The analysis here shows that this interpretation—though widely circulated and accepted—is in fact wrong on two counts. First of all, though many conservative Republicans have long opposed—and continue to oppose—an active federal role in education, Republican presidents have played an important role in nationalizing the politics of education, and the two Bushes significantly broadened the scope of federal influence over schools. Second, Clinton's push for national standards in education with Goals 2000 was opposed and resisted by many of his fellow Democrats, particularly in Congress. So in this sense, the struggles *within* the Democratic and Republican parties were as important as the struggles *between* the Republican and Democratic parties.

14. Stone, Henig, Jones, and Pierannunzi, *Building Civic Capacity*, 50.

15. The debate over federal education policy over the past twenty years was between not two different visions of school reform, but three—a liberal vision, a conservative vision, and a centrist vision that was embraced by moderates from both the Democratic and Republican parties. Liberals sought to increase federal funding and programs in education and to protect disadvantaged groups through the imposition of federal mandates on schools. Conservatives sought to roll back federal influence in education as a means of both preserving local and parental control and improving school performance—they viewed federal involvement as unconstitutional and counterproductive. In the wake of *A Nation at Risk*, a group of business leaders joined with moderate Democrats and Republicans (including a number of governors) and began to call for federal leadership in pushing academic standards, tests, accountability measures, and governance reforms. It is this third vision that forms the basis of NCLB and the new federal education policy regime.

16. Only time will tell how long the broader political dynamics that have accorded such importance to swing issues and encouraged party leaders to embrace centrist positions on them will persist. But the recent debate over Medicare reform was illuminating in this regard. President Bush and the Republican Congress in 2003 added a $400 billion prescription drug benefit for seniors on Medicare, which was the largest expansion in the program's history. The new federal investment was made contingent on the introduction of a number of market reforms, including a pilot program to have Medicare compete with private insurers in a number of cities.

17. Harris and Milkis observed, for example, that the nature of the regulatory process had "sheltered regulatory policy from broader democratic influences such as the presidency or electoral politics." *The Politics of Regulatory Change*, 51. See also Martha Derthick, *Policymaking for Social Security* (Washington, DC: Brookings Institution Press, 1979), and Gary Mucciaroni, *Reversals of Fortune* (Washington, DC: Brookings Institution Press, 1999).

18. For a collection of contemporary essays that reveal the different sides of this debate, see Jeff Manza, Fay Lomax Cook, and Benjamin Page, eds., *Navigating Public Opinion* (Oxford: Oxford University Press, 2002).

19. The most recent version of the view is expressed in Lawrence Jacobs and Robert Shapiro, *Politicians Don't Pander: Political Manipulation and the Loss of Democratic Responsiveness* (Chicago: University of Chicago Press: 2000).

20. The shifting terrain within the interest-group community also proved crucial, as the support of the business community (and later some civil rights groups) for standards-based reform from the 1980s on provided a counterweight to groups oriented to the status quo.

21. See, for example, Jennifer Hochschild and Bridget Scott, "Trends: Governance and Reform of Public Education in the United States," *Public Opinion Quarterly* 62, 1 (Spring 1998): 79–120; Carl Kaestle, "The Public Schools and the Public Mood," *American Heritage* 41 (February 1990): 66–81; and Tom Loveless, "The Structure of Public Confidence in Education," *American Journal of Education* 105, 2: (1997): 127–159. On NCLB specifically, see Lisa Dotterweich and Ramona McNeal, "The No Child Left Behind Act and Public Preferences," paper presented at the American Political Science Association Conference, August 2003.

22. See Lowell Rose and Alec Gallup, *The Annual Phi Delta Kappa/Gallup Survey of the Public's Attitudes toward the Public Schools*, various years, available online at http://www.pdkintl.org/kappan/k0309pol.pdf.

23. Paul Pierson, *Politics in Time* (Princeton, NJ: Princeton University Press, 2004), 1–2.

INDEX